CONSERVATION AND ECONOMIC EFFICIENCY

An Approach to Materials Policy

CONSERVATION AND ECONOMIC EFFICIENCY

An Approach to Materials Policy

TALBOT PAGE

Published for Resources for the Future
by The Johns Hopkins University Press
Baltimore and London

Library of Congress Catalog Card Number 76-22846

ISBN 0-8018-1904-0

ISBN 0-8018-1951-2 paper

Library of Congress Cataloging in Publication Data will be found on the last
printed page of this book.

RESOURCES FOR THE FUTURE, INC.
1755 Massachusetts Avenue, N.W., Washington, D.C. 20036

Resources for the Future is a nonprofit organization for research and education in the development, conservation, and use of natural resources and the improvement of the quality of the environment. It was established in 1952 with the cooperation of the Ford Foundation. Part of the work of Resources for the Future is carried out by its resident staff; part is supported by grants to universities and other nonprofit organizations. Unless otherwise stated, interpretations and conclusions in RFF publications are those of the authors; the organization takes responsibility for the selection of significant subjects for study, the competence of the researchers, and their freedom of inquiry.

This book is a product of the Quality of the Environment Division, which is directed by Walter O. Spofford, Jr. It was edited by Ruth B. Haas, Joan R. Tron, and Sally A. Skillings.

RFF editors: Herbert C. Morton, Joan R. Tron, Ruth B. Haas, Jo Hinkel, Sally A. Skillings

Contents

LIST OF TABLES

LIST OF FIGURES

Foreword

ONE OF THE GREATEST CHALLENGES that mankind currently faces, and will continue to face during the next several decades, is to provide and maintain a reasonably high material standard of living for all and at the same time provide and maintain a decent natural environment within which humans can enjoy their varied and many activities. Debate continues on whether or not it will be possible to achieve, and then to maintain, specified levels of material well-being. The concern generally expressed involves the continual erosion of a finite natural resource base and whether or not technological improvements can keep pace with the rapidly increasing demands for goods and services. But this concern does not represent the whole story. A spectrum of other related problems confronts our technologically oriented society as well. An increasingly important set involves the detrimental side effects of the production technology used to win increasing outputs from both renewable and nonrenewable natural resources. These by-products range from despoiled landscapes and pollution to toxic materials in the environment. Although some are limited in scope to degraded recreational and aesthetic attributes of the environment, others are more global in character and may even threaten those natural systems that are essential for the support of life. The latter, more severe, impacts appear to be associated with some of the newer technologies. Material well-being and the quality of the natural environment are integrally related, and policies established to address one will ultimately have an impact on the other. Clearly, the provision of goods and services and the uses and quality of the natural environment must be considered as a whole, and tradeoffs between them will be necessary. These complex interrelationships by themselves would be sufficient to confuse and concern our modern society, yet there is still another dimension of the natural resource utilization issue which requires our attention. Resources, wealth, and income, both among and within sovereign nations, are unevenly distributed, and the gap in income and well-being between groups of nations continues to widen. This continued growth in the gap between have and have-not nations raises both moral and ethical issues and in addition threatens world order and stability.

For the world as a whole, the levels of per capita material wealth that will eventually be possible depend upon a number of interrelated factors, among them: the size of the human population, its rate of increase, and its geographic distribution; the levels, patterns, and product mixes of human consumption, levels of consumption of virgin materials, and the rate of exhaustion of a fixed resource base; the reuse and recycling of materials, and the durability of products; the substitution of materials and technological change; the kinds and quantities of wastes generated and subsequently discharged to the environment; and the socially acceptable limits placed on the environmental side effects of the various production technologies. The future state of our natural and environmental resources ultimately depends on the policies that are adopted with respect to the utilization of materials (especially of the nonrenewable resources) and to the protection of the natural environment. Collectively, these policies constitute a materials policy.

Talbot Page addresses the range of issues that need to be considered in establishing a materials policy. First, he examines a materials policy based on a criterion of economic efficiency. In this context, he investigates the factors affecting the competition between the uses of virgin (primary) materials and recycled (secondary) materials and attempts to assess the impact on their relative use levels of three commonly cited market failures: (1) differing taxes and tax allowances on primary and secondary materials, (2) differential freight rates for primary and secondary materials, and (3) the failure to include waste disposal costs in the price of goods and services.

Second, Page examines the intertemporal (long-term) distributional implications of a materials policy that is based on the criterion of economic efficiency and judges this criterion to be insufficient to guarantee fairness to future generations. Here, Page introduces the notion of equity and fairness based on John Rawls' "original position." Page suggests that representatives of the future would be unlikely to accept today's market allocation of virgin material extraction, recycling of scrap material, and the stimulus of technological substitution. They would be likely to insist upon active provisions in materials policy to keep the resource base intact. These ideas are closely related to the conservationists' concern that the resource base should be left intact, or renewed, for the use of future generations. A second criterion, a conservation criterion, is developed to introduce equity and fairness into the economics of natural resources.

Finally, Page attempts to reconcile these two diverse positions by combining the best properties of each. In doing so, he points out that there is no automatic mechanism in the market to balance the tendencies of technological substitution, resource depletion, and waste generation from an intertemporal point of view; that resource depletion and the future long-term quality of the natural environment are *not* market failure problems, but distributional problems, and that they should be dealt with using macroeconomic policy instruments similar to those with which we treat unemployment and income distribution. Page advocates using the market and microeconomic policy instruments to enhance and maintain an efficient utilization of natural resources, and macroeconomic policy and government intervention to ensure an equitable distribution of the resource base into the distant future. This is a fundamental point in Page's argument. Equity and efficiency are the two basic strands of economic thought pursued by Page. Brought together, they form a basis for the discussion and development of a materials policy.

Materials policy, broadly stated, has been the focus of much of the research conducted at Resources for the Future since its inception in 1952. Indeed, Resources for the Future was established as an outgrowth of President Truman's Materials Policy Commission (also known as the Paley Commission) primarily for the purpose of assessing the adequacy of the nation's natural resources. RFF's early materials policy studies focused on the supplies and scarcity of natural resources. In their now-classic study, Harold Barnett and Chandler Morse (*Scarcity and Growth: The Economics of Natural Resource Availability,* 1963), based on the data series constructed by Neal Potter and Francis Christy (*Trends in Natural Resource Commodities: Statistics of Prices, Output, Consumption, Foreign Trade, and Employment in the United States, 1870–1959,* 1962), pointed out that the real unit costs and relative prices for most resource materials, except timber, remained stable or declined from 1870 to 1957. They noted that it appeared that the market had adjusted for scarcity by encouraging technological change and the substitution of less scarce materials for those more scarce. In their assessment of the long-run productivity of the resource base, environmental costs were not directly taken into account, although they did suggest that there appeared to be a reduction in the quality of life generally.

Conservation of the resource base received relatively little attention in RFF's research except in studies of fisheries resources and of the preservation of natural landscapes. There the focus was on the use of the resource for recreational, including wilderness, experiences and on the preservation of unique natural areas.

Recently in RFF's history, during a period when considerable emphasis was placed on the issues of environmental quality management, interest in materials returned, but this time it focused on reuse and recycling as an alternative for reducing the growing quantities of waste materials to be disposed of. Most of these studies stressed, to a greater or lesser extent, the systems nature of the residuals (waste) management problem and employed the criterion of economic efficiency in their analyses. The primary concern of all these studies was the failure of the market to reflect waste disposal costs and environmental damages associated with alternative disposal patterns in the prices of final goods and services.

The establishment of a materials policy requires the interaction of a number of complex, interrelated factors and issues, some of which have been addressed in previous research efforts at RFF. Page builds upon these studies in addressing the many interrelated issues systematically. In bringing together the ideas of intratemporal efficiency and intertemporal fairness, two of the fundamental considerations necessary in establishing a sound materials policy, Page has developed a new perspective and synthesis.

This study was begun while Talbot Page was on the staff of the Quality of the Environment Program, then directed by Allen V. Kneese, and was completed while the author was on the staff of the Natural Environments Program directed by John V. Krutilla. Dr. Page is currently on the staff of the Quality of the Environment Division.

December 1976   Walter O. Spofford, Jr.
                                                Director, Quality of
                                                the Environment Division

Preface

I BEGAN THIS STUDY five years ago with the question of recycling. Several pieces of major legislation—including the National Environmental Policy Act and the Resource Recovery Act—had declared recycling to be a national goal. But how much recycling, which materials, what incentives? It soon became clear to me that questions of "optimal" recycling are tied to questions of optimal durability, exhaustion of the resource base, and the distributions of long-lived wastes generated by materials use: that is to say, recycling policy belongs in the broader context of materials policy.

In order to define the "optimal" balances between materials use and conservation and material waste generation and protection of the future from these wastes, some of which are extremely long-lived, it is necessary to know how to value the long-run costs of depletion and waste generated. At first this appears to be a straightforward problem to be handled by the discounting of future costs. But the problem becomes more complicated when one assumes, as I do in the latter part of this book, that the resource base is owned jointly across generations (here the resource base refers not only to the positively valued resources "in the ground" but also to the negatively valued material wastes generated by materials use). Once the resource base is recognized as belonging to all generations, it becomes clear that we must ask what is a fair or equitable intergenerational use of the resource base. As I will try to illustrate, this question goes beyond choosing a discount rate and using it.

Discussion of the fair use, intertemporally, of the resource base is not a new discussion. It is the principal focus of much of the conservationist literature. In the economics literature on natural resources, however, the focus has been quite different. The focus has been on the efficient workings of markets. While there has been considerable discussion of the appropriate rate of discount, there has been little effort to go beyond discounting and market efficiency to consider the question of intertemporal fairness. In fact, I found these two strands of thought, efficiency and conservationist, had frequently been used one in opposition to another. It appeared to me, nonetheless, that instead of conflicting, the efficiency and conservationist strands of thought could be fitted together so that one contributed to the other. And in considering the narrower question of market inefficiencies, I found inconsistencies and confusions relating to materials use and policy. I decided to work toward a conceptual unification of the materials policy area.

The resulting book should be of use to those interested in materials policy issues by bringing many of these issues and individual studies together under a single conceptual structure. The economics of natural resources and materials use is presently large, amorphous, and rapidly growing. As more empirical work is done, much of it narrowly focused, I expect that our knowledge will become more precise and solid. This is not primarily an empirical book; while there are a number of empirical statements in it, I have hedged many of them against the expectation of more narrowly focused future empirical work by others. There is an increasing amount of work being done on scarcity, materials substitution, the structure of materials industries, taxation of virgin and scrap materials, and residuals management. Rather than trying to be exhaustive or definitive, I have attempted to provide a guide through this increasingly dense thicket. In doing so I hope I have not added too many inconsistencies and confusions of my own. Parts of the book are more technical than others. Where the discussion is mathematical I have tried to paraphrase it in nontechnical terms. The first and last chapters may be read as a nontechnical overview of the book as a whole.

I wish to thank Allen V. Kneese, Blair T. Bower, Chandler Morse, Clifford S. Russell, Ezra Mishan, Taylor Durham, Richard Speigleman, James Sawyer, Jr., Frederick J. Wells, Mark F. Sharefkin, John V. Krutilla, Walter O. Spofford, Jr., Theo Page, Philip Mause, Robert Anderson, Fred Lee Smith, Sterling Brubaker, and Harold J. Barnett. Several of these people read the manuscript in several versions, and each helped in one way or another to unscramble the text. Others, including Johannes Linn, Anthony C. Fisher, V. Kerry Smith, Peter Pearse, and Arthur Wright were helpful on specific chapters. I also wish to thank my editors,

Ruth B. Haas, Joan R. Tron, and Sally A. Skillings, who labored over various versions of cut and taped drafts. I must add, however, that on a number of points my readers did not agree with each other, or with the author. The author has a certain advantage on such occasions, and he absolves his commentators from what remains.

December 1976   Talbot Page

CONSERVATION AND ECONOMIC EFFICIENCY

An Approach to Materials Policy

1

Introduction: Toward a
Materials Policy

> *Upon our own generation lies the responsibility
> for passing on to the next generation the prospects
> of continued well-being.*
> —Paley Commission Report, 1952

> *I do not believe there is either a moral or any
> other claim upon me to postpone the use of what
> nature has given me, so that the next generation
> or generations may have an opportunity to get
> what I myself ought to get.*
> —Senator Henry Teller,
> former secretary of the interior, 1909

FOR MANY YEARS there have been two approaches to the formulation of materials policy, one associated with the traditional thinking of resource economists and the other with that of conservationists. An important purpose of this book is to develop a unifying conceptual structure to join together these two approaches. In carrying out this purpose, the book is divided into three principal parts. Part One discusses material flows, and some of their determinants, as they enter and exit from the economy. Part Two considers three short-term failures of markets to efficiently balance material uses. And Part Three, from a long-term perspective, develops efficiency and conservation criteria as a foundation of materials policy.

In the past, national policy has followed the assumption that the more we extract and use our natural resources, the faster we build up the economy. The larger the volume of materials we process, so the idea has gone, the richer and more secure we become. Instead of letting our

1

mineral resources lie fallow in the ground, they should be turned into productive assets, benefiting future generations as well as our own. For example, for two centuries the United States favored mineral extraction on its national lands, codifying the practice in the 1872 mining law. The extraction of minerals, including energy minerals, was encouraged by depletion allowances and other tax preferences; energy consumption was encouraged by a promotional price system that gave volume discounts for larger consumption. The ostensible cost of energy and materials was reduced by ignoring the environmental costs associated with extracting and processing them.

This exploitative policy toward natural resources does not appear to have been entirely intentional. Nor has it been completely uniform. Large areas of land have been preserved from development. The control of gas prices by federal regulation has discouraged exploration and development. Yet the bias toward development and exploitation is pronounced. In the past this policy may have made sense; resources appeared limitless; pollution and other environmental costs associated with their extraction were relatively small and localized; and our comparative advantage in relation to other countries lay in the abundance of our natural resources.

During World War II, enormous quantities of material resources were used up, and the resulting concern over the adequacy of the materials resource base led to the establishment of the Paley Commission, in 1951, "to study the materials problem." This commission concluded that the age of abundance for the United States was over, but that shortages in materials could be met through increased foreign trade. (The President's Materials Policy Commission, *Resources for Freedom.*) Today, however, policies encouraging the use and consumption of materials, many of which are strategic militarily, would also increase our import dependence, and perhaps, therefore, lessen our security. Moreover, if other countries emulated our pattern of materials use, would they be able to satisfy their demand through increased imports? Material extraction and processing tends to be heavily polluting; could the earth's environment assimilate all the wastes from many countries following the U.S. pattern of materials use? Could the United States sustain its own use pattern? Would there be enough for the future?

In the past few years these questions have been brought home in various ways: by the Arab oil embargo, by worldwide material shortages in 1973 that temporarily increased many prices severalfold, and by models and projections of future scarcity of materials and increases in pollution. Consequently, in the past few years considerable rhetoric has been expended on the need for conservation and increased physical efficiency in the use of materials. Indeed, increased conservation and efficiency might mitigate many of the problems simultaneously.

By materials we mean here the basic raw materials of the economy— minerals, metals, and nonfood fibers. In 1972 the United States consumed 290 million tons of forest products, 140 million tons of metals (mostly iron), 1.9 billion tons of fuel minerals, and 2.1 billion tons of nonmetallic, nonfuel materials (mostly stone, sand, and gravel).[1] The relative values of these materials in 1972 are shown in figure 1. Energy minerals clearly dominate over other materials in value, even before the recent price increases in fuels.

Taken together, these materials are inconspicuous in the gross national product (GNP) accounts; they represent less than 4 percent of the GNP.

Figure 1. Material consumption by dollar value, per capita, 1972

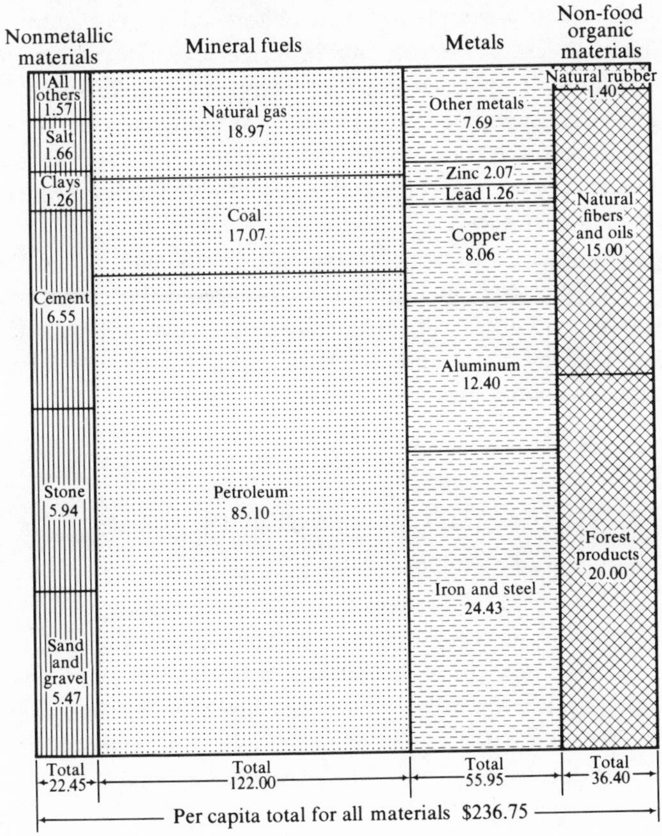

However, materials' percentage of GNP is a deceptive measure of their importance. Materials are like water in Adam Smith's paradox of water and diamonds. Water is cheap compared with diamonds but if worse comes to worst people will pay all they have for a little water, not so for diamonds. Nonfuel materials comprise about the same fraction of the GNP as does the airline industry. With some adjustment we could do without the airline industry, but there is no way that we could do without materials.

The consumption of materials has doubled every thirty-five years since 1870.[2] This is bound to change, for we cannot go through many more doubling periods. Much of the growth in materials consumption is driven by population growth, and historically the growth in consumption of materials has been about 0.3 percent greater than the growth in population. Thus, some of the increase in materials consumption is likely to melt away automatically and painlessly as population levels off. And some of the growth will be attenuated, however painfully, if we move into an era of sharply higher costs for both energy and materials. Whatever changes take place, our historical experience remains built into our economic structure, and our economy still favors extraction and use over conservation. Perhaps the most basic question of materials policy formulation is this: After two centuries of favoring materials extraction, should we now take active steps toward a more conservative materials policy, and if so, how?

By what standards do we judge the best, or optimal, balance between depletion and conservation of materials, between disposal and recycling, durability and original cost, maintenance and new production? These questions lead directly to another: How should we account for the very long-run costs which may be associated with materials depletion and waste generation?

Efficiency Criterion

The market itself provides a standard of sorts[3] in that the market defines a balance between depletion and conservation, recycling and disposal, and durability and initial cost. Market forces lead to a certain flow of material through the economy, extending from extraction to discharge into the environment (or material throughput). In the exploitative view, the extraction of virgin materials is an engine of economic growth and development, so that extraction should be encouraged beyond what the market would do by itself. Opposing this view is the belief that markets do not provide adequately for the future, so that provision for the future, in the form of conservation, should be encouraged beyond what the market would do by itself. It is interesting that both the exploitative and conservationist views are largely justified in terms of benefit to the future, yet they recommend opposite materials policies.

Generally, economists have taken a more neutral view. The market is indeed flawed, they agree, but if the flaws were corrected, there would be no need for a national materials policy; the market would provide the right balance between depletion and conservation, disposal and durability, and so forth. In this view, recycling is neither good nor bad in itself; it is the correction of market failures that is important. If the market failures cannot be corrected, or if upon examination they turn out not to be failures at all but "distortions" to bend market allocations toward worthy and intended policy goals, then the market can still be used as a standard to measure by. By this view, we estimate what the market would do in the absence of distortions, calculate the gaps by examining what the market is actually doing, and choose materials policy goals on the basis of closing these gaps. To follow this prescription is to act under the *efficiency criterion*. This criterion, which can be used as a basis for materials policy, says that material flows *should* be arranged as if they were operating in a perfect market.[4]

There are four causes of market inefficiencies that are important for our purposes and that manifest themselves in imbalance between prices and marginal costs. These are (1) monopoly pricing power; (2) the market system's inability to include environmental and disposal costs in product prices; (3) distortions in the federal tax system; and (4) price systems, such as freight pricing, which discriminate among products on the basis of what the traffic will bear.

1. Elementary economic theory tells us that monopolies tend to restrict output in order to raise prices and increase their profits. With the increased prices, the marginal costs of production would be less than the price charged, indicating a potential social gain from increased production. Although industries processing virgin materials, or primary industries, are not pure monopolies, they are typically dominated by a few large firms that show some evidence of the power (and will) to influence prices. Does this mean that in order to keep prices high these industries act like conservationists, slowing down the rate of extraction

beyond what would occur in a competitive market and beyond what would be consistent with the efficiency criterion? As we shall see in chapter 3, it is not clear that the power of primary industries to influence price is used to decrease the rate of virgin material extraction below that indicated by the efficiency criterion.

2. Costs generated, but not borne by a producer are called external costs, while the costs borne by the producer are internal costs. The most obvious examples of external costs (or externalities) are environmental costs, including air and water pollution. Markets fail to transfer these costs to the responsible firms; instead, they fall on society as a whole. The private incentive of a firm is to increase production to the point where the internal marginal costs equal price. But to satisfy the efficiency criterion, the environmental costs must also be internalized. Some ways to accomplish this are effluent taxes, and restrictive standards or other regulations. Transferring social costs to the responsible firms could serve two purposes: It could lead the firm to reduce the polluting aspects of its activities or, as the internalized costs are passed on in higher prices, it could signal consumers to shift away from pollution-intensive products, or both. It is sometimes suggested that pollution and other environmental costs should not be passed on in higher prices but should come out of profits or should be subsidized by governments. But even if environmental costs reduce profits in the short run, the criterion of economic efficiency tells us that, in the long run, prices should reflect environmental costs as well as private costs. Otherwise, the appropriate market signals will not exist. Failure of the price system to include solid waste disposal costs in product price is the solid waste counterpart of the failure of the price system to internalize the costs of air and water pollution. In the past, local governments have paid the cost of municipal waste disposal, just as society as a whole has paid the costs of breathing air polluted by incinerators. The market system fails to incorporate these disposal costs in a product's price. To satisfy the efficiency criterion, all the marginal costs (disposal costs and environmental costs, as well as private internal costs) must be taken into account in a firm's production decisions.

3. Another way of distorting prices is through the tax system. If one sector is taxed more lightly than the rest of the economy, resources will tend to flow into that sector. The tax advantage may first be translated into initially higher profits, and then into lower prices and additional products sold. Although any tax system will distort the allocation of resources somewhat, the efficiency criterion says that the distortion

should be minimal: The tax system should be as neutral as possible. It is hard to ensure neutrality, and easy to promote nonneutrality. The simplest way to guarantee nonneutrality is to tax one sector of the economy lightly and another sector heavily. For forty years economists have argued that the extractive sector is taxed lightly relative to other sectors, leading to too much extraction, too much material and energy throughput, too much solid waste, and not enough recycling. Now it is gradually becoming apparent that the previous nonneutrality of the tax system has been an important cause of the solid waste problem.

4. An example of the fourth factor affecting marginal costs and prices is transportation rates. The cost of transporting a raw material is a large fraction of its price. Thus differences in transportation costs will be reflected in product prices. There is some evidence that transportation rates, particularly railroad freight rates, are not related to the actual cost of shipment and that scrap materials headed for recycling pay higher rates than virgin materials. In fact, it appears that some virgin materials pay less than the marginal cost of shipment. If the efficiency criterion were applied, rates would be based on marginal costs, resulting in a more balanced flow of virgin and scrap materials.

Do Markets Provide for the Future?

Correction of the last three market inefficiencies described in the preceding section would lead to more recycling and less material throughput. And if the market failures cannot be corrected directly, there is a case, following the efficiency criterion, for policy measures in the conservationist direction. Is this enough? Is the efficiency criterion sufficient as a basis for a materials policy? Would even perfect markets provide adequately for the future?

There is little doubt that markets do provide for the future. Investments are made that bear fruit in the future, and resources are set aside for future use. While it is a common and accurate perception that markets weigh the well-being of the present more heavily than the well-being of the future, there are nonetheless market forces that tend to "renew" depletable resources. Consider a "nonrenewable" resource such as oil. Resource holders, seeing a limited stock of their resource and anticipating a future scarcity, would feel the incentive of higher future prices to reserve some of their stock from the market, even if the oil industry were perfectly competitive. Today's reservation of resources resulting from speculation on future price increases leads to higher prices today. The difference between today's price with, and today's price without, resource reservation and anticipation of future scarcity is today's scarcity value of the resource. Today's higher price encourages substitutes and the development of new technology to replace the resource being depleted. Competitive firms in an industry exploiting a depletable resource have the incentive to reserve resources to the point where the growth in scarcity value equals the market interest rate.[5] Not only is this optimal from the point of view of the firm, but, under a particular criterion of social welfare, it is also optimal from the point of view of society. In other words, the market mechanism of resource reservation is consistent with the efficiency criterion and is a needed mechanism for its satisfaction.

Of course, resource reservation is just one factor among many market forces, and it may be submerged in the complications and distortions of actual markets. Many depletable resources are located in underdeveloped countries and are exploited by multinational or foreign firms. Such firms may not weigh today's resource price against tomorrow's higher price. Tomorrow the firm may be nationalized and the profits go to someone else. Insecure tenure is not conducive to resource reservation. However, as countries gain control of their resource bases, they may not act like competitive firms, but try to form cartels to control their markets. If they are successful, they may raise prices, slowing the rate of extraction. If only partially successful, they may destabilize the market, inducing large swings in price and material flows.[6]

On public land in our own country mineral rights are acquired upon the discovery of the mineral in the same way that fish become owned upon their capture. This rule of capture, stemming from the 1872 mining law, tends to promote more mineral exploration and exploitation than the efficiency standard calls for, just as does the rule of capture in ocean fishing. For minerals on public lands, exploration may be undertaken on a preemptive basis in order to prevent a competitor from obtaining a claim first. Once the claim is established, mineral exploitation may have a higher priority than other uses of public land.[7] However, in recent years the preemptive uses of federal lands for mineral and timber extraction have increasingly been challenged, and a large amount of land has been set aside from these uses.

Resource reservation depends upon estimating future potential profits and weighing them against the opportunity of present profits by means of a market interest rate or discount rate. It is possible that a large timber firm may look ahead forty to fifty years and compare its present and future possibilities consistently with the efficiency criterion. But the firm's own timber managers may have a much shorter time horizon. A manager may realize that he must prove himself in just a few years and may want tangible results. He may discount the future at a much higher rate than the firm does, and his decisions may greatly determine the harvesting as well as the replanting rate.[8] Thus resource reservation, which tends to provide for the future by buying time through giving the present a higher incentive to develop substitutes and new technology, has complications and market failures of its own.

Suppose that these problems were somehow eliminated, along with distortions resulting from the tax structure, transport rates, and the inability of the market to internalize disposal costs. Would this idealized market provide adequately for the future?

Intertemporal Fairness

Markets can be expected to allocate resources more or less efficiently relative to a given distribution of wealth or market power (a hypothetical ideal market would actually achieve efficiency). But markets cannot be expected to solve the problem of what is a fair or equitable distribution of wealth, either among different people at a point in time (intratemporally) or among different generations (intertemporally). The questions of depletion and generation of long-lived wastes are fundamentally questions of equitable distribution of burdens across generations. The problem of a fair intertemporal distribution arises because the material resource base is potentially long lived, as are some wastes (the plutonium waste generated by reactors has a half-life of 24,500 years). Thus the same materials must be shared among many generations.[9]

Sometimes these distributional aspects of resource use are obscured by the assertion that depletion resulting from market forces will automatically benefit the future as well as the present. Resources in the ground are sterile, the argument goes, and the future will be better off if resources are extracted so that they can be turned into productive capital. The obscuration arises because "can be benefited" is different from "will automatically be benefited." Market forces channel most material, perhaps 90 percent of it, into short-lived consumer goods rather than productive capital. If iron ore is taken from the ground, mixed with tin, and then made into soft drink cans that are used once and scattered along the roadside, the future is not benefited. The future would have been better off if the iron and tin had been left in the ground, even if they had been growing in scarcity value at "only" 2 percent. Quite often in manufacturing cycles, materials are changed from more to less usable forms. The rule "deplete up to the rate where the growth in scarcity value equals the interest rate" is an efficiency condition of today's market and a condition met more or less automatically by the market. Whether or not the future is damaged by today's depletion is another question entirely. The answer depends on whether or not there is enough growth in technology, substitutes, and discoveries to "renew" the resource base. The increasing prices that result from growing scarcity value encourage technological and other substitutions without guaranteeing renewability of the resource base.

It is sometimes assumed that future generations will be better off than the present one, even taking into account future burdens from long-lived wastes and depleted resource stocks. The assumption is usually derived from extrapolations of past trends in capital formation and other economic aggregates. In the past it was often assumed that increases in knowledge were always net benefits and that capital accumulation was always a homogeneous good thing. Under such assumptions, with knowledge and capital growing, the only intertemporal welfare problem is how much saving the present generation should do and how fast the future should be made better off. Under the assumption that the future is going to be better off no matter what, the question of intertemporal equity is not a pressing matter.

However, the costs of long-lived material wastes or material resource depletion are not certainties or even mathematical expectations. The burdens associated with resource use that we are placing upon the future are largely risk burdens. With respect to both material wastes and depletion, the equity question is: What is a fair distribution of risk to impose upon the future? For many long-lived wastes, we have exceedingly little idea of the intertemporal distribution of risk. And in order to judge the distribution of a depletion burden, we would first have to forecast the strengths of each of the price determinants of the major material resources. Clearly this is a very difficult thing to do and involves a great deal of uncertainty in the assessment of risk.

While technology is ultimately the only way of renewing "nonrenewable" material resources, it adds to the legacy of risk to be bequeathed to the next generation. Technological solutions are not inevitable. As the flows of "nonrenewable" resources become larger for the United States and increasingly so for other countries, our dependence on technological fixes becomes greater. The power of technology itself becomes greater, with uncalculated and perhaps unmanageable side effects. Thus, the burden as we use up oil is the risk burden that we will not come up with a substitute technology in time. Alvin Weinberg has called one alternative, nuclear power, a Faustian bargain.[10] More generally, the present is in the process of imposing many Faustian lotteries upon the future. Our legacy to the future is not homogeneous and is not composed entirely of benefits. Intertemporal equity emerges as an important problem because there is no easy way to add up the costs and risks along with the benefits and no way to guarantee that the future is going to be better off than the present.

Obviously, there are great uncertainties in trying to estimate the distribution of the depletion burden and the burdens associated with generation of material wastes. On top of this there is the difficulty of deciding what is a fair distribution of these risk burdens. Finally, there is the task of persuading the present generation to take preventive actions, if appropriate, to avoid imposing unfair burdens upon the future. Basing even part of a materials policy on considerations of intertemporal fairness may seem an overwhelming task, but certain practical steps may be quite manageable.

Some policy instruments may impose little net burden upon the present generation but may have substantial effects on the condition of the resource base forty or fifty years hence. As we have seen, resource reservation works through a price effect. There are two other means of achieving direct price effects that are of considerable importance in this book. The first is the severance tax; this is simply a tax on virgin material extracted from the ground or environment. It may be based either upon the dollar value of the material extracted (ad valorem) or upon the weight or quantity of the material extracted (specific). Severance taxes increase the nominal scarcity of virgin materials, from the point of view of users and consumers. Severance taxes also slow down the rate of extraction, buying time to develop substitutes and increasing their payoff. In the past the severance tax has been levied principally at the state level, but in this book the tax is considered at the national level as an instrument of intertemporal fairness.

The second means of achieving direct price effects, other than resource reservations, is the percentage depletion allowance. As will be seen later, this provision is almost a mirror image of a severance tax and is nearly equivalent to a subsidy per unit of material extracted. Not only is it the best known provision favoring mineral industries and a direct price effect, but in addition its close relationship with the severance tax makes it instructive for our purposes. Percentage depletion allowances began in 1926 and have grown over the years largely in ignorance of their long-run effects. It appears, but it is by no means clear, that the short-run effects of percentage depletion allowances are not highly disruptive but the long-run effects may be substantial; the same may be true of the severance tax. In the long run, measures such as percentage depletion allowances and severance taxes affect the renewability of the resource base, especially when we think of technological change as a method of renewing "nonrenewable" resources.

It is sometimes argued that a move toward materials conservation would not be possible without a cut in the standard of living. Occasionally one runs into a statement that reducing consumption of virgin materials would soon put us back into the eighteenth century. But this view is too pessimistic. The Federal Energy Administration has estimated that four European countries, each with about the same standard of living as ours, produce each dollar of GNP with half the amount of energy that we do. International comparisons of material consumption of metals, nonmetal minerals, timber, and energy minerals per dollar of GNP show enormous differences among countries (see appendix A). There is a great deal of flexibility in the use of materials. Moreover, examination of present market inefficiencies shows certain slacks in the present market allocations of materials uses. Because of these slacks, it may be possible to undertake policy objectives toward intertemporal fairness with little or no net sacrifice on the part of the present generation.

Keeping the Resource Base Intact

The problem of intertemporal fairness becomes greatly simplified when the resource base is kept essentially intact over time. Suppose, for example, that as we are forced to use less rich ores, say ½ instead of 1 percent copper ore, technology progresses, allowing the cost of copper per unit extracted (including the environmental costs) to remain constant. Then it is a matter of indifference which generation one is born into, at least with respect to the copper resource. Copper is being managed on a "sustainable yield" basis. In such a case, at least with respect to the materials base, there would be a world of equals between generations. It might be an attractive goal, as a matter of intertemporal fairness, to keep the resource base essentially intact, but it is not a goal that markets can be expected to achieve automatically, even if they were perfected.[11]

The weakness of the market as an allocator of long-lived resources can be illustrated by the following analogy. Consider the ocean fisheries stock, which is jointly valued by many nations, just as the material resource base is jointly valued by many generations. One method of allocation, a nonmarket one, might be to establish compacts among the nations to ensure that each got an "equitable" catch and that the stock as a whole was not overfished. Another way of allocating the fisheries resources might be to give control and full rights for the entire resource stock to Japan for one year, to the United States for the next year, to Russia the third year, and so forth. In a rough way this is analogous to the fact of market life: total resource control and full rights vested in each generation, one-by-one serially. One could make the analogy incorporate overlapping generations by assuming that someone living in one country has relatives in a "successor" country (descendants) and that there is a probability that one might oneself move to a successor country (survive into another generation).[12] In the fisheries analogy, management of the stock would depend on the "present generation's" inability to exhaust the resource in a single year and upon its altruism toward the "next generation." The altruism would be selfish in the sense that the presently controlling nation would save for its successor nation only to the degree that the saving benefited the controlling nation. Relying on the altruism of previous nations would doubtless make successor nations feel uneasy. Yet this is roughly the situation intertemporally when the market is the sole mechanism by which the resource base is managed.

Conservationists have long held it an important goal to keep the resource base essentially intact from generation to generation. And when the resource base appears threatened, as it now does with respect to fossil fuels, preservation of this base becomes an important goal for society as a whole. Economists will recognize this goal as a macroeconomic one, and the severance tax, in this context, as a macroeconomic policy instrument. Economists often recommend macroeconomic policies on employment, inflation, interest rates, and the balance of payments. These policies are designed to establish a context within which market forces can interact on their own to the advantage of society at large.

In the past, economists have not included preservation of the resource base in their list of macroeconomic goals needing explicit policy measures. They have relied on the invisible hand of the market to match new technology against depletion, much as, before the Depression, they counted on the invisible hand to eliminate unemployment. But now, as material flows are becoming enormously larger, lead times shorter, and the environmental and technological effects more pervasive, it is time to make preservation of the resource base an explicit policy issue.

Several questions in this book about joining the views of traditional economists and those of conservationists guide the inquiry. What are the institutions and market forces that determine the actual pattern of material uses and flows? What should be the balance between virgin material extraction and conservation, between material disposed of as waste and recycling, between longer product life and greater original cost, and so forth? And what are possible instruments to implement policy changes implied by criteria chosen for materials policy?

The book is not meant to be a comprehensive treatment of materials policy. Little is said, for example, about other countries' materials problems and policies, international trade, bargaining, and national defense, although for a comprehensive basis of materials policy, these considerations must be taken into account. We have made a beginning conceptualization in terms of economic efficiency and intertemporal fairness; we believe that once this conceptualization is made, other considerations underlying the formulation of materials policy will fall more easily into place. It seems clear, for example, that considerations of economic efficiency and intertemporal fairness apply to countries other than our own, and perhaps with greater force to those countries dependent on one or a few depletable resources.

The three parts into which this book is divided may be thought about in terms of a nineteenth century sailing ship. In Part One, we look at which ropes are connected to which sails; we look at some of the interactions involved in materials use and how material flows are organized by primary and secondary materials industries. Further, we ask how we know when the sails are in balance one with another at a given time, and we note that the efficiency criterion offers a definition of balance of the various types of material uses and flows. In Part Two, we focus in detail on three possible sources of inefficiency that may cause the sails to be out of balance one with another. Part Three focuses on the long-term aspects of intertemporal fairness in contrast with Part Two's emphasis on the near term. In Part Three, we consider the course of the ship as a whole: markets like sails may be in balance, but we may still ask where the economy as a whole is heading and which way the rudder is set. Adjusting the rudder in Part Three involves considerations quite different from those of adjusting the sails in Part Two; one sets the sails according to the wind; the rudder, according to the destination. So too in the case of materials policy: The considerations underlying economic efficiency are quite different from those of intertemporal fairness.

Notes

1. Extrapolated from figure 2.3 of National Commission on Materials Policy, *Materials Needs and the Environment Today and Tomorrow: Final Report* (Washington, D.C., U.S. Government Printing Office, June 1973) pp. 2–6.

2. Neal Potter and Francis Christy, Jr., *Trends in Natural Resource Commodities: Statistics of Prices Output, Consumption, Foreign Trade, and Employment in the United States, 1870–1957* (Baltimore, Md., Johns Hopkins University Press for Resources for the Future, 1962) p. 8.

3. A product's price measures its marginal benefit in terms of a consumer's willingness to pay for it. Its marginal cost is a measure of the cost of one extra unit of the product. The marginal cost at a production level of X units per month (or whatever unit of time) is the difference in total costs for a production level of $X + 1$ units and the total costs for a production level of X units (for the same unit of time). The market tends to balance the marginal benefits with the marginal costs of production.

4. A perfect market is said to be efficient; that is, it satisfies the condition that there is no possible way to change the allocations of goods and services to make some people better off without hurting at least one person. In a perfect market there are no price distortions so that economic activities are carried out to the point where marginal cost equals price. The cost and benefit are matched, on the margin, for each product, and there is no way to improve one person's economic well-being without hurting another's. Where there are institutional constraints, in a world of "second-best," this condition of price equal to marginal cost can be quite complicated, taking into account indirect costs.

5. Harold Hotelling, "The Economics of Exhaustible Resources," *Journal of Political Economy* vol. 39 (April 1931) pp. 137–175.

6. Actually, it appears that several developing countries with newly nationalized oil deposits are more concerned about resource reservation than the previous resource managers, the international oil companies. The motive does not appear to be speculation on future price increases (in a competitive market) as discussed above. The motive appears twofold: to increase the rents on the present flow of oil and to provide a more stable economy over the next few decades. The trade-off between present and future welfare is explicitly a policy issue for several developing countries with raw material deposits.

7. Mason Gaffney discusses this point in his "Editor's Conclusion" of *Extractive Resources and Taxation* (Madison, Wisc., University of Wisconsin Press, 1967) pp. 391–399; the point is also discussed in a Ph.D. dissertation by Frederick Peterson, "The Theory of Exhaustible Natural Resources: A Classical Variational Approach," Princeton, N.J., 1972.

8. See, for example, Robin Marris, *The Economic Theory of "Managerial" Capitalism* (New York, Basic Books, 1964).

9. In another very long-run sense, depletion can be considered quite generally to include the extinction of genetic stocks.

10. Alvin Weinberg, "Social Institutions and Nuclear Energy," *Science* vol. 177 (July 7, 1972) p. 33.

11. Of course maintaining the resource base intact is not by itself adequate provision for the future. If we maintain our forests and other resources intact, but the population triples in the next fifty years, we have still passed on a much increased resource problem.

12. The assumption underlying this analogy is that future generations do not have the market powers to earn and trade for the resource base; they inherit it. To the extent that later generations have their own labor and hence market power to trade with overlapping previous generations, the analogy needs modification.

PART ONE

MATERIAL FLOWS
AND USES

2

Virgin Material Intensity

and Waste Management

We find it useful initially to view environmental pollution and its control as a materials balance problem for the entire economy.
—Robert Ayres and Allen Kneese

IN RECENT YEARS, depletion and waste accumulation have emerged as serious material problems in the public perception. And because it works directly toward the conservation of virgin materials and directly against the accumulation of waste materials, recycling has received considerable attention. In spite of the fact that it is essentially a piecemeal effort, increased recycling has been proclaimed a national goal in several recent pieces of national legislation.

However, there are at least three other means toward conservation and waste control. 1. *Durability.* For the same product and same product service, it may be possible to increase the product's lifetime, decreasing the amount of virgin material consumed and waste generated per unit product service. 2. *Material embodiment.* For the same product service, it is sometimes possible to decrease the amount of material embodied in the product. There have been striking gains in material saving in the communications and information-processing industries. A first-generation computer, filling a large room, had about the same capacity as a modern hand calculator. Design changes that decrease the material embodied per unit product service do not, however, always go along with increased durability, to judge from a comparison of modern hand calculators with their apparently indestructible mechanical predecessors. 3. *Waste generation in production.* Material saving in the product itself, nonetheless, can be quite misleading. Often the material embodied in a product is small in quantity compared with the waste generated in its production. Shrinkage of a product may be gained at the expense of increased material waste in production. A great deal of conservation of virgin material can be achieved in the production processes themselves.

These three factors, plus the amount of recycling, determine the degree of conservation and waste generation in the economy. They depend in turn upon technology, economic incentives, life style, and product specification. In regard to the last, often an enormous amount of waste can be avoided by making the specification less stylistic and more utilitarian. For example, a paper towel may be either bleached (white) or unbleached (brown) and otherwise have the same properties of softness, absorbency, and so forth. The stylistic preference for whiteness carries with it a doubling of the sulfur dioxide generation, a fourfold increase in biological oxygen demand (BOD), and a more than fourfold increase in dissolved solids.[1]

A measure of the composite effect of durability, material embodiment, waste generation in production, and recycling (or reuse) upon conservation and waste accumulation is *virgin material intensity*. This is defined for the economy as a whole as the quantity of virgin material consumed divided by the gross national product. (For an application of this, see appendix A.) How do we know when we have the right degree of virgin material intensity in the economy, or the proper rates of depletion and waste accumulation? Inasmuch as this question involves consideration of the fairness of long-run costs and risks, I defer it in favor of the following question, immediate in its time frame: How do we know when the above four factors are in proper balance one with another at a given moment in time? The efficiency criterion gives us a definition and tells us that to the degree that market inefficiencies are eliminated, these four factors will simultaneously be brought into proper balance one with another. Another way of putting the matter is that whether we want a lot or a little conservation of virgin materials, we would like an efficient balance among recycling, durability, embodiment, and waste generation.

Waste generation and recycling are directly measurable, physical concepts, in contrast with durability and embodiment per unit product service, which are more elusive. When we turn our attention to material flows leading to waste generation and perhaps recycling, we find that much of what we would like to know about the other two factors can be inferred from this discussion.

Material Flows

The pattern of material flows is schematized in figure 2, which shows the basic path of materials in the mining and timber industries as they are extracted from the environment, moved through various stages of processing and use, and finally disposed back into the environment. While the throughput of material from the environmental source to the environmental dump may be slowed by increased durability in

Figure 2. Schematic of material flows

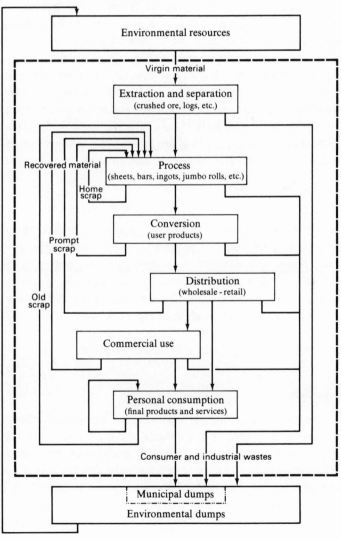

products or convoluted by recycling loops, the 4½ billion tons of new materials produced annually—produced at a growing rate—are destined to become waste deposited into the environment, along with the contributions of earlier years and later ones. The different stages sketched in figure 2 are often associated with different material forms and different material wastes.

Extraction

At the extraction stage, ores are taken out of the ground and trees are harvested from the forest. Materials are separated by crushing, heating, and chemical treatment. (The value of materials at the separation stage, just after extraction, is used as the basis for calculating percentage depletion.) The resulting virgin materials are relatively homogeneous at this stage. But in the separation of virgin materials, many waste materials are generated: these include air and water pollutants, tailings, slag, timber slash, and so forth. Many of these waste materials are quite unlike the virgin materials being produced. The products at this stage are crushed and beneficiated ores, logs, and so forth.

Process

Processing carries materials to the stage of basic shapes: sheets, bars, ingots, jumbo paper rolls. In processing there are cuttings, trimmings, and other scrap materials that are of the same composition as the virgin material stock. Most of this material is too valuable to throw away; much of it is "home scrap" that by definition never leaves the "roof" of the processing firm. Instead, it is put back with the virgin material stock and reprocessed as new material. Other processing materials are treated as waste and deposited into the environment.

Conversion

In conversion operations the basic shapes are formed, clipped, cast, and otherwise fabricated into products. At this stage the scrap materials generated are often of the same composition as the original material. Often these scrap materials substitute directly for virgin materials. Because they do not require mining, cutting from the forest, or the rest of the steps that produce virgin material, many scrap materials generated in converting operations by and large take care of themselves.

Distribution

Distribution carries products from the manufacturing to the wholesale and retail levels. Value added here comes not from changes embodied in the material products themselves, but from transportation and marketing services. Still, there are some materials generated at this stage that have recycling potential. These materials tend to be obsolete intermediate products, not intended for consumption by consumers. For example, corrugated shipping containers are often collected by supermarkets and kept separate from the waste stream for recycling.

Commercial

Many commercial establishments consume material products in producing services for the final consumers. In this way a bank may generate a large and steady volume of IBM punch cards in the production of banking services. Such "waste" materials are sometimes reprocessed instead of thrown away.

Personal Consumption

One may think of consumption as the final act in turning virgin material into waste material. However, in terms of material flows for many products, more waste material is generated in producing a consumer good than is embodied in the final product. The final consumption product may be compared to a small tail on a large dog—in this case the virgin material. Most postconsumer material is thrown away; some finds its way into secondhand markets; and some is recycled as old scrap. The term "old" or "obsolete" distinguishes this material from scrap material generated in industrial or commercial enterprises. The latter form of scrap, especially when it is generated in quantity and in homogeneous quality, and when it has not had a long service life, is called prompt scrap.

Residuals, Waste, and Scrap

There is a confusing variety of terms describing materials at their various stages of use and disuse. At one level the situation is simple. In figure 3, material resources flow into a production process and material

Figure 3. Simple view of material flows in a production activity

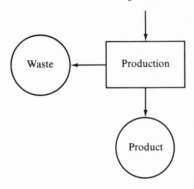

products and wastes flow out. The difference between the two is that products can be sold at positive prices while the waste flows cannot. But to provide definitions useful for our purposes, it is necessary to disaggregate figure 3 into figure 4.

The purpose of a production activity, as seen by the engineers who design it, is to produce one or a few main products, as noted by the heavy arrow. Incidental to this purpose, cuttings, trimmings, and many other nonproduct outputs are generated (the circle labeled "nonproduct output" in figure 4).[2] Some nonproduct outputs, such as the trimmings generated in the rolling of aluminum sheet, are valuable. If such materials disappeared from existence, the profits of the activity would go down. If the material is similar in composition to the virgin material stock, it is reprocessed as home scrap in the original production activity (direct recycling) or sold as prompt scrap to other firms (indirect recycling). Or it is further processed and sold as by-products.

Other nonproduct outputs, such as sulfur dioxide, are valueless from the point of view of the production manager; worse than that, they are typically costly to dispose of. If these materials disappeared from existence, the profit of the activity would go up, for disposal costs could be saved. These latter materials are labeled "residuals" or "waste." For these materials, the cost of recovery is more than the value of the recovered material. One can distinguish residuals or waste from other forms of nonproduct output by a hypothetical word test: "If the production manager had a magic wand, he would wave them from existence." The traditional view toward such material is to figure out the least costly method of treating the waste and then disposing of it into the natural environment. However, the least costly method of disposal may not be immediate discharge into the environment; some form of material recovery may be cheaper. Moreover, material recovery and by-product production become more attractive with increasingly strict requirements for environmental control. Waste generated is not the same as waste discharged into the environment.[3]

Figure 4. Material flows in a "typical" production activity

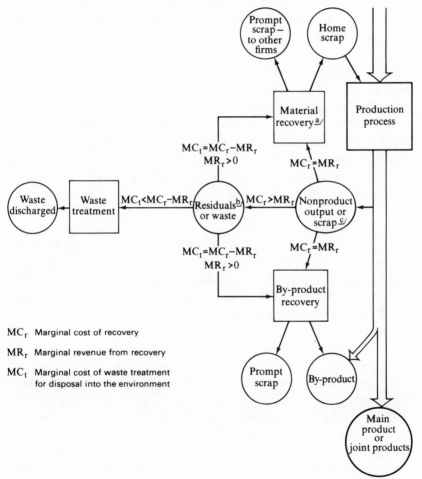

MC_r Marginal cost of recovery

MR_r Marginal revenue from recovery

MC_t Marginal cost of waste treatment
        for disposal into the environment

[a]/ Recovery may refer to any of four activities: material recovery from nonproduct output, material recovery from residuals, by-product recovery from nonproduct output, or by-product recovery from residuals. The marginal costs of one may be different from the marginal costs of another, and the same goes for revenues.

[b]/ "Residuals" can be used interchangeably with "waste materials" or waste.

[c]/ Sometimes "scrap" is used to refer to that part of nonproduct output with positive value; in this book the term is used interchangeably with "nonproduct output."

Cost Characteristics

Whether it is sooner or later and whether or not the material is to be recycled, processed into a by-product, or thrown back into the natural environment depend upon its existing form and physical location.

In *Recycling: The Alternative to Disposal,* Thomas Quimby identifies four physical and locational characteristics that in large part determine the path taken by a residual.[4] The characteristics tend to vary with the stage at which the residual is generated and apply to the extractibility of virgin material as well. They are mass, dispersion of mass, contamination, and homogeneity.

1. Mass. A residual must be generated in sufficient quantity to be worth recovering. Just as it is not worth the effort to send a truck to pick up a single old newspaper, it is not worth mining even the richest ore if the deposit is too small.

2. Dispersion of mass. The mass or quantity of newspapers generated in an apartment building and deposited at one place is more recyclable than the same mass generated in a hundred separated houses, in the same way that one large deposit of ore is more extractible than the same quality ore and same quantity of desired metal scattered in several small deposits.

3. Contamination. A desired material mixed with some foreign material may be more or less contaminated, depending on the nature of the contaminant. Paper fiber in old newspapers is contaminated with ink, but this is not much of a problem because the ink can be easily washed away. On the other hand, old newspapers mixed with other household refuse pick up grease and dirt, rendering the fiber nearly unrecoverable as fiber. In the same way, two ores containing the same percentage of aluminum may be quite different in extractibility, depending on the other material in the ore. It is comparatively easy to extract aluminum from bauxite; it is more difficult to extract aluminum from certain clays.

4. Homogeneity. A residual which changes in form and quality from batch to batch is usually less easy to handle than one of constant and known quality. When the contaminants vary or the desired residual varies in grade, there must be special monitoring equipment and more flexible processing equipment. It is usually easier when the process can be fine tuned to a particular quality of material and particular form of contamination. In the same way, a homogeneous ore may be easier to handle than one that varies in its mineral properties.

Added to these cost characteristics are the usual considerations such as transportation cost to markets. The type of residual and its cost characteristics depend in large part on the type of economic activity in which the material is generated. Residuals from conversion operations tend to score well in the four characteristics and tend to be amenable to recycling, while postconsumer wastes tend to score poorly and are more difficult to reuse, particularly because of problems of contamination.

Location of Policy Interventions and Market Inefficiencies

The effect of a policy intervention or a market inefficiency depends upon its location in the economic system. One market inefficiency, the failure of the price system to include the costs of waste disposal, can be located at the lower boundary between the economy and the environment in figure 5. Economic theory suggests disposal charges to rectify this market inefficiency or externality. Such charges would form a little barrier where consumer wastes and manufacturing wastes are discharged from the economic system into the environment. Without a barrier at *CW* and *MW* representing disposal costs, the economic pond drains too quickly of its materials, according to the efficiency criterion. The material flow through the economy from *VM* to *CW* and *MW* (throughput) is too swift, leaving the back eddies of recycling (*OS, PS,* and *HS*) too weak, and drawing in too fast a flow of virgin material, again according to the efficiency criterion. In the process, material becomes too cheap and durability too short. What happens to material embodiment is less clear, because the cheapening of materials and ease of disposal work in opposite directions.

A second inefficiency, the subsidy of virgin materials, can be located at the top boundary between the economy and the environment. Overstimulating the flow of virgin material, according to the efficiency criterion, a subsidy on *VM* compounds the problem of material throughput, further speeding the flow of material through the economy, retarding recycling (which is less able to compete with virgin material), and decreasing durability.

Market inefficiencies involving monopoly power and other departures from marginal cost pricing can be located inside the economic sector. As we shall see later, the direction of these effects is less clear. One policy intervention, the severance tax, can be located at the top of the bound-

Figure 5. Factors determining virgin material intensity

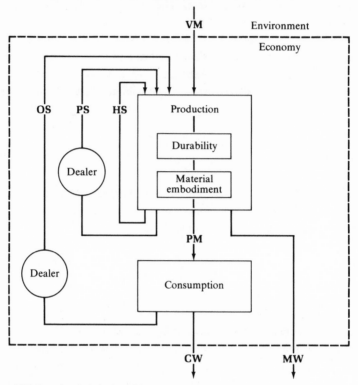

VM Quantity of virgin material
CW Quantity of consumer waste discharged to environment
MW Quantity of manufacturing waste discharged to environment
HS Quantity of home scrap
PS Quantity of prompt scrap
OS Quantity of old scrap
PM Quantity of material in final product

ary, retarding the flow of virgin material into the economy. This intervention would tend to increase the rate of recycling, increase durability, decrease the material embodiment per unit per product service, and decrease waste generation, thus decreasing the virgin material intensity through all four factors. A second policy intervention, often discussed, would be a direct subsidy to purchasers of scrap materials. This would encourage material "flywheeling" around the economy, diverting some of the wastes otherwise destined for the environment, but perhaps leading to lower durability and increased material embodiment. Another direct subsidy to scrap material is the donation of voluntary effort promoting recycling. Because it has involved enormous public participation in recent years, we shall consider this example of specific intervention in some detail.

Failure of Volunteerism. The most obvious thing to observe is that by donating time and effort to collect and recycle newspapers, bottles, and so forth, this effort singles out one of the four factors determining virgin material intensity, thereby leading to an inefficient balance among the four. Besides this imbalance, the interaction of market supply and demand often frustrates voluntary efforts to increase the flow of old scrap. Consider the case of old newspapers where it appears that supply, through the hands of dealers, is more responsive to its price (price elastic) than demand, which jumps around according to economic conditions other than its own price. (See appendix B for the definition of elasticity and its geometry.) The supply and demand for old newspapers are shown in figure 6. Assume that the market has equilibrated with a price of old newspapers of p_1 and quantity flow of q_1 per unit time. A volunteer group, thinking that q_1 is too small a flow of recycled newspaper, organizes itself to collect and sell to dealers q_2 quantity of old newspapers, no matter what the market price is (figure 7). This new source of supply is added onto the original source to form an aggregate supply schedule SS' in figure 8. The total amount of recycling does increase slightly from q_1 to q_3; but the new contribution from the volunteer effort q_2 is almost completely offset by a decline in the traditional source of supply from q_1 to q_4. The reason is that the new source of supply, the volunteer effort, has softened the scrap price from p_1 to p_2, and this price fall has discouraged the traditional source of supply.

This is one important reason why we cannot expect volunteer efforts, by themselves, to increase recycling very much. It is also a reason that

Figure 6. Supply and demand for old newspapers

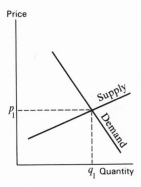

Figure 7. Volunteer supply—insensitive to price

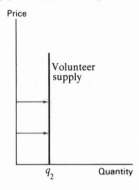

secondary industries look upon voluntary efforts with great ambivalence. They tend to see voluntary efforts as displacing their own.[5] There are two other reasons for not relying on volunteer efforts as the social policy to promote recycling. First, it is inequitable; the small numbers who respond to appeals "in the public interest" in effect subsidize the many who do not. And second, it is ineffective; the number who respond is too small to make even a small dent in the total solid waste stream.

Already many of the recycling centers that sprang up in response to Earth Day are withering away as volunteers realize these facts. At their peak, there were perhaps 3,000 recycling centers in the country, of which about 2,000 were voluntary citizen efforts. By the summer of 1974 there were about 1,500 centers run by volunteers. However, in the past several years many volunteer efforts have been taken over by local governments.[6] Some centers may survive as they become more like

Figure 8. Aggregate supply and demand schedule

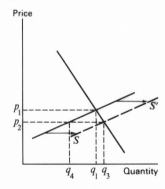

ordinary businesses with paid staff. And so will certain of the centers subsidized by some industries, established for the admitted purpose of heading off "ban-the-can" legislation, until the issue of mandatory deposits is decided one way or another. In wartime, patriotism can be, and has been, a sufficient motive to make voluntary recycling work. But at present, volunteer effort is not the answer to recycling. Voluntary efforts to change the structure of incentives—for example, the tax structure—are likely to be more effective. It is one thing to adjust an intake valve to a reservoir, quite another to attempt to empty the reservoir by hand.

Disownership

The dashed line in figure 5 separates the economic sector from the environmental sector. Although it is something of a simplification, it is useful to imagine that as materials cross the upper part of this boundary, they are appropriated from the environment and fall into private ownership. It is at this boundary that we ask what is the proper amount of conservation, what are the obligations of mining companies to reclaim stripped land, and how do we decide between retaining land as a wilderness area or the preemptive alternative of timber and mineral extractions?

At the bottom of the figure, waste materials are disowned and flow back into the environment. At this boundary solid waste takes on the fundamental characteristics of a pollution problem. Costs are transferred from those who benefit by ridding themselves of unwanted material to those who happen to be in the way or who otherwise bear the burdens. The trend from returnable to nonreturnable bottles is a well-known example of a shift of costs from those who benefit (the beverage consumers and manufacturers) to the public at large. Similarly, "convenience packaging" is convenient to the individual consumer who transfers the cost of disposal to the public agency that picks up litter or collects a larger volume of municipal solid waste. The most obvious recipients of burden are the local taxpayers who pay for collection and disposal of solid waste. The public is also burdened by the remnants of the solid waste and litter after disposal, although these costs do not show up as tax payments.

When a waste is generated, its price, from the point of view of the owner, dips to zero or below. In this case, the owner would have the material removed at zero cost, if that were possible. The next easiest course is to leak the unwanted material into the environment in order to minimize management costs. Such disowning happens all the time. Consumer litter varies from candy wrappers to automobiles; producers disown material by means of smokestacks and discharge pipes; in the agricultural sector, pesticides and fertilizers are disowned through runoff and other entropic processes; and in the mining sector enormous quantities of material are disowned by smokestacks and acid mine drainage. A basic rule of thumb is: whenever in a long chain of material flows price dips to zero, the material is subject to a push into the environment.

It is often recommended that laws, fines, and charges control this process of disowning material into the environment. As ways of adjusting the structure of incentives, such controls have the effect of enforcing negative prices on the dumping of material into the environment, and hence are barriers to dumping. There are two important difficulties associated with this effort. First, there is no market to set and collect the charges; nor are there easily workable ways to administer anti-dumping laws. Second, negative prices carry with them the incentive for evasion; with negative prices there is an incentive to dump surreptitiously.

Inside the dashed line boundary in figure 5 the situation is quite different. Economic materials are valuable and command positive prices. And with positive prices there is no incentive to disown a material; each owner clings to his material because he knows he can get a positive price for it. Ownership is maintained throughout a chain of flows.[7]

As we have seen, materials flow through many paths on their way to becoming environmental wastes. How useful materials become in their embodiment as final products, how long they last, and how often they are recycled before discharge into the environment depend upon their cost characteristics and locations, as well as on consumer preferences or consumer demand. We have focused on the flow paths of virgin and scrap materials partly because these flows are observable. We have suggested the possibility that factors other than recycling—durability, embodiment, and waste generation in the production process—may take care of themselves when scrap and virgin materials are brought into efficient balance, if the policy interventions are suitably located and combined. Next, we consider the balance between virgin and scrap materials, but this time from the perspective of primary and secondary material industries, their structure and interaction.

Notes

1. Blair Bower, "Studies of Residuals Management in Industry," E. C. Mills, ed., *Economic Analysis of Environmental Problems* (New York, National Bureau of Economic Reseach, 1975).

2. The definitions follow those by Blair Bower in "Studies of Residuals Management in Industry"; see also Blair Bower and Daniel Basta, *Residuals–Environmental Quality Management: Applying the Concept* (Baltimore, Md., Johns Hopkins University Center for Metropolitan Planning and Research, October 1973) p. 2; and Allen Kneese and Blair Bower, "Residuals–Environmental Quality Management—Economic, Technological, Ecological, Institutional Aspects of Residuals Management: Report on a Research Program" proposed Resources for the Future publication, chapter 1.

3. For the materials with positive prices in the "nonproduct output" circle in figure 4, recovery by either path takes place until the marginal cost of recovery equals the marginal revenue of recovery. Materials for which the marginal cost of recovery exceeds the marginal revenue have negative prices and move to the circle labeled "waste generated." From here, if the marginal cost of recovery minus the marginal revenue from recovery is less than the marginal cost of waste treatment and discharge into the environment, then there still is an incentive to recover the material. Otherwise the material takes the third exit, discharge into the environment.

4. Thomas Quimby, *Recycling: The Alternative to Disposal* (Baltimore, Md., Johns Hopkins University Press for Resources for the Future, 1975). There is an earlier version of this list of characteristics in a statement by Blair Bower in *Hearings before the Subcommittee on Fiscal Policy of the Joint Economic Committee*, 92 Cong. 1 sess. (Nov. 8-9, 1971) pp. 118–133.

5. "In the absence of expanded markets—if steel mills and foundries cannot be encouraged to use more scrap—there is every reason to believe that the metallics coming from public recycling centers would replace material now coming from scrap processing plants." Frederick Berman, president of the Institute of Scrap Iron and Steel, Inc., in the *American Metal Market* (May 3, 1972) p. 9.

6. Interview with Pat Taylor, Environmental Action, fall 1974.

7. These observations suggest another basis or rationale for severance taxes. Negative prices are not self-administering; they encourage leaks into the environment. A second-best solution to this problem may be to shift the entire price system for materials upward; a kind of affine transformation. The proper amount of the shift occurs when the gain by having less negative prices equals the loss from distortions in price ratios.

3

Competition Between Primary and Secondary Industries

> —*Rep. Yates: There is no question that the fabricating part of your business is the part that makes money.*
>
> —*Richard Reynolds: And it takes less investment.*

THE VERY ACT of regarding the interaction of virgin and scrap material flows from the perspective of industry structure and competition raises basic questions about pricing. Do virgin material industries use their potential monopolistic power to act as conservationists, restricting output as they raise prices? Or do virgin material firms behave like managerial capitalists, reaching out for the growth of "their material" through low prices? As we shall see, it is difficult to observe the actual prices of materials let alone understand the underlying pricing behavior. While much remains uncertain about industry behavior, it is possible, nonetheless, to make explicit some of the economic conditions underlying the competition of scrap and virgin material. Analyzed in terms of perfect and imperfect substitutes, case studies by Sawyer and by Russell and Vaughan suggest that long-run impacts from changes in cost or policy interventions can be large.

The purpose of this introductory look at the complicated pattern of material industries' interaction and competition is to set the stage for later discussion of market inefficiencies, or market failures, and policy interventions. We shall not treat in detail all, or even any, of the material industries, although we do include a brief illustration of the primary and secondary aluminum industries as being in some ways typical of other material industry pairs.

Primary and Secondary Industries

Firms extracting and processing virgin materials are primary firms or primary producers; collectively they make up the primary industry for each material. Firms processing scrap materials are secondary firms, and, along with dealers who collect and trade these materials, they make up the secondary industry for each material.

In the past, primary producers tended to be located near forests and mineral deposits, away from population concentrations, while secondary producers tended to be located near population centers, their source of supply. But now primary producers are using more prompt and old scrap so that the distinction between primary and secondary industries is becoming blurred. Nevertheless, the distinction is still useful. The output of the secondary industry is comparable to the product of the primary industry at the level of basic shapes—ingots, rods, bars, sheets, jumbo rolls, and so forth—and the two industries are in direct competition. While both primary and secondary industries produce the same basic shapes, they are not symmetrical in structure. While primary firms are moving more into the traditional sources of supply of secondary firms, secondary firms are not moving into virgin material sources of supply.

Most primary industries are dominated by a few large corporations that are often vertically integrated. Alcoa, for example, owns its own bauxite mines and produces some of its own electricity, refines its own ore, extracts aluminum from it, mills its aluminum, and even fabricates its own pots and pans. Secondary industries tend to be considerably smaller than their primary counterparts, so that a few primary firms dominate the combined primary and secondary market for a given material. In addition, because the actions of each of a small number of primary firms have an effect on the market price of a material, primary firms have pricing policies.

In many cases the secondary industry, in terms of sales volume, is considerably smaller than the primary industry. Moreover, for many materials, the secondary industry is composed of small firms,[1] and most secondary producers are smaller and weaker financially than their primary competitors. Many secondary firms began as family businesses, and some remain so. Typically, secondary firms are too small, compared with the combined primary and secondary industry, to influence the market price, and hence they act as price takers, without pricing policies. In the secondary industry, the dealers buy, separate, and accumulate scrap materials and then sell them to secondary processors. Secondary dealers often act like commodity traders, which in fact they are. Inventories build and shrink on a large scale in passive response to prices, which tend to be more volatile than prices in the primary industry. Most secondary industries tend to be labor-intensive while primary industries tend to be capital-intensive. In the past, as labor has become more expensive compared with the cost of capital, secondary industries have increasingly suffered in competition with primary industries; however, at present the situation appears to be changing somewhat as secondary industries become more capital- and less labor-intensive. In the past, primary industries, which tend to be energy-intensive as well as capital-intensive, have benefited from low-cost energy and a pricing structure incorporating volume discounts. This situation too is changing as we move into an era of higher cost energy.

There are frequent misunderstandings about the nature of the interactions of primary and secondary industries. Sometimes it is argued that because the ups and downs of scrap market prices are large compared with the average cost of processing scrap, a small change in some factor—such as the depletion allowance for virgin material or in relative freight rates—would make little or no difference in the amount of old scrap processed.[2] While the variance in scrap prices is large, it is the mean or average price that mainly determines material flows over "long" periods; in the case of secondary industries this is only a few years. We shall take a look at some of the reasons for this large variance, which leads to inventory holding and commodity speculation on the part of secondary firms. It is a mistake to confuse the variance in price with a change in the price mean. The variance in price has important effects, but they are different from those of a change in the price mean.

Because the cost of basic materials is a small fraction of most product prices, it might appear that a small change in a material price will not make a noticeable difference in the market for scrap and virgin materials. For example, in 1971 the stumpage value[3] of Louisiana Southern Pine was about $6 per ton; a jumbo roll of paper sold for about $255 a ton, so that a change in the tax status of virgin timber might have affected the paper product price by less than 1 percent.[4] But it is erroneous to conclude from this observation that a change in the price of virgin material that leads to a much smaller change in the product price will have little or no long-run effect on the secondary market for old newspapers. The effect of the price of one material on a competing substitute is largely determined by the substitutability of the materials, and the smallness of effect on product price can be quite misleading.[5]

The Question of Pricing

In economic theory, a monopolist restricts output in order to raise prices and profits. According to this theory, a monopolist in an extractive industry would maintain higher prices for virgin materials than would otherwise occur in a competitive situation and would thus act as a conservationist, slowing down the depletion of virgin materials and aiding the secondary industries with the umbrella of his higher prices. However, in the extractive industries, the situation is not one of pure monopoly, but oligopoly. The market is shared by a few or several large firms. A single oligopolistic firm has the ability to affect market prices by its output and pricing policies, but it knows that it will in turn be affected by the actions of rival firms. If one firm in an oligopoly raises prices and the others do not go along, its market may dry up. If its price increase does not hold, or "stick," it may have to back down from its costly mistake. If one firm lowers prices, it may increase its market share, unless all the other firms follow suit, leaving the relative market shares the same but the industry worse off. Or, one firm's price cutting could lead to further price cutting by other firms, resulting in a price war—a disastrous event from the industry viewpoint. In short, what is best for one firm in an oligopoly depends on the strategic behavior of the other firms. The situation is difficult to analyze and perhaps little can be said in general since actual behavior may be determined in large part by particular institutional features of the oligopolistic industries and the attitudes of the managers of the firms. It is generally agreed, though, that oligopolistic firms are cautious about changes in price, up or down. In time of general inflation, this may mean that prices in the extractive industries are chronically low, compared with prices that might be expected under monopoly power.

In a particularly simple theory of oligopoly pricing for the aluminum industry,[6] the firm with the lowest price preference sets the price. Other firms, wishing for higher prices, must match the low price preferrer, but they have no incentive to go below that price. The low price preferrer can increase his price, knowing that the higher price preferrers will follow, moving in the direction of their own desired prices, and the lowest price preferrer can hold prices constant or even cut them, knowing that the other firms must follow.

An Illustration: The Case of Aluminum. Until World War II, aluminum was a textbook example of a monopolized industry. But after the war, Judge Learned Hand ordered that aluminum reduction plants which had been built by the government during the war and operated by Alcoa be divested and formed into new aluminum firms. In this way Kaiser and Reynolds were formed. Later a few other primary aluminum firms, including some foreign ones, entered the American market for primary aluminum.

Most of these firms were, and are, integrated from the mining to the fabrication stage. Bauxite mining and aluminum processing require a large amount of capital and great size to realize economies of scale, and this large capital requirement constitutes a severe entry barrier for firms that might wish to join the primary aluminum industry. However, an assured supply is a strong incentive to vertical integration backward, toward the source of supply. Other extractive industries also tend toward vertical integration, probably for much the same reasons as the aluminum industry.[7]

Flows for the primary and secondary aluminum industries are sketched in figure 9. The primary industry can process its material all the way to finished products or, with less processing, sell sheets and ingots to independent fabricators and foundries. The primaries' most important product lines are to their own fabricators. Casting is traditionally a secondary market, for reasons we shall see in a moment; conversely, fabricators using extrusion processes are mainly the province of primaries; but both industries compete to some degree in both markets.[8] In the process of milling and fabricating, large amounts of new scrap are generated.

Most of the feedstock for the secondary aluminum industry comes from new scrap, but there are large amounts of old scrap as well. Because of the problem of undesirable alloy ingredients, most of the secondary metal is formed into high-silicon alloys and sold into the casting industry. The casting process, using molten aluminum, is more tolerant to undesired trace alloy ingredients than the milling process, which squeezes metal between rollers. Virtually none of the secondary output goes to rolling mills. Extrusion processes stand midway between casting and milling in this acceptability of secondary alloy metal, and some of the secondary metal goes to the independent fabricators for

Figure 9. Material flows in the primary and secondary aluminum industries

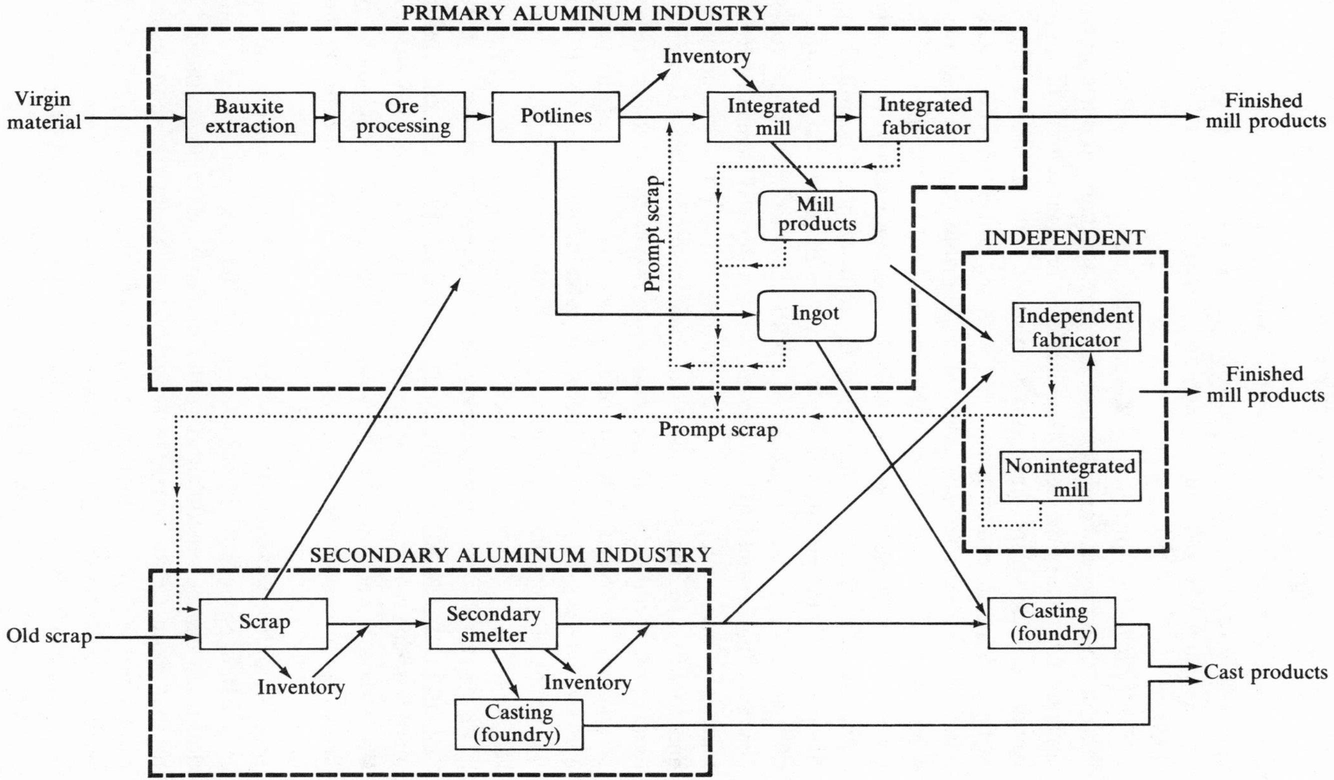

extrusion. But about 80 percent of the output of the secondary industry goes to the foundries for casting, with the rest going to the independents for extrusion and other uses, such as an oxidizing agent for steel production.

To follow the primary and secondary industry interaction, first imagine that the demand for castings and for mill products has been constant for some time and the ultimate or original sources of supply—bauxite and old scrap—have also been stable, with all the material flows in figure 9 in an equilibrium, along with the prices associated with the flows. From this reference point of equilibrium, imagine that there is some shift in demand: for example the demand for mill products picks up, perhaps because of an upturn in the housing industry. In a textbook competitive market there are two main adjustments. One would expect the price of mill products to be bid up, an increase that would choke off part of the demand increase. With the increased price for mill products there would be an increase in the derived demand for virgin material. One would expect to see the price of bauxite bid up as well, and to see a second adjustment, an increase in the flow of virgin material. One would expect to see these same two adjustments, in price and in quantity, mirrored in the secondary industry. In fact, if the primary and secondary products were perfectly substitutable, one would expect the prices of secondary and primary products to move in step, equal all the way.

In the actual aluminum market there are complications. A potline that reduces the virgin aluminum material, alumina, into primary aluminum ingot is built to run at full capacity, twenty-four hours a day seven days a week. It is an expensive piece of capital equipment, with large capital costs to be borne when it is not run at full capacity. Once down, it is expensive to restart. Thus, flexibility in production in the primary industry comes at a high cost.[9] A secondary smelter, however, is a batch process. It is not designed to be run continuously and its downtime can be scheduled more flexibly. Simple economic theory tells us that more capital-intensive activities tend to be run more continuously, and it appears to be a pattern that the more capital-intensive primary firms tend to use three shifts a day for their basic processing activities while secondary firms use one, two, or three depending on short-run economic fluctuations.

In figure 10, monthly production of primary and secondary aluminum firms are plotted. As can be seen, relative to their average production volumes, secondary production fluctuates month to month considerably

Figure 10. Aluminum ingot production, January 1967–March 1973

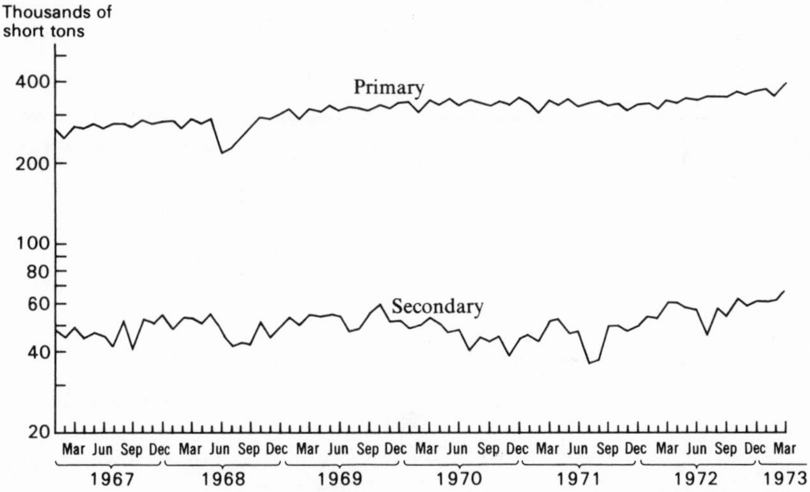

more than primary production. Thus far reality conforms to simple economic theory, at least for the six-year period from which this interval was excerpted.

As for the first adjustment, the price adjustment, it is often stated that primary firms try to ride out fluctuations in demand with stable prices. One such statement and rationale for it goes back to I. W. Wilson's testimony in the Monopoly Power Hearings: "We attempt to hold that price [of primary aluminum] as steady as we can because we believe that will insure the maximum development of the aluminum industry."[10] It is also often stated that the month-to-month price fluctuations of secondary aluminum ingot are considerably greater than those for primary ingot. Unfortunately there is no way to check out the proposition that secondary prices are more volatile than primary prices by looking at published or list prices. In figure 11 we see published prices for primary and secondary ingot. These prices show remarkably little month-to-month fluctuation. It is generally agreed, however, that these prices are not the ones at which transactions take place. From the list prices there are discounts and premiums that are more or less secret.[11] For many materials, the lack of trustworthy published price data greatly increases the difficulty of understanding the interactions between primary and secondary industries.

Nonetheless, from time to time estimates of actual transactions prices are obtainable. Figure 11 also includes estimates of actual prices of

Figure 11. Listed and estimated actual prices for primary and secondary aluminum, 1970–1971

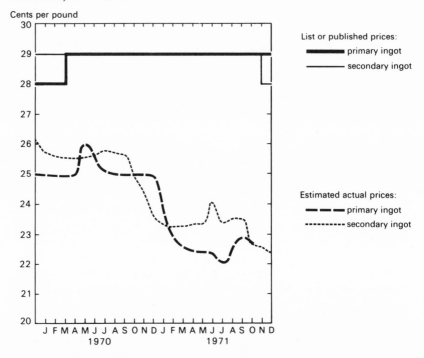

Cents per pound

List or published prices:
━━━━ primary ingot
──── secondary ingot

Estimated actual prices:
▬ ▬ ▬ primary ingot
·········· secondary ingot

J F M A M J J A S O N D J F M A M J J A S O N D
1970   1971

primary and secondary ingots. It can be seen that the plots do not, for the period for which they were obtainable, support the idea that secondary prices are more volatile than primary prices at the ingot level. Without further comparative price data, we are left with the common wisdom that secondary prices fluctuate more than primary ones. The matter is not resolved by figure 11, although this glimpse at transactions prices does not confirm the common wisdom. Figure 11 does show, however, the danger of relying on published or list prices.

One reason for the difficulty in obtaining primary ingot prices is that much of this metal is not sold but is further processed inside the integrated primary firms. The same problem in obtaining price information occurs for bauxite: Although list prices exist for bauxite for tax purposes, very little bauxite is sold on the open market. Presumably an imputed price of bauxite would be less volatile than the price of scrap.

Besides price and production there is a third factor of adjustment, inventory change. Primary firms maintain large inventories often of six months to a year's production which they deplete when demand increases and which they add to when demand falls. In this way primary firms can react to shifts in demand, while maintaining production and prices stable.

It appears that, in response to changes in demand, primary firms specialize more in inventory changes, while secondary firms use all three forms of adjustment; further, primary firms adjust inventories in a countercyclical way to dampen price changes, while secondary firms act more as commodity speculators in their short-term reactions to price and demand changes.

As to pricing policy, spokesmen for firms in the primary industry have stressed their desire for low aluminum prices. Although a skeptic might feel that such statements are made for their reassuring sound, we shall see in a moment that one school of economic thought finds plausibility in the position. In the Monopoly Power Hearings, I. W. Wilson offered the classic reason why a primary industry might want to use its market power to promote low rather than high prices: "the whole objective of Alcoa over the whole period of years has been to keep the price trend down, so as to broaden the market [in its competition against copper, steel, and, later, plastics]."[12] Such a pricing policy would tend to make it harder for secondary firms to compete against primary ones.[13]

According to one strand of economic thought, large firms, and not just extractive ones, are not short-term profit maximizers, or even the maximizers of the present value of profits.[14] These firms are controlled by managers and not by the owners of capital. The managers seek goals that benefit themselves: stability of the firm and the industry, predictable growth, high salaries, and so forth. Instead of maximizing the present worth to shareholders, it is in the interest of the managers to provide sufficient return to the shareholders to keep them quiescent—to keep them from dumping their stock or trying to take over the firm—and no more. Instead of restricting output and raising prices, the policy of these managers is more likely to penetrate the market with "reasonable" prices and to control it.

In an elaboration of the managerial theory of the large firm, the economy is divided into a "planning" sector, composed of large corporations in oligopolistic markets, and a "market" sector, composed of many small competitive firms.[15] For much of the economy the planning sectors are somewhat isolated from the market sectors, for example, the automobile industry on one side and the food franchise industry on the other. But for most materials the two sectors are directly juxtaposed, with a secondary firm in the marketing sector competing against a primary firm in the planning sector, both for the same material.

How well this managerial theory of the firm applies to materials industries is not clear. It will be hard to establish or refute this theory without better price data and a firmer empirical base.[16] But even from this limited discussion it appears too simple to conclude that primary firms will exercise whatever monopoly power they may have to raise prices, slow the flow of virgin material, and in doing so shelter secondary firms.

Modeling the Material Flows

The preceding sections indicate some of the complexity and unanswered issues associated with the competition of primary and secondary industries. Some of the interaction, nonetheless, can be described in terms of simple models of supply and demand. The purpose of this section is to show how the economic "parts" fit together while at the same time illustrating some definitions that will be useful later in the book.

Perfect Substitutes

After reprocessing, not many scrap materials are interchangeable with their virgin material competitors. However, the case of perfect substitutes, in which the processed scrap material is interchangeable with a raw material competitor, is the simplest case, and we begin with that.

For perfect substitutes, small changes in relative costs can bring about enormous changes in the balance between scrap and virgin material flows. In the case of perfect substitutes, the prices of the two materials tend to be equalized in the market, and, in a perfect market, they must be equalized. A small increase in the price of the virgin material caused, for example, by a decrease in the percentage depletion allowance, would lead to a substitution of scrap for virgin material limited only by the eventually rising cost of supplying additional amounts of scrap material. More and more scrap would be brought into the market until the cost of finding new sources of scrap was driven up sufficiently to restore the equality between scrap and virgin prices. The relationship between the rising cost of additional supplies of scrap brought into the market and the total amount of scrap marketed is conceptualized by the *supply curve,* which by definition specifies the amount of scrap brought into the market for a given market price. For a given price, additional scrap is brought into the market until the cost of the farthest away and worst grade equals the market price.

When scrap material and virgin material are perfect substitutes, the supply curves can be drawn on the same diagram. For example, panel A in figure 12 incorporates some of the typical conditions in the scrap and virgin materials markets. For typical market prices the amount of scrap supplied is small compared with the amount of virgin material. About 4 percent of the total supply of aluminum is from old scrap and about 80 percent from virgin material (the rest comes from new scrap, which we neglect here). About 20 percent of the total supply of copper is from old

Figure 12. Perfect substitutes

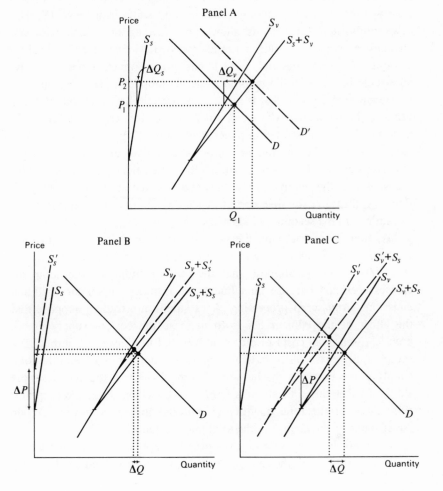

scrap. Panel A pictures the two ultimate or original sources of supply, virgin material and old scrap. New scrap, which is roughly a fixed fraction of new production "flywheeling" around in the system, is omitted.[17] The total supply of material (new scrap) is derived by adding horizontally the supply of old scrap (S_s) to the supply of virgin material (S_v). The market is quite literally "thin" in old scrap $(S_s$ is a thin wedge next to the y-axis compared with $S_v)$, and the total old scrap makes little difference in the total supply schedule $(S_s + S_v)$. Since the two materials are perfect substitutes, users do not care from which source they draw their supply, and the market equilibrium is shown at the intersection of the total supply curve and the (total) demand curve (D). In this case the equilibrium quantity cleared in the market is Q_1 at price P_1. Now suppose that the demand for material increases, perhaps because of a general upturn in the economy, and demand shifts from D to D'. The new equilibrium price P_2 is shown in the diagram, along with the changes in scrap and virgin material traded. It is true that the absolute amount of virgin material (ΔQ_v) has grown much more than the minuscule increase in the amount of scrap supplies (ΔQ_s), but in relative terms the scrap market is more volatile than the virgin material one because the percentage change is much greater for scrap than for virgin material. This is illustrated in panel A of figure 12 by drawing the scrap supply curve to be substantially more elastic than the curve for virgin material supply.[18] For a small firm in either the primary or the secondary industry, it is the relative, percentage changes that are most meaningful. Panel A illustrates the first step in explaining the old saw that it is "feast or famine" in the secondary industries.

In panel B we start with the same original supply and demand relationships $(S_s, S_v$ and $D)$ and suppose that the change occurs in the secondary industry. Suppose that the cost of supplying old scrap increases, perhaps because an effluent tax is placed upon air pollution emissions from scrap processing. As a simple illustration, suppose that the effect of the effluent tax is to increase the cost of supply (more precisely, marginal cost) of old scrap by ΔP, for all levels of output. The scrap supply curve shifts vertically up by amount ΔP to S_s', and the total supply curve becomes the horizontal sum of the two sources of supply $S_s' + S_v$. But this time there is hardly an effect on the market equilibrium price or the total quantity of material traded. Minuscule ΔQ in panel B shows the change in the total market quantity.

Alternatively, suppose that the cost of supplying virgin material increases. Starting with the same original supply curves S_s and S_v for scrap and virgin material in panel C, suppose that the effluent tax falls on the primary industry instead of the secondary. Supposing that the effect of the tax increases the cost of production by the same amount as previously, the supply curve of virgin material shifts upward by the same amount ΔP, implying a new total supply curve $S_v' + S_s$. This time the equilibrium price is significantly affected, with the change in total quantity illustrated by ΔQ in panel C. In the first case the primary industry hardly noticed the misfortune of the secondary because the market price is almost unaffected. But in the second case the secondary industry benefits from the general market price rise resulting from the tax on the primary industry, and trades a larger quantity. Thus we can illustrate by panels B and C the truism that "everything is determined by the primary industry and nothing by the secondary."

At this simple level of analysis just three parameters summarize the workings of the scrap–virgin material market for changes at a given price level: the elasticities of supply for scrap and for virgin material and the elasticity of demand. Surprisingly little is known about any of these three parameters. In the very long run the supply curve depends, of course, upon cumulative extraction. Knowledge about the very long-run supply schedule for virgin material would be equivalent to knowing the effects of depletion on the prices of virgin materials, and this depends upon forecasting new discoveries and new technologies. Economists seem to have given up the very long-run supply curve as imponderable; but further, there have been few estimates of shorter run elasticities of supply of virgin materials. In the short run (one or a few months), the supply of virgin material is generally considered inelastic. Opening new mining sites and installing new capital for processing usually takes two to five years. In the middle-run period the supply of virgin material is usually considered much more elastic.

There are perhaps even fewer estimates of the supply curve for old scrap, and these do not inspire confidence. Sawyer cites estimates for one grade of steel scrap that range over three orders of magnitude.[19] One method of estimation is econometric techniques, using statistical analyses on historical data of prices and quantities. Without commenting on particular analyses, it can be said in general that it is difficult to tailor econometric analysis to scrap markets because of several special features of these markets: (1) the poor quality of price and quantity data for scrap and virgin markets; (2) the dynamic short-run nature of the supply for scrap; (3) the role of changing technology, which is very important for some secondary industries and which is difficult to take into account econometrically; and (4) important nonlinearities (which are also hard to model econometrically) in the supply of scrap.

An alternative to econometric analysis is to model the secondary industry from an engineering point of view. This approach takes into account specific technologies. Using this approach, Sawyer found that a change in technology, the introduction of the shredder, was the most important factor influencing automobile scrap flows.[20] Sawyer also found that the short-run supply of scrap depended upon the history of prices. If prices had been high in the past, the region would be picked clean, so that supply depended entirely on new deregistrations inside the radius of collection. In this case the short-run supply curve might look like *A* in figure 13. The supply becomes inelastic for high prices as the supply is limited by the number of deregistrations, which become fewer as the radius of collection grows (and as shredder territory begins to overlap).

With a history of low prices, hulks accumulate, even within the calculated radius of collection, because collection costs are not homogeneous.

Figure 13. Elasticities of supply

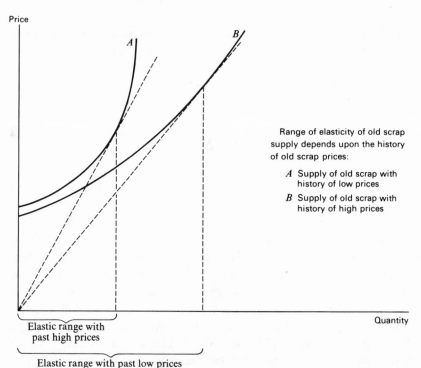

Price

Range of elasticity of old scrap supply depends upon the history of old scrap prices:

A Supply of old scrap with history of low prices

B Supply of old scrap with history of high prices

Quantity

Elastic range with past high prices

Elastic range with past low prices

In this case the supply is elastic over a longer range (*B* in figure 13). This has been the normal case until recently. Part of the supply is met out of inventory, which is stored partly in junkyards of dealers who act like commodity speculators awaiting higher prices, stored partly in back-yards of owners who do not want to pay to have their cars towed away, and "stored" as litter along the roadside. Changes in inventory as a result of price history and anticipations about future prices are one aspect of the dynamics of the scrap market.

Compared with econometric estimates, estimates based on engineering considerations tend to yield much higher values for elasticities. In the case of shredded steel scrap, after weighing engineering and economic factors, Sawyer estimated the short-run supply elasticity to be very elastic, in the range of ten.

Imperfect Substitutes

The effect of the price of one material on a competing substitute is determined in large part by the substitutability of the materials. The more perfectly virgin and scrap materials substitute for each other, the more important a small change in the relative prices of virgin and scrap materials will be in affecting the amount of recycling. This is true even though material costs are often only a small part of the total cost of a product. However, although products from new scrap are essentially perfect substitutes for products from virgin material, most products from old scrap materials are not perfect substitutes.

Contamination and homogeneity, mentioned in chapter 2, are major problems confronting secondary metals industries. Mixed in with the desired metal are traces of other metals (called tramps in the steel industry). Most of the reprocessing of scrap aluminum is done by melting and blending. Heavily contaminated old scrap is diluted with purer new scrap and sometimes brought to specification by the further dilution with virgin ingot. Depending on the mixes of scrap available for processing, batches of melt are made into various alloys. Some uses of aluminum, particularly casting, are more tolerant of undesirable traces than other uses, and the secondary industry specializes in such markets. Variability from one batch to the next, along with contamination, means that secondary industries need to analyze carefully their sources of material.[21] Contrary to their image of industrial backwardness, some secondary firms use highly sophisticated and modern techniques for monitoring their stock and assuring quality control.

Notwithstanding, some scrap materials have especially desirable properties. Scrap steel has melt properties that improve the performance of some furnaces. Scrap glass (cullet) also has superior melt properties. For these two cases, and others besides, scrap material has desirable properties of its own; however, even in these cases old scrap must still compete with new scrap.

When scrap and virgin materials are not perfect substitutes, demand for one material is separated from demand for the other, and it is no longer appropriate to add the two sources of supply as in figure 12. The situation for imperfect substitutes is illustrated in figure 14. The linkage between the two markets (the scrap market is still "thinner" than the virgin material one) depends on the degree of substitutability between the two materials. If there is little substitutability,[22] what happens in the virgin material market will have little effect on the scrap market. But if there is substitutability, a change in price in the virgin material market will affect the demand in the scrap market. In figure 14 the entire demand curve for scrap material is dependent on the price in the virgin material market. [The notation $D_s(P_v)$ means that the whole demand curve for scrap is a function of P_v, the price of virgin material.] Suppose that the demand for mill products, which is dominated by the primary aluminum industry, picks up, shifting the demand for virgin aluminum ingot upward from D_v to D_v', so that the equilibrium price in the virgin material market moves from P_v to P_v'. In consequence, the demand for scrap aluminum shifts from $D_s(P_v)$ to $D_s(P_v')$, and the equilibrium price in the scrap market moves from P_s to P_s'. As it is drawn, the price change in the scrap market is somewhat less than the price change in the primary market.

Figure 14. Imperfect substitutes and the cross-elasticity of demand

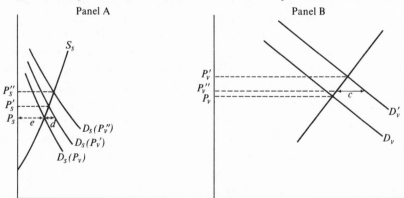

The question is how much the demand curve for scrap jumps in response to a change in price in the primary market. In actual markets, the jump in the demand curve for secondary material might be large in comparison with the price rise in the primary material. Suppose that individual primary aluminum companies do not passively let the price of primary ingot rise to its market clearing level P_v', but slow down deliveries and ration demand. The shortage, presumably a short-term one allowed for the purpose of leveling out fluctuations in price in the primary market, is shown as c in panel B of figure 14. In this case, demand spills over into the secondary market as a factor in pushing out the demand curve D_s, and in this case the price rise in the primary market $(P_v'' - P_v)$ is smaller than the price rise in the secondary market $(P_s'' - P_s)$. In order to write the secondary demand curve as a function of the price of the primary materials, we would have to know the pattern of rationing and price response on the primary side. In either case, with rationing or not, the parameter that describes the relationship of primary material price to secondary material demand is the *cross-elasticity of demand*. This parameter is defined to be the percent change in demand in one market resulting from a 1 percent change in price in another market, other prices being equal. In figure 14 if the change in demand in the primary market had led to a 1 percent change in the price of virgin material $(P_v' - P_v)/P_v = 0.01$, then d/e in panel A would measure the cross-elasticity of demand for scrap aluminum with respect to the price of primary aluminum. This is one more parameter about which very little is known. Presumably the cross-elasticity of demand is greater in the short run than in the long run because of the temporary nature of product rationing and inventory depletion in the primaries' response to increased demand. In the long run, the degree of substitutability determines the cross-elasticity of demand.

The same problems which encumber econometric estimation of supply curves plague econometric estimation of the cross-elasticity of demand; moreover, there seem to have been fewer attempts to estimate this parameter than the supply elasticities.[23] As in the estimation of supply elasticity, there is the alternative of simulating the market relationships from an engineering point of view in order to estimate the cross-elasticity of demand. Using linear programming techniques, Russell and Vaughan have simulated a large steel firm that has both an electric arc furnace and a basic oxygen furnace. These two furnaces will accept various mixes of scrap and iron ore charges, the most profitable depending in part on the prices of scrap and ore. For a given price of scrap corresponding to a horizontal S_s in panel A of figure 14, Russell and Vaughan varied the price of ore in order to generate the kind of information summarized in the cross-elasticity of demand.[24] (See figure 15.) To translate figure 15 into cross-elasticities of demand (there is a different one for each price of scrap), one would have to make assumptions about the size of the secondary market and perform the exercise for different scrap prices. One would have to go beyond simulating a hypothetical primary firm to make assumptions about the size of the entire scrap industry. The result in figure 15 is enough to show a remarkable sensitivity of the demand for scrap steel on the price of virgin ore. In the model, this sensitivity is not a short-run one but a "permanent" long-run effect.

Factors Affecting Supply and Demand

The demand for scrap and virgin materials is derived from the pattern of consumer preferences for products and passed back through manufacturers as demand for materials of different types and prices, as illustrated in the diagrams in this chapter. Of course, the pattern of

Figure 15. Estimated demand for scrap steel as a function of the price of ore

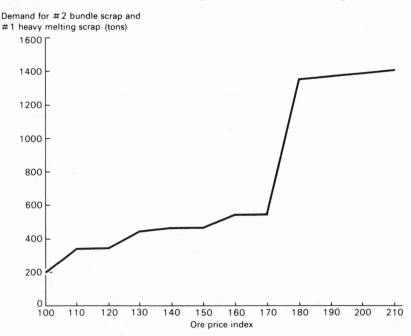

consumer preferences may not be an immovable first cause, but may in turn be influenced by advertising, marketing practices, and changes in "life style." Going further, we may find that changes in life style may be more responsive in the long run to changes in the price structure than to exhortations to change. For example, a tax on low-mileage cars may do more to change habits and conserve gasoline than direct appeals.

The factors determining supply are various types of costs. At the beginning of this discussion, we mentioned differences in capital, labor, and energy intensities of primary and secondary industries. As the prices of these factors of production change, the supply curves of scrap and virgin materials will be affected differently. In the same way, changes in technology will affect the supply curves of the two types of materials differently, as has happened in the case of iron and steel.

For example, the possible ups and downs in relative value of scrap and virgin material are well illustrated in recent iron and steel developments. As the high quality ore deposits of the Mesabi Range became depleted, scrap steel became relatively more attractive. But when the technological advance of pelletizing was introduced, it had the effect of upgrading poor quality ores, and scrap suffered in consequence. On top of this technological change, the basic oxygen furnace began to replace the old, less efficient open hearth. Since the open hearth furnace could take a charge of up to 70 percent old scrap and the basic oxygen furnace only 40 percent, this innovation in steelmaking was a severe blow to the scrap steel industry.

But then, in the beginning of the 1960s, the automobile shredder was introduced. This innovation lowered the cost of processing car hulks and provided a more homogeneous and usable feedstock for the steel furnaces, giving new life to the scrap steel industry. The shredder, in turn, hastened the spread of another innovation, the electric furnace, which can accept a 100 percent old scrap charge and can be built on a small scale near shredder markets. In the long run, technology is influenced by, as well as influences, scrap prices.[25]

While federal expenditures represent only a small fraction (in many categories less than 2 percent) of total domestic spending for commodities, the government nevertheless can affect the balance of supply and demand through procurement specifications and tax policies. Because its procurement specifications are often models for state and local governments, the federal government's approach to reuse of materials is more important than indicated by its fraction of the market. In the past, federal specifications required the use of virgin materials even when technically equivalent secondary materials were available. The General Services Administration, for example, often required for government paper 100 percent groundwood stock, which would imply virgin material. Now, however, governmental units are switching to specifications more appropriately based on performance. The switch is a partial one, because in many cases it is harder to administer, test, and control specifications based on performance than simpler specifications based on pedigree.

In this discussion we have seen that little is known about the actual magnitudes of changes in scrap and virgin material flows resulting from changes in supply and demand relationships. We have seen at a minimum, however, that it is naïve to conclude from the volatility of scrap prices or the small fraction of the cost of some material in the total cost of a product that such changes will have little or no effect. In fact, from the studies of Sawyer, and Russell and Vaughan, we have preliminary evidence that the effects of such changes may be very large. Moreover, in 1973 there was direct evidence of price effects for the supply of secondary materials. Higher prices for scrap materials, resulting from shortages for primary ones, were quickly translated into booming scrap markets.

The conclusion of this discussion is that prices matter, and for close substitutes, which is often the case for materials, they may matter a great deal. In Part Two we turn to market failures associated with demand pricing, particularly freight rates; the inability of the price system to incorporate disposal costs in product prices; and the tax structure, particularly in its treatment of virgin materials. These market inefficiencies affect material use and material flows through prices. They, along with the common perception that we have "too much" waste generation and "too little" recycling, do not suggest that the price system does not work; it works, but in response to the structure built into it.

Notes

1. See Battelle Memorial Institute, *A Study to Identify Opportunities for Increased Solid Waste Utilization, Volume I: General Report* (for the U.S. Environmental Protection Agency [Columbus, Ohio] 1972, distributed by the National Technical Information Service [U.S. Department of Commerce] Springfield, Va.) pp. 30–45.

2. Interstate Commerce Commission, "Ex Parte No. 281, Increased Rates and Charges, 1972" (Draft Environmental Impact Statement, March 6, 1972) p. 3.

3. The value of the standing tree before cutting.

4. Emil Sunley, "The Federal Tax Subsidy of the Timber Industry," in Part 3

of *The Economics of Federal Subsidy Programs,* a compendium of papers submitted to the Joint Economic Committee, U.S. Congress, 92 Cong. 2 sess. (1972) p. 328.

5. If an equivalent amount of product can be made with varying mixes of scrap and virgin materials, the situation can be described by isoquant curves, with scrap material on one axis and virgin material on the other, and with the degree of substitutability measured by the elasticity of substitution. If the scrap and virgin materials were perfect substitutes, the isoquant would be a straight line segment so that a small change in the relative price between scrap and virgin material could lead to a switch from a total specialization in one material to a total specialization in the other.

In *The Best and the Brightest* (New York, Random House, 1972) p. 231, David Halberstam gives a vivid example of the impact of small cost differentials upon close substitutes. When Robert McNamara was at the Ford Motor Company, the company made it a practice to buy the latest model Chevrolet and break it down part by part to see how its rival shaved costs. If a small aluminum casting were found to be doing the job of a small steel Ford part but for a tenth of a cent less, it could mean a total switch in material for that part involving hundreds of thousands of pounds. Small differences in the prices of materials can have large effects upon material flows, with negligible effects upon car prices.

6. Merton J. Peck, *Competition in the Aluminum Industry 1945–1958* (Cambridge, Mass., Harvard University Press, 1961) pp. 35–62.

Because of differences among the several firms in an oligopoly, some firms will do better with higher prices, some with lower prices. The one which does the best with the lowest industry price is the low price preferrer. For the years Peck studied, Alcoa was usually the low price preferrer; it was large enough so that its pricing decisions could not be ignored. In that period most of the price changes were first announced by Alcoa and then quickly matched by the other firms in the primary industry. Since 1960, different firms have been the low price preferrer at different times and have initiated price changes.

In the extractive industries there are obvious ways of minimizing the uncertainties of being a price leader. Industry leaders can make statements in the trade journals that the present price is "too low" and state that it should be changed by some amount. Other firms can react to such statements about the current market price. In this way a firm can find out if indeed it is the low price preferrer and can minimize the hazards of price leadership.

7. The problem of assuring supply may be more important for extractive industries than for most other industries. Because mineral deposits are geographically located in very different qualities and quantities and because transportation costs are a very important part of the cost of virgin material extraction and processing, there are strong tendencies for "local" monopoly power. This leads to vulnerability of a firm buying from a single source and is an incentive to integrate vertically to assure supply.

8. The products are not perfectly substitutable: primary ingot is generally 99 percent pure, secondary ingot 97 percent pure.

9. This is not meant to say that there is no flexibility. Even at full capacity, potlines can be run more or less intensively, by using more or less electricity. And during times of protracted decline in demand, the potlines may be run at less than capacity.

10. Monopoly Power Hearings quoted in Peck, *Competition.* In a personal communication with the author in August 1975, John Stamper, the commodity specialist for aluminum at the Bureau of Mines, agreed that primary firms still try to keep prices steady, but that now it is probably harder to do so.

11. One method for discounting is to vary the allowance for the freight charge. See Charles River Associates, *An Economic Analysis of the Aluminum Industry* (Washington, D.C., General Services Administration, March 1971) pp. 4–42. The existence of secret prices indicates that transactions are taking place at differ-

ent prices. This is in contrast to a textbook competitive market, where everyone has the same information and there is one market price.

12. Quoted in Peck, *Competition*, p. 58.

13. This tendency would be strengthened by what might be called a cheap ingot policy. This policy, the existence of which is problematical, would price ingots cheap and fabrications dear. A presumed reason for this policy on the part of established primary firms would be to steer competition of new entrants in the primary aluminum industry from extraction, where market control may be most critical, to fabrication, which is dependent on ingot supply.

John Douglas, a commentator on the aluminum industry, wrote that at one time "the price structure [in the primary industry] placed the profit center in fabrication." In congressional testimony in 1954 Richard Reynolds of Reynolds Aluminum had the following interchange with Representative Yates. Yates: "There is no question that the fabricating part of your business is the part that makes money." Reynolds: "And it takes less investment." However, Douglas wrote in the same article that the profit center had been shifted back from fabrication toward extraction. See John Douglas, "Aluminum Roller Coaster: Critical Review of a Dynamic Industry," Aluminum Mill Products Report in *The American Metal Market,* May 19, 1971, Section 2, pp. 1A–6A.

14. Marris, *Economic Theory.*

15. John Galbraith, *Economics and the Public Purpose* (Boston, Houghton Mifflin, 1973).

16. For a lively but malicious discussion of some of the issues, see Robert Solow, "The New Industrial State or Son of Affluence," John Galbraith, "A Review of a Review," and Solow, "A Rejoinder"—all in *Public Interest* no. 19 (Fall 1967); and Robin Marris, "Galbraith, Solow, and the Truth about Corporations," and Solow, "A Comment on Marris"—both in *Public Interest* no. 11 (Spring 1968). Also see John Galbraith, *Economics and the Public Purpose* (Boston, Houghton Mifflin, 1973).

17. In a long-run sense old scrap also "flywheels" around in the system. The point is that new scrap is a by-product of production and sufficiently valuable to be used over a wide fluctuation of material prices. Old scrap often lags years behind new production, and its supply on the market depends very sensitively on price. Thus it makes sense to include old scrap and exclude new scrap in this example of supply and demand analysis. While conceptually useful, however, the distinction between price sensitivities between old and new scrap is not clear cut: there are marginal sources of new scrap, certain cuttings and borings for example, that might be lost to the materials system from a dip in prices.

18. Note that S_s in figure 12 cuts the vertical axis before the horizontal, while S_v in both figures cuts the horizontal axis first; thus the supply of scrap is elastic and the supply of virgin material is inelastic, which implies that $\Delta Q_s/Q_s > \Delta Q_v/Q_v$. See the geometry of elasticity in appendix B.

19. James Sawyer, *Automotive Scrap Recycling: Processes, Prices, and Prospects* (Baltimore, Md., Johns Hopkins University Press for Resources for the Future, 1974) chapter 7. The estimates were from 0.01 to 10.

20. In the region around Philadelphia, Sawyer calculated the shredding and collecting costs for given distances from the shredder to the hulks. Then for a given price of shredded steel scrap, he calculated the radius of collection at which the scrap processors would just break even. (Price is determined on the extensive margin in a literally Ricardian way.) Within this feasible circle of collection, he calculated the number of new hulks made available each month from "deregistrations"; this depended in large part on population densities. Starting with typical scrap prices and a typical collection radius of 50 miles, Sawyer then considered the effect of a 1 percent increase in price. This price increase permitted collection of hulks an extra 8 miles out. The increase in radius of course leads to an enormous increase in feasible territory of profitably collected hulks. But the great responsiveness of new territory to increased radius of collection is somewhat offset

by three factors: (1) deregistrations become less frequent farther away from the shredder (shredders are located near population centers), (2) the cost of collection increases per hulk as the hulks become more dispersed, and (3) one shredder territory begins to overlap with another.

21. Sawyer found that one of the reasons for the success of the shredder was that it produced a more homogeneous source of steel scrap.

22. or complementarity, which is important for certain kinds of steel furnaces.

23. The Environmental Law Institute has made some econometric estimates of the cross-elasticity of demand, on a monthly basis: the cross-elasticity of paper stock (waste paper) with respect to the price of wood pulp, 0.13; the cross-elasticity of prompt and obsolete iron and steel scrap with respect to a six-month Almon lagged pig iron price (BLS price index of list prices), 0.28; cross-elasticity of lead obtained from obsolete and prompt lead scrap with respect to the price of refined common pig lead, 0.64. See econometric chapters by Taylor Durham and Richard Speigleman in Robert Anderson, Taylor Durham, and Richard Speigleman, "Federal Tax Policy and Depletable Resources: Impacts and Alternatives for Recycling and Conservation," Environmental Law Institute study for the U.S. Environmental Protection Agency, forthcoming.

24. A description of the model can be found in Clifford Russell and William Vaughan, *Steel Production: Processes, Products and Residuals* (Baltimore, Md., Johns Hopkins University Press for Resources for the Future, 1976).

25. See Blair Bower, *Economics of Residuals Use*, Hearings before the Subcommittee on Fiscal Policy of the Joint Economic Committee, 92 Cong. 1 sess., (November 9, 1971).

PART TWO

INTRATEMPORAL EFFICIENCY

4

Discriminatory Pricing

*The public interest is best served when the rates
are so apportioned as to encourage the largest
practicable exchange of products.*
—Interstate Commerce Commission

DISCUSSIONS OF depletable resources and waste management are
often confined to problems of market inefficiencies and how to remedy
them. The first inefficiency concerns discriminatory practices in pricing.
Thus, if freight rates favor the shipment of virgin materials over secondary ones, the theory is that the rate structure should be changed to
eliminate the discrimination; if the tax system favors industries using
virgin materials over other industries (including those using secondary
materials), then the special tax preferences toward the extractive industries should be removed; somehow the market system should be adjusted to internalize the cost of disposal. Correct the market failures,
the idea goes, and the market system becomes neutral with respect to
material flows; neither virgin nor scrap material is favored. Material
flows are then compatible with economic efficiency. As mentioned in
the Introduction [and discussed more fully in chapters 7, 8, and 9 (Part
Three)], there are shortcomings in this approach. Nonetheless, the
approach is useful in understanding how markets work and how market
allocations may be distorted. In the main, this is the approach in the
discussions of Discriminatory Pricing and Disposal.

An important condition for economic efficiency is for price to equal
marginal cost. But as we shall see, there are times when it is not possible
to meet this condition or when it may not be desirable to meet it.
Here, we examine cases in which there is debate about the desirability
of price–marginal cost equality. For the most part, the chapter is devoted
to the case of railroad freight rates. These prices have received con-

siderable attention in discussions about recycling. Then we look briefly at energy prices, which incorporate the same principle found in freight rates. Both transportation and energy pricing have a promotional impact on the throughput of materials (in the case of energy pricing the initial impact is on energy materials).

The First Example: Railroad Freight Rates

Each time the railroads would like to increase their freight rates,[1] they must submit the proposed changes to the Interstate Commerce Commission (ICC). The ICC allows comment and petition from the affected industries and then decides whether or not to permit the changes. Since no shipper wants to see rates for his commodity increase, there are often protests, and intricate reasons are found why a particular commodity should not have a rate increase, or at least should have a smaller increase than requested.

For years, two trade associations for secondary materials, the National Association of Recycling Industries (NARI)[2] and the Institute of Scrap Iron and Steel (ISIS), have argued that rates discriminate in favor of virgin materials. The scrap industry has actively participated in the rate proceedings—filing petitions and verified statements, and making legal comments—with quite mixed results. Sometimes scrap rates were held down in the midst of a general rate increase, or the rate increase was less than the railroads requested, but often the railroads got what they asked. Recently the scrap industry has been more successful in keeping the percentage rate increases for scrap in line with or even lower than the percentage rate increases for the competing virgin commodity.

The secondary industries allege three major inequities in their freight rates. First, they argue that they pay higher rates on average for a comparable shipment.[3] Second, the ICC practice of allowing equal percentage increases in the rates for virgin and scrap materials "pyramids" the gap between virgin and scrap materials. (If the rate increases were purely inflationary—all prices going up by the same percentage—this increase in gap would not be of any significance; but if transportation cost were an increasing fraction of total cost, the increase in gap would be an increased relative burden on the secondary industries.)[4] And third, they argue that freight rates are a larger fraction of the total value of scrap materials than they are for virgin materials. This would imply that equal percentage increases in the rates for both virgin and scrap materials would relatively favor the primary industries.[5]

There are several counter arguments. One is that scrap and virgin materials do not compete. While this view does not accord with the discussion in chapters 2 and 3, on occasion the ICC has sanctioned it. With no competition, the argument goes, there can be no discrimination, and comparison of scrap and virgin material pairs is pointless. A more convincing point is that a comparison of a small number of rates is unlikely to be representative. To pursue its own interest, the scrap industry can be counted on to select pairs of rates most favorable to its position. A further argument, which is more important for our purposes, is that differences between rates for scrap and virgin materials are based upon differences in the costs of shipment, and hence are not discriminatory.

Without a better idea of the nature and practice of discrimination, there is no way to untangle claims and counterclaims relating to discrimination and shipments of scrap and virgin materials. For the following discussion, therefore, discrimination will be defined as a departure of price from marginal cost.

Discrimination

There are several opportunities to practice price discrimination in rate making and while it is in general illegal,[6] the Interstate Commerce Act does not prohibit all forms of discrimination, only "unjust discrimination." The act prohibits at least two forms—discrimination by location and discrimination by shipper.

1. *Discrimination by Location.* Suppose (as in figure 16) that two railroads connect *A* and *B* but only one connects *A*, *C*, and *B*. Before the Interstate Commerce Act, railroad 2 might (and railroads in this situation frequently did) charge more to move a ton of freight from *A* to *C* than from *A* to *B*. Railroad 2 had to meet the rate of railroad 1 in order to ship from *A* to *B*, but over the route *AC*, railroad 2 was free

Figure 16. Long-haul, short-haul discrimination

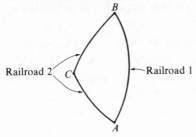

to charge what the traffic would bear. Before the Interstate Commerce Act, in fact, railroad 2 would often charge what the traffic would bear for both *AC* and *AB*. It set rates for each route such that a slight increase in the rate would diminish traffic sufficiently to lower net revenue. This calculation would take into account both the costs of shipment and the sensitivity of the demand for transportation in response to its price (the freight rate).

But suppose a railroad believes that its total capacity is fixed in the short run and that the out-of-pocket costs, if not spent on one route, would be spent on another. Then the railroad might be tempted to maximize its total revenue by maximizing its revenue over each route. We shall see that maximization of total revenue is good neither from the railroad's point of view nor from society's, but nonetheless railroads have tended in some degree to follow this idea in their rate making. A railroad that maximizes its total revenue by charging what the traffic will bear neglects the costs of shipment and focuses entirely on demand considerations. A railroad maximizes its revenue when it sets the rate for each route just high enough so that the elasticity of demand for transportation over that route is 1. At that level, a 1 percent increase in the rate would induce a 1 percent decline in shipments, leaving the revenue constant. For a higher level, where demand is usually more sensitive to price changes,[7] a 1 percent increase in the rate induces a decline in volume that is greater than 1 percent and hence a fall in revenue.

In terms of figure 16, competition over route *AB* means that traffic, from the point of view of railroad 2, will be more elastic at a given rate than traffic over *AC*. Railroad 2 charges what the traffic will bear in both routes, but route *AB* will bear less of a charge than *AC*.

Shippers of freight over the short routes were angered to see freight move over the same route and more at a lower rate. This highly visible form of discrimination became a political issue and "long-haul, short-haul discrimination" was prohibited by the Interstate Commerce Act. It should be pointed out, though, that the act did not prohibit all forms of discrimination by route, but only the most blatant.[8]

2. *Discrimination by Shipper.* Another form of discrimination that aroused public hostility was discrimination on the basis of the shipper. Large shippers could respond to lower rates with larger volumes, and their size gave them alternatives unavailable to small shippers. Because small shippers had less bargaining power and fewer alternatives, their demand for transportation, for the same rate level, was often less elastic than for large shippers. The railroad's adjustment of rates to equalize

elasticities meant that large shippers were given lower rates than small ones, many of whom in the early railroad days were farmers. To avoid a public outcry, this sort of personal discrimination was practiced under the cover of secret rebates. The bargaining power of large shippers was enormous. Stories are told about Standard Oil's collection of a rebate not only on oil it shipped, but also a rebate on its competitors' oil shipped by the same railroad.

As in the case of discrimination by location, personal discrimination is based on demand elasticity. Larger shippers had a higher elasticity of responses to freight rates than smaller shippers, and consequently benefited from lower rates. After 1887 secret rebates were outlawed and rates were required to be public.

3. *Discrimination by Commodity*. Just as the elasticity of demand for transportation varies from person to person and from location to location, it also varies from commodity to commodity. (It is the same elasticity of demand in all three cases. Characteristics of each commodity, its route, and its shipper jointly determine the elasticity.) There are two factors which determine a commodity's elasticity of demand for transportation. One is the elasticity of demand for the product itself and the other is the fraction that freight rates contribute to the price of the final product. Suppose that the fraction of transportation cost in the total cost of a commodity is f and that the elasticity of demand for the commodity is e. Then a 1 percent increase in the freight rate would increase the total commodity price by f percent; as a 1 percent increase in the commodity price leads to an e percent decline in demand, an f percent increase in commodity price leads to an ef percent decline; hence a 1 percent increase in the freight rate leads to an ef percent decline in commodity demand. Thus the elasticity of freight shipments of a commodity with respect to freight rate is simply defined as the product of the fraction of transportation in total product price and the commodity's own price elasticity of demand (ef).[9]

As a discriminating railroad increases its freight rate for a particular commodity, e increases and f tends to increase. When the product ef is driven up to the value of 1, any further increase in the freight rate would lead to a decline in the railroad's revenue. In taking the out-of-pocket costs of the commodity's shipment into account, a railroad would maximize its total net revenues by increasing rates until ef is somewhat higher than 1.[10] However, squeezing the last penny of net revenue from a single commodity might be short sighted. By increasing the costs of one commodity, a railroad might lower the demand for transportation of other commodities. A farmer who sells less wheat because of high freight charges might buy, and have shipped, less furniture. Taking into account demand linkages, a railroad is likely to maximize total net revenues by not squeezing a commodity as hard as would otherwise appear in its interest.

Instead of prohibiting this third type of discrimination, the Interstate Commerce Act expressly sanctioned it, giving it the less pejorative name "value of service." Commodity discrimination meant that for commodities with the same demand elasticity (e) the rate should be a constant fraction of the products' prices. As a rule of thumb, commodity discrimination meant higher rates for more valuable commodities. The ICC defended "value of service" rate-making on the grounds of the public interest.[11]

For a given list of commodities, it is much easier to estimate f than e. It is possible, though, to find elasticities of demand estimated by economists in other studies. While for some commodities where f is a large fraction of cost—for bituminous coal, for example, f is ⅔—the product ef appears to be close to 1.[12] For most commodities, ef appears to be considerably less than 1. It seems plausible that the gap between ef and 1 may result, not from the railroads' failure to maximize their revenues but from a difficulty in measuring the appropriate elasticity. While an economist will try to compute the demand elasticity for aluminum in general, the discriminating railroad will consider aluminum from each source to each destination a separate commodity. With this narrower definition, a commodity will be more sensitive to price changes because the opportunities for product substitution are much greater. Suppose a mill can buy steel scrap from locations X, Y, or Z. If the price of scrap from all three sources goes up by 1 percent, the effect on scrap from A will be considerably less than if the price on scrap from A alone goes up by 1 percent. The economists' elasticity of demand for the commodity in general is not the appropriate elasticity for a discriminating railroad. A discriminating railroad will use the higher elasticities of commodities narrowly defined by locations. With these higher e, the products ef may in fact be close to 1. In other words, discrimination by commodity includes an indirect discrimination by location.

To summarize, all three forms of price discrimination exploit the elasticity of product demand; in fact, exploitation of the demand is the economists' definition of price discrimination. In framing the Interstate Commerce Act, Congress chose to prohibit discrimination by location and by person and to sanction discrimination by commodity. However, being so closely related, it is difficult to keep the three forms of discrimination separate, as we have just seen.

Compared with manufactured goods, value-of-service pricing favors secondary materials, which are low valued. However, value-of-service pricing also favors primary materials, which are low valued as well. If value-of-service pricing favors primary materials more than secondary ones, then commodity discrimination, on balance, may discourage the shipment of secondary materials. One result of value-of-service pricing is, judged by the efficiency criterion, too much material throughput in the whole economy, with overcapitalization at the two points of extraction, the mines and the dumps.

Three Rationales for Rate Making

In the controversy over rate making as it applies to materials, three points of view have emerged. Rate making can be based on concepts of marginal cost pricing, demand discrimination or value of service, or "equivalency."

MARGINAL COST CRITERION. By the economists' definition—a definition explicitly used above—discrimination exists whenever rates depart from marginal costs. This means that whenever there is rate discrimination, the efficiency criterion is being violated. With rate discrimination, shippers receive the wrong price information on the social cost of transporting their commodities.

Advocates of marginal cost pricing recognize that rates set equal to marginal costs may not generate total revenues sufficient to cover total costs. If railroads are required to be financially self-sufficient, the following policy is often recommended: let the freight rate for each commodity be the sum of the marginal cost plus a surcharge. Set the surcharges so that their sum over all commodities just eliminates the deficit and so that each commodity's surcharge as a percentage of the entire rate is in the same inverse proportion to that commodity's elasticity of demand for transportation.

Suppose that a railroad has N markets, one for each commodity or commodity class and for each route, and let p_i be the freight rate in the ith market, characterized by some particular commodity and route. Then the recommended rate for the ith market is chosen so that

$$\frac{p_i - MC_i}{p_i} = k/e_i \qquad (4.1)$$

where k is a constant chosen so that the sum of the surcharges $p_i - MC_i$ over all of the railroad's markets is just big enough to eliminate the deficit. This policy is recommended by economists because it minimizes the total cost customers have to pay to meet the railroad's self-sufficiency revenue requirement.[13] Often a pricing scheme following equation (4.1) is called "optimal discrimination."

It is possible to think of the surcharge as equivalent to a tax. Suppose that a railroad is required to follow marginal cost pricing but that this leads to deficits that the government makes up with taxes on freight shipments. The government knows that taxes generally distort the allocation of resources and it wishes to set the taxes so that the distortion is minimized in the sense of minimizing the social burden of the misallocation. For each unit of commodity i shipped it levies a tax equal to the surcharge $p_i - MC_i$, and it follows equation (4.1). The idea is that levying a higher tax where a commodity's sensitivity to price is less and a lower tax where a commodity's sensitivity is more minimizes the distorting effect of the tax. Under this policy there would be a lower surcharge for scrap (elastic with respect to freight charges) than for manufactured goods (inelastic). The rate is based mainly on cost considerations with just enough commodity discrimination to eliminate deficits.

The economists' attempt to minimize social burden through tax discrimination is closely related to the revenue-maximizing behavior of the railroad (or other discriminating monopolist). A revenue-maximizing railroad, neglecting the marginal costs of shipment, would set MC_i equal to 0, and with the constant k equal to 1, would follow equation (4.1).[14] Equation (4.1) would then require each price to be set so that the elasticity for each market e_i was equilibrated to 1. This version of a revenue-maximizing railroad represents a polar case for which there are probably no pure examples.

Yet it does appear that railroads have neglected cost considerations and overemphasized demand considerations in their rate making. In an 1890 case the ICC stated that "[t]he cost of transportation of any one article of commerce can never be disposed of with any accuracy."[15] Because there are so many joint costs and products involved in transportation networks, the statement still applies. In view of the difficulty in allocating capital costs among many users, it is not surprising that railroads have to some extent neglected cost considerations in rate making. Nevertheless, the ICC has been faulted for not trying harder to establish accounting methods that would better allocate costs.

Whitten points out that railroad accounting procedures grew up in a period when the railroads were largely held by banking houses.[16] He suggests that in the banking houses' own ledger sheets the cost side was rather fixed and boring, while the revenue side inspired ingenuity and imagination. In any case, for railroad accounting, costs were classified on a financial rather than a functional basis. Apparently, in this fluid period cost accountability was much less important than attention to revenue-maximizing possibilities, hence the refinement of the various forms of discrimination. The ICC adopted the railroads' system of accounting, and the last major codification of the present Uniform System of Accounts was in 1907. Since then, the ICC accounting system has been a graveyard for economists trying to estimate marginal costs of various services.

Suppose, however, that a railroad kept useful functional accounts and was able to discover the cost structure of each type of service [and thus the marginal cost $MC(q_i)$ of each commodity shipment service]. Then it would be much more attractive to the railroad to maximize its net revenue, which is its profit, than its total revenue. In doing so it would follow equation (4.1) but with k equal to 1.[17]

The close relationship between a railroad's discriminatory rate making and the government's financing of a deficit by least-distorting taxation suggests that there are certain attractive features to the natural tendency of the railroads to use "value-of-service" pricing. Granted that the first purpose of commodity discrimination is to increase railroad revenues rather than expand traffic, there appears to be a certain rough equity in this form of discrimination. "Let the more valuable products pay more" sounds a little like the ability-to-pay principle of the progressive income tax. Because most cheap bulk commodities moved east-west while most manufactured commodities, more valuable and hence discriminated against, moved within the already developed East, value-of-service pricing was viewed as a development policy for the West and seen in the national interest.[18] In the early railroad days there were great economies of scale to be realized by further development. Marginal cost pricing would have led to deficits while value-of-service pricing led to larger profits and expansion.

Here there is a conflict. To be consistent with a neutral materials policy, marginal cost pricing is desirable. In no other way can we transmit the proper price signals on the social costs and benefits of materials use and conservation, and ensure the proper mix between scrap and virgin materials. At the same time, if the railroads need to expand to realize their potential economies of scale or if they run chronic deficits, there is a case for commodity discrimination. There is no easy choice. We are forced to compromise between what may be best for a materials policy and what may be best for a transportation policy. If there is no other workable way of making up a railroad's deficit, it may be necessary to preserve a substantial element of value-of-service pricing and adjust materials policy somewhat to offset the "incorrect" price signals emerging from the transport of virgin and scrap material.[19]

But the case for value-of-service rate making should not be pushed too far. While the mathematics of a profit-maximizing railroad is much the same as the mathematics of a least-distorting tax, it is not quite the same, and the implicit conditions underlying equation (4.1) may not be realistic or desirable.

To arrive at (4.1) it is assumed that the railroad has a fixed stock of capacity (its track, and so forth) and is adjusting its variable operations to maximize net profit. But in fact its profits from different operations will lead to new investment and the abandonment of some old lines. These profit signals are different with different elasticities of demand and may not coincide with inherent comparative advantages over other modes of transportation. Value-of-service pricing has a tendency to lead to inefficient patterns of railroad, truck, and barge transportation.[20] Moreover, the least elastic shippers may be the smaller firms, and individuals, who are poorer and have fewer alternatives. Thus value-of-service pricing may bear down hardest on the poor in a socially undesirable way.

Finally, there is a major difference in the role of the constant k. For minimum-burden taxation, k is chosen just large enough to eliminate the deficit or to fulfill some other socially defined purpose. It is not generally equal to 1. For the railroad using $k=1$, condition (4.1) guides the railroad to maximum profits, which may be far in excess of the socially desirable level. In the late nineteenth century, resentment against the railroads' "excessive profits" was a strong impetus for regulation.[21]

Although there is a case for value-of-service pricing, most economists appear to believe that the railroads and the ICC have relied too much on this pricing policy in the past and that they should move toward marginal cost pricing. It appears that in the past few years there has been a move in this direction.

VALUE-OF-SERVICE CRITERION. As we have seen, the ICC sanctions rather than prohibits commodity discrimination. There are times, however, when the ICC is willing to sustain the protests of shippers who charge that their commodity is being discriminated against in favor of some other commodity. This is the case when the commodities in question are direct and obvious competitors. There is a rough consistency in this point of view. Suppose the two commodities in question were perfect substitutes. In this case they would both have the same price and same product elasticity. Value-of-service pricing would dictate the same fraction of the rate in the price of each and hence the same freight rate for each. Thus if a shipper found that a perfect substitute for his commodity was traveling at a lower rate, his commodity would bear an "unjust" rate according to the value-of-service criterion. By the same criterion, if two commodities are not perfect substitutes, but still close competitors, the rates should be correspondingly close.

This has been written as though value of service were the ICC's only consideration in rate making. This is indeed not the case; there are at least two other factors. Over the years, cost considerations have grown in importance, though a serious consideration of cost still awaits a better system of accounting. Secondly, rates are sometimes set to harmonize with "the national interest." In the 1930s, for example, when agriculture was a severely depressed industry, the ICC found it in the public interest to keep rates low for agricultural commodities. The public interest was expressly sanctioned as a basis for rate making by the Supreme Court in 1953 when it refused to bar rates lower than costs for some commodities.[22]

Nonetheless, the question of whether or not scrap is being discriminated against in favor of primary commodities has been judged by the ICC to depend upon the prior question, "Are they direct competitors?" In the case of scrap iron and steel, the ICC has wavered over this question of competition. According to McEwen, in 1959 the ICC accepted the argument that scrap iron does not compete with iron ore. Under this precedent-setting decision the ICC reasoned, if no competition, then no discrimination. However, in 1967, in an ICC hearing over a 3 percent rate increase (*Ex Parte* 256), the ICC decided that competition does exist between scrap iron and iron ore. But then during *Ex Parte* 262–267 on selected rate increases, which took three years to conclude, the ICC drifted back to its original position of no competition.[23]

EQUIVALENCY CRITERION. Under these ground rules the Institute of Scrap Iron and Steel (ISIS) has spent a great deal of time and effort in the rate proceedings trying to establish the competition between scrap iron and iron ore. The ISIS approach has been to bring in metallurgists to explain how the substitution is made. Over a period of time, a kind of compromise position has evolved. ISIS agrees that a ton of iron scrap is not a substitute for a ton of iron ore, but maintains that a ton of scrap substitutes for one ton of metal content of iron ore plus enough coal to reduce it. Because a ton of scrap is "equivalent" to a package of iron ore and coal, the rate for scrap should be the sum of the rates of the substitutable iron ore and coal.[24] It seems that if the ICC will accept the idea of equivalency, ISIS will throw in coal free for the ride. As can be seen, this is an argument of pure commodity discrimination (value-of-service) and one quite independent of cost considerations. In this equivalency argument it does not matter that scrap often travels in single car shipments while ore often travels in efficient unitized train loads, that gondola cars for scrap are smaller than ore cars, or that scrap travels, on average, farther than ore. All these are higher cost factors for scrap shipments. Nor does it matter that scrap shipments do not imply backhauls of empty cars, while ore shipments usually do—a lower cost factor for scrap.

Of the three rationales for rate making, value of service and equivalency require much less information about the costs of shipment than does the economists' marginal cost pricing with "optimal discrimination." The economists' rationale is an expression of the efficiency criterion and makes the most sense in terms of efficient allocation of materials. But with its heavy demands upon cost information it is unclear how far this rationale can be applied in practice. Two sources of cost information that could potentially clarify the question of rate making for materials have been developed in recent years. These are the Interstate Commerce Commission's environmental impact statement for freight rates for scrap materials and the ICC's "burden studies."

Freight Rates and NEPA

The National Environmental Policy Act (NEPA) declares "it is the continuing responsibility of the Federal Government . . . to . . . enhance the quality of renewable resources and approach the maximum attainable recycling of depletable resources."[25] Because the ICC considers the "national interest" as a legitimate basis for rate making, one might think that this statement in NEPA might have an effect on ICC rulings. But this policy statement was not to be the principal impact of NEPA on the rate making procedure. Another section of the Act requires federal agencies to write a "detailed statement" on "federal actions significantly affecting the quality of the human environment," concerning in particular "[a]ny irreversible and irretrievable commitment of resources which would be involved in the proposed action. . ."

At first the ICC ignored the Act. After all, the ICC does not take actions like building dams or cutting forests; it merely sets regulations and prices for railroads and other transportation industries. Various environmental groups, including a group of law students and the Environmental Defense Fund, disagreed, arguing that NEPA required an environmental impact statement analyzing the effects of proposed rate increases on recycling and hence on the use of virgin materials. In response, the ICC asked the railroads to submit environmental impact statements. These were not to be taken as formal statements by the responsible federal agency, because according to the ICC, this was not required. After the railroads' statements were criticized by the Council on Environmental Quality and the Environmental Protection Agency as inadequate, the ICC wrote its own "informal" statement.

In its cursory six-page statement, the ICC suggested that the proposed rate increase, which was 2½ percent, was too small compared with month-to-month fluctuations in the price of scrap to make a difference. As discussed in chapter 3, this assertion neglects the institutional and market forces that lead to high short-term variance in the prices of scrap materials. It was also previously noted that with high elasticities of substitution, a small change in the long-term average prices of scrap and virgin materials can lead to large differences in the mix of scrap and virgin material usage, even in the presence of large short-term fluctuation in the prices of scrap materials. Comparing a permanent increase in the average price with the variance in price makes little sense. In its comment on the ICC draft impact statement, the Environmental Defense Fund correctly noted the basic ingredients for an analysis of the impact of freight rates on recycling: the fraction of transportation cost in the prices of scrap and competing virgin materials and the supply and demand sensitivities of scrap and virgin materials with respect to their prices.

Just before the SCRAP case, as it was called, was settled by the Supreme Court, the ICC released its final environmental impact statement. As before, the ICC concluded that freight rate charges for scrap would not adversely affect the environment. On the contrary, it argued that holding down rate increases would affect the health of the railroads and consequently harm the environment. The statement did not include any estimate of the effects of rates upon recycling. Specifically, it did not compute the fraction of transportation in the cost of recycled and competing commodities, nor did it estimate the elasticities of demand (or elasticity of substitution).

Nonetheless, the ICC went far beyond its previous statements by including a long defense of the present rate structure and, by implication, the proposed rate changes. In its second draft statement, the ICC listed several bases for rate making,[26] which boiled down to three mentioned before: (1) the cost of shipment, roughly out-of-pocket costs or marginal costs; (2) demand for the commodity (value of service); and (3) public interest, either on a local level or a national level.

Although the ICC maintained that there are several bases for rate making, it justified differences in rates between primary and competing secondary commodities almost entirely on the basis of differences in cost of shipment. It is unfortunate that the environmental impact statement did not develop new information on costs which would help untangle the question of competition between virgin and scrap materials, and the effects of transport rates upon the use, generally, of materials in the economy.

ICC Burden Studies

In its environmental impact statements the ICC discussed at some length, though without quantification, factors determining different costs for scrap and virgin material shipments. The ICC concluded that scrap did not bear a disproportionate share of the burden of cost. However, this conclusion conflicts with two of its own previous cost studies.

In these studies, called burden studies, the ICC divided the rate into two parts: variable costs of shipment of a particular commodity, and contribution to overhead. (See appendix C for further detail.) The idea is that rate differences between primary and secondary commodities might be justified on the basis of cost, in terms of differences between variable costs—roughly MC_i in equation (4.1)—and differences in their contribution to overhead—roughly $P_i - MC_i$ in (4.1).

The variable costs, which roughly correspond to out-of-pocket costs and the economists' marginal costs, were computed to reflect the average switching conditions and average train operations of the territories in which the traffic moved, the average weight of load, the average length of haul, the type of equipment, and the empty-return movement of the equipment.[27] The ratio of revenue received (rates) to variable costs is, then, a measure of the contribution to overhead. Results of the two ICC studies are shown in table 1.

For both years in table 1 and for nearly all cases, scrap commodities contributed more to overhead than primary commodities did. According to the commission's data, many primary commodities did not even pay their own way (their variable costs). While paper waste paid 123 percent of its variable cost of shipment, pulpwood logs, on average, paid only 80 percent of the variable cost of shipment. If the commission analysis is correct, secondary materials were, and presumably still are, in effect subsidizing primary commodities.

The commission saw no reason why primary commodities should subsidize secondary ones:

to attempt to hold the rates and charges on recyclable commodities at depressed levels, upon some theory that it is socially desirable that their movement be encouraged, would cast a burden on the rates and charges applicable on the remaining commodities that the railroads transport or, as some of the parties suggest, the primary materials. In effect the shippers of such commodities would be asked to underwrite or partially subsidize the transportation of the recyclable commodities.[28]

Table 1. ICC Burden Studies
(revenue as a percentage of variable cost)

	1966	1969
Iron and steel scrap[a]	155	142
Iron ore	143	130
Beneficiating grade ore, crude	62	99
Paper waste and scrap[a]	123	115
Primary forest products	83	75
Pulpwood and other wood chips	84	83
Pulpwood logs	80	69
Waste and scrap, aggregated except ashes[a]	144	140
Copper ores	114	176
Crude copper ores	45	151
Lead and zinc ores	144	134
Bauxite	111	111
Manganese ores	128	137
Dimension stone, quarry	152	119
Crushed and broken stone	92	86
Sand	89	80
Gravel	80	75
Phosphate rock	75	72

Source: Interstate Commerce Commission, *Ex Parte No. 270 Investigation of Railroad Freight Rate Structure,* served Nov. 11, 1971 (the data from *Ex Parte 270* were compiled from the ICC Waybill Sample).
[a] Secondary commodities.

There is an inconsistency here. When the ICC sanctioned lower rates for agricultural commodities in the national interest, other commodities were in effect subsidizing the agricultural ones. If primary materials should not subsidize scrap materials, even though national legislation says that it is socially desirable to recycle more scrap, why should the ICC permit scrap to subsidize virgin material, as is implied by the burden studies?

Value of service as a basis for rate making, as defined by equation (4.1), does not allow the rate to go below the marginal cost of shipment, yet there appear to be many such cases underlying the statistics of the virgin materials included in table 1. Hence, table 1 suggests that the railroads are not following value-of-service rate making. Allowing rates to fall below variable costs is in the interest of neither the railroads nor economic efficiency. And as one of the groups of commodities paying part of the cost of shipment of virgin materials, scrap material is paying a disproportionate share, in terms of either value-of-service or marginal cost pricing, contrary to the ICC's position in its environmental impact statement. Some progress toward understanding the rate system and its effects on the transportation industries and material flows might be made if the ICC reconciled the results of its two burden studies with the conclusions from its environmental impact statement.[29] It does appear that in the past few years the ICC has not only moved toward marginal cost pricing but also toward allowing rate changes encouraging scrap compared with virgin materials.

The Second Example: Energy

As we have seen, the opportunities for price discrimination by railroads are particularly intricate. In the absence of regulation and neglecting the railroads' own administrative costs, each commodity, each route, and each shipper offers an opportunity for a separate rate guided by equation (4.1). Although some of the forms of discrimination are prohibited and there are other important factors in rate making, the finely divided market for freight transportation has led to many billions of individual rates (many of which are now inoperative because of simplified class rates).

Besides railroads and their competitors which have adopted value-of-service pricing, there are other examples of discriminatory pricing, the most important for the consumer being the electric and gas utilities. For electric utilities—many of the comments to follow will also apply to gas utilities and other discriminating monopolies—the markets are not so finely divided as with railroads. Instead of thousands of commodities, an electric utility sells only one, electricity, and discriminatory pricing takes a simpler form. Discrimination has been mainly by customer or customer class. Large customers still bargain individually with the utilities for lower rates.[30] Again, larger customers are often more elastic in their demand and receive lower rates.

The most common system of discriminatory pricing for utilities is the declining block rate system. All the customers in a given customer class receive the same rate schedule: for the first so many kilowatt hours consumed in a billing period, the rate is so many mills; for the next block of kilowatt hours, the rate declines to some lower amount of mills per kilowatt hour, and so forth. In this way a large user pays a lower rate for his marginal consumption (which is the rate that counts for the customer's allocative decision) and a lower rate on average. The system is equivalent to volume discounts for larger customers. There are other mechanisms for setting lower rates for customers with more elastic demand. Large customers are given lower rates for "interruptible" power that in the past was rarely interrupted. (Recently things have changed and interruptible power is no longer such a good proposition.) Larger users are put into special customer classes with lower rate structures over all the blocks.

As before, the justification for pricing in accordance with equation (4.1) is that it encourages a larger system, spreads fixed costs over more consumption, and achieves economies of scale. Even for elastic customers with low rates, by (4.1), $p > MC$, so that they still contribute to overhead and lower the costs for less elastic customers.[31]

However, the traditional rationale for discriminatory pricing—to promote usage in order to achieve economies of scale—is no longer unquestionably appropriate. Recently there have been signs that the economies of scale for energy utilities have been exhausted. Very large grid systems are hard to manage and sometimes break down; transmission costs increase with the grid size; new sites are much more expensive than old ones because the best sites have been preempted, and with the spread of population it is harder to locate away from people; new transmission lines are also increasingly expensive to site for the same reasons. Incremental sources of energy materials, whether coal, gas, or oil or the more nontraditional sources, are much more expensive than the old contracted sources. Part of the increased cost of new capacity reflects inflation and the private benefits to utilities of being locked into old contracts, but much of the increased cost for new capacity reflects true increased long-run marginal costs at higher levels of energy supplied per unit of time.[32] With the growing evidence that there are no longer economies of scale to be realized, most if not all of the rationale for the traditional form of discriminatory pricing evaporates.

In the case of railroads, discriminatory pricing affects the total amount of railroad service initially and incidentally, but it has an even more important effect on the flows of virgin and scrap materials. In the case of electric utilities, the product is electricity and so discriminatory pricing affects the flow of energy supplies directly. At a time when new sources of energy are costly in terms of private resources, the environment, and political vulnerability, the present promotional policy is highly questionable.

The opposite of this policy is an increasing block rate system that would promote conservation. Such a system tends to minimize the social burden of sudden belt-tightening. The more elastic customers who have more substitutes and alternatives are induced to cut down proportionally more than less-elastic customers. The burden of conservation is carried more heavily by the rich, who are larger users; the poor, who may use only the first block, are largely unaffected by an inversion of the block rate structure. In other words, the first block of usage, which is the most essential for each customer, rich or poor, remains cheap, while the following blocks, which are more of a luxury, are made more expensive. As a conservation measure, Japan has moved toward an inverted block rate system.

Unlike the railroads, which cling to value-of-service pricing as a way of increasing badly needed revenue, the present declining block rate system is likely to generate less revenue than marginal cost pricing, because incremental units are very expensive. In this case a move to marginal cost pricing is attractive to the utilities, which have a strong incentive to move in this direction, and in fact there is such a trend. Already we can observe a move from declining block rates to flat rates and a move toward peak pricing. Frederick Wells has suggested that marginal cost pricing may generate so much revenue as to become a problem. For many systems, Wells suggests that one way of obtaining more of the efficiency effect of marginal cost pricing without generating so much surplus revenue is to use inverted block rates.[33]

For utilities the most often proposed reform in the direction of marginal cost pricing is peak load pricing. This would mean charging more for customers using electricity in peak hours (and in peak months too). This reform would also be conservationist in the sense that it would tend to allocate capital more efficiently, slowing down the growth in new plant and equipment.

If we establish national goals to recycle scrap material and conserve virgin material, including energy material, then raising the freight rates for virgin material while holding down the rates for scrap material and instituting inverted block rates for utilities are specific policy measures toward these goals. But are these measures too specific, the focus too narrow? As we have just seen, the ICC objected to having the transport industry singled out to bear the burden of promoting recycling through its rate structure. As an alternative a national severance tax on virgin materials would work toward the same goals but at a more general level. Such a tax would spread its impact, and burden, throughout the entire economy. With more general policy instruments available, it would appear that the ICC is correct in its objection. More neutral policies, in the direction of marginal cost pricing, would be more appropriate than special rates for materials transport and inverted rates for utilities.

However, more generalized, or macroeconomic, policy instruments may not be readily available, and we might have to fall back temporarily upon "second best" measures. In the short run it may be desirable to run equation (4.1) "backwards" with higher freight rates for virgin material and inverted block rates. Moreover, even if the more generalized policy instruments were available, "second best" elasticity discrimination for conservation might be appropriate for short-term adjustment. The "optimal" severance tax may be a small tax that makes itself felt over many years—it may best be set to have a long period of adjustment. But elasticity discrimination may work best for short periods of adjustment—the rates being set to achieve quick conservation in a few years with minimal social pain.

In the foregoing discussion, we have seen that marginal cost pricing is complicated by revenue constraints, possible economies of scale, difficulties in cost estimation, and needs for adjustment in the use of resources. A move toward marginal cost pricing for both transport and utilities would lead to a greater efficiency in the use of material and to greater conservation in material use. But, when the complications are taken into account, we may have to settle for something less than full marginal cost pricing with its equation of price and marginal cost. Even if marginal cost pricing were possible it might not be desirable. In chapter 5, the situation is perhaps a little simpler. There marginal cost pricing is clearly desirable; unfortunately, however, it may not be possible.

Notes

1. The term "rate" is something of a misnomer because freight rates are not charges per ton mile or per some other unit. For each route and for each commodity or class of commodities, a separate rate is established. In other words, a freight rate is a total charge for, or price of, a transportation service.

2. Previously known as the National Association of Secondary Materials Industries (NASMI).

3. See, for example, the middle table on page 37 of *Hearings before Subcommittee on Fiscal Policy,* Joint Economic Committee (Washington, D.C., U.S. Government Printing Office, 1972).

4. *Hearings before Subcommittee on Fiscal Policy,* p. 40.

5. For an illustrative comparison see table 31 of Moshman Associates, *Transportation Rates and Costs for Selected Virgin and Secondary Commodities,* a study prepared for the U.S. Environmental Protection Agency (Washington, D.C., 1973).

6. John Meyer, Merton Peck, John Stenason, and Charles Zwick, *The Economics of Competition in the Transportation Industries* (Cambridge, Mass., Harvard University Press, 1960) p. 179.

7. We can use the geometric discussion in appendix B to show that elasticity of demand tends to increase as the price increases. With demand for the commodity D, the elasticity with price P_1 is $\dfrac{AB}{BC}$ and the elasticity with price P_2 is $\dfrac{XY}{YZ}$. As the demand curve is drawn $\dfrac{AB}{BC} < \dfrac{XY}{YZ}$ and so the elasticity is larger for a higher price.

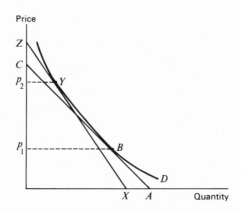

8. Discrimination by location depends not only on the differences in availability of alternative rail lines but also on the availability of alternative means of transportation.

9. The above is a simplification. There are other characteristics of a commodity that influence the elasticity of demand for transportation. There are differences among commodities in their flexibility to change in the distribution system. Some commodities may be more or less easily stored, for example. I am indebted to Jack Ventura for this and other comments.

10. Meyer, *Competition in Transportation,* pp. 196–199.

11. "The public interest is best served when the rates are so apportioned as to encourage the largest practicable exchange of products . . . this can only be done by making value an important consideration, and by placing upon the higher classes of freight some share of the burden that on a relatively equal apportionment, if service alone were considered, would fall upon those of less value. With this method of arranging tariffs little fault is found, and perhaps none at all by

persons who consider the subject from the standpoint of public interest." *First Annual Report of the Interstate Commerce Commission,* p. 36, cited in Ann Friedlaender, *The Dilemma of Freight Transport Regulation* (Washington, D.C., The Brookings Institution, 1969) p. 12.

12. Meyer, *Competition in Transportation,* table 41, p. 198.

13. William Baumol and David Bradford, "Optimal Departures from Marginal Cost Pricing," *American Economic Review* vol. LX, no. 3 (June 1970) pp. 265–283. There are various versions of the revenue constraint; also, the above formulation is limited by the prohibition against long-haul, short-haul discrimination.

14. $(p_i - 0)/p_i = 1 = k/e_i$. With $k = 1$, we have the rule: set each price p_i so that $e_i = 1$.

15. Meyer, *Competition in Transportation,* pp. 179–180.

16. Herbert Whitten, "Recyclamation," a study for the U.S. Department of Transportation, December 8, 1971, p. B3.

17. Under an accounting system that properly measures the effects of one activity on the costs of other activities and under fairly normal circumstances, a profit-maximizing monopolistic railroad will do so by maximizing the profit, or net revenue, in each of its markets. For the ith market, characterized by a particular commodity (q_i) and route, the railroad will set its rate (p_i) and offer transport services to maximize total revenue minus total cost $TC(q_i)$. As total revenue is $p_i q_i$, the railroad maximizes $p_i q_i - TC(q_i)$ by setting the derivative equal to zero: $(dp_i/dq_i) \cdot q_i + p_i - TC'(q_i) = 0$. With $MC(q_i) = TC'(q_i)$ and slight rearranging, we have

$$[p_i - MC(q_i)]/p_i = [(-dp_i)/(dq_i)](q_i/p_i)$$

The right hand side is $1/e_i$ and so we have equation (4.1) with $k = 1$.

18. Incidentally, the politically powerful Grange farmers were twice benefited when the Interstate Commerce Act prohibited long-haul, short-haul discrimination and preserved commodity discrimination.

19. The "correct" ones being defined by marginal costs of shipment.

20. Meyer, *Competition in Transportation,* p. 194.

21. Pricing by exploitation of demand conditions may encourage market instability, collusion, cartelization, and cartel cheating. Kolko wrote that the railroads' desire to stabilize their cartel, which was unmanageable on its own, was a principal force leading to the Interstate Commerce Act. Gabriel Kolko, *The Triumph of Conservatism* (New York, Free Press, 1963).

22. The Court maintained that "As long as rates as a whole affect railroads' just compensation for their overall services to the public ... the fixing of non-compensatory rates [rates lower than cost] for carrying some commodities when the public interest is thereby served [is not barred]." Baltimore & Ohio Railroad Company et al. vs. The United States et al., 345 U.S. 146 (1953).

23. Larry McEwen, "Issue Paper—Freight Rates," EPA memorandum, Sept. 13, 1972, Exhibit I.

24. Herschel Cutler, "Role of Transportation in Disposal of Obsolete Metallic Waste One Year Later," *Waste Age* vol. 2, no. 4 (July-August 1971); see also *Waste Age* vol. 1, no. 4 (July-August 1970).

25. According to the discussion in chapters 1 and 2 in this book, the goal to maximize recycling is inefficient policy.

26. Interstate Commerce Commission, *Ex Parte No. 281, Increased Freight Rates and Charges, 1972 (Environmental Matters)* March 13, 1972, pp. 19–39. This was the first extensive environmental impact statement.

27. The ICC felt that "recognition of these transportation characteristics in the application of the costs is sufficiently representative of the costs incurred by the carriers for transporting the major portion of the commodity classes." Interstate Commerce Commission, *Ex Parte No. 270, Investigation of Railroad Freight Rate Structure,* served November 11, 1971, Appendix B, p. 3.

28. Interstate Commerce Commission, *Ex Parte No. 281,* pp. 177–178.

29. Compared with the impact statement, which is a discussion without numerical analysis, the burden studies are much more thorough. However, the burden studies have been criticized in turn, because of their method of cost allocation. A few of the difficulties in cost allocation are mentioned in appendix C. In arguing against the need for a cost study in its environmental impact statement, it was stressed that the ICC was undertaking a thorough examination of the rate structure in another *Ex Parte* proceeding. Perhaps this study will resolve the unanswered questions raised in the impact statement and the burden studies.

30. Unlike freight rates, these rates are per unit service consumed, e.g., 1.3 mills per kilowatt hour.

31. Firms with higher load factors (using more nearly the same amount of electricity all the time) also receive lower rates. But this practice is defended on the basis of lower costs rather than the elasticity of demand and "spreading fixed costs," as is the practice of charging less to larger users with lower average distribution costs.

32. It is highly doubtful that increasing national electricity consumption from 1.9×10^9 megawatt hours to 2.0×10^9 megawatt hours would achieve economies of scale, except in isolated instances. In other instances there are likely to be diseconomies of scale.

33. Wells points out some of the assumptions and problems of this possibility, which has its own inefficiencies but may be more efficient than the present system of declining block rates. Frederick Wells, "In Defense of Inverted Block Rates," draft (Washington, D.C.: Resources for the Future, March 1973).

5

Disposal

We strongly object in the most clear terms possible to the philosophy that a product should bear the costs of its own disposal.
—Norman Dobyns,
vice president of the American Can Company

A SECOND SOURCE of market inefficiency is the price system's failure to incorporate disposal cost in product price. There is a certain alchemy in traditional economic theory. Economic systems are modeled in which goods are produced, consumed, and then vanish. What allows this to happen is the assumption that unwanted material can be disposed of at zero cost. Of course materials do not really vanish, but unwanted materials do "vanish" in an economic sense if they can be disposed of at zero cost. Correspondingly, there is little inefficiency when disposal costs are very low.

A century ago the disposal of solid waste may well have been indeed virtually costless for many persons living in the countryside. But with growing urbanization a larger fraction of solid waste was generated in cities, where it was less easy to handle. More waste was generated per person, so that even in rural areas there came to be problems of selection and maintenance of disposal sites and significant transportation costs. At the same time the solid waste stream grew more complicated, with more toxic substances and less-degradable materials. The costs associated with solid waste include not only those of waste collection and treatment before disposal into the environment but also the on-site costs of storage and processing prior to collection, and the residual environmental costs after disposal. As these costs increase, the assumption of free disposal becomes more and more strained. And when the costs of disposal grow to 10 or 15 percent of a product's sales price, a serious inefficiency emerges in the price system when these costs are neglected.

We can interpret the inefficiency associated with individual behavior and municipal solid waste as follows. Consider an individual about to dispose of a unit of trash. The price of disposal is the burden *to him* of disposal. This burden is mainly the effort of taking the object to the trash can or other receiving medium; the price to him also includes the effect on him of additional municipal taxes, but this is negligible. The price to him is the sum of his internal costs. For many individuals disposing of solid waste, the price has not changed over the years—it remains virtually zero. But the marginal cost has changed, and this is a source of distortion in the market system. The marginal cost of disposal (often called social marginal cost) is the difference in total cost, internal plus external—waste storage, collection, processing, disposal, and environmental cost after disposal—of the entire waste stream with the extra unit of material and the total cost of the entire waste stream without the extra unit. The market system is unable on its own to incorporate the full marginal cost of disposal into the product's price. Only a few of the costs are incorporated into the product itself, and these by definition are called internal costs.[1]

As a matter of economic principle it is desirable for products to bear their own disposal costs in order that product prices reflect the associated external costs. In the case of solid waste disposal, however, the problem is not what is desirable but what is practicable. It is not clear what are the best ways of internalizing the costs of disposal and it is not always clear that the effort at internalization is worth the administrative costs entailed. In this chapter we look at the costs of disposal and the internal price of disposal to the disposer. This price, as we shall see, is not in all cases virtually zero, and in other cases it need not be zero.

Municipal Solid Wastes

In this chapter we are mainly interested in the example of municipal solid wastes. There are of course enormous quantities of solid wastes generated outside this category—piles of spoil from mining, slash from timber operations, and wastes from feed lots, to name a few sources. Much of this material is disposed of on-site and the associated costs are internal to the degree that they do not spill over to affect neighboring land, either visually or physically.[2] Within a municipality there are many generators of solid wastes—residences, offices, gas stations, manufacturing plants, and so forth. Even within city boundaries, much solid waste is disposed of on-site or is removed by the generator himself. Often the generator contracts with a private firm to remove and dispose of solid waste. Perhaps 65 percent of the solid waste generated in a city is handled by the city government. The municipality either collects and disposes of the waste itself or contracts with private firms to do so. And while municipalities charge user fees for the collection of solid waste from some commercial and industrial sources, much of the collection is "free" from the point of view of the disposer.[3]

The Environmental Protection Agency (EPA) estimates that in 1973 the total volume of municipal solid waste destined for municipal dumps, whether or not handled by city governments, was about 135 million tons.[4] Although the composition of this waste varies by region, EPA's estimate of the composition in the aggregate is shown in table 2. As can be seen, "mixed solid waste," as municipal solid waste is often called, is more paper fiber than anything else.

Most municipal solid waste is dumped, incinerated, or landfilled. For each of these three basic methods there is much the same method of collection, by truck. The collection costs vary widely by region but, as a national average, costs of collection, processing, and disposal are about $26 a ton.[5] The traditional rule of thumb is that 80 percent of the municipal expenditure on solid waste is for collection and only 20 percent goes for processing and disposal, but this breakdown is a little out of date and weighs the rapidly rising processing costs too lightly.

Table 2. Nation's Cities, Municipal Solid Waste Composite, 1969

Composition	Percentages by weight
Newspapers	10.34
Magazines	7.47
Other paper	11.33
Containerboard	25.70
Boxboard	3.95
All metals	7.52
Glass	8.49
Plastics and textiles and "other"	5.85
Wood	2.52
Food wastes	9.24
Yard and garden wastes	7.58
	99.99

Source: McKinsey & Company, Inc., A Recycling Incentive Tax, November 1971, p. 3-2. Composited from typical compositions for research purposes. Adapted from Irwin Remson, A. Alexander Fungaroll, and Alonzo W. Lawrence, "Water Movement in an Unsaturated Sanitary Landfill," Journal of the Sanitary Engineering Division, Proceedings of the American Society of Civil Engineers, vol. 94, st. 2, April 1968. Cited in Jacquelin Burke and Weston Fisher, Realities of Recycling (Minneapolis, Minn., Minnesota Pollution Control Agency, 1973), p. 4.

The time-honored method of solid waste disposal is open dumping. Despite an EPA campaign to close 5,000 open dumps, most municipal solid waste is still disposed of in this most primitive of ways. Refuse is either dumped into open pits or into water bodies. For this traditional method of disposal the 80–20 breakdown in costs is still roughly applicable. But while the budgetary expenditures are rock bottom, environmental costs are often high. In growing recognition that waste management decisions should be made on the basis of total costs—budgetary plus environmental—open dumping has fallen into disfavor.

In the past several years many communities upgraded their dumps into sanitary landfills, "sanitary" expressing a hoped-for degree of improvement over dumps. The refinement is to bury solid waste in roughly 2-foot compacted layers with 6 inches of earth between each layer. The principal virtue of the method is that it is simple and cheap, adding only $2 to $4 a ton to the basic costs of collection and hauling that are required even with the open dumping. On top of these processing costs is the cost of land: sanitary landfill is comparatively land-intensive, and many municipalities are running out of landfill sites. Another drawback, held in common with open dumping, is that noxious materials may leach into the groundwater unless additional costs are incurred to prevent leaching. Because the solid waste stream has grown vastly more complicated, leaching of harmful substances has become a serious problem in some areas.

Many communities have opted for incineration as an alternative to various forms of dumps and landfills. But while incineration is land saving, it is a great deal more capital-intensive. Consequently, the processing costs are much increased, ranging from $8 to $15 a ton. Incineration reduces solid waste volume by somewhat more than half its weight and in the process trades a solid waste problem for an air pollution one. Air pollution control devices are most successful in trapping large particles and some specific gases in the smokestack. Unfortunately, many of the "exotic" trace materials get through an incinerator's smokestack, and the process of combustion itself may yield other harmful substances, such as hydrochloric acid. As more is learned about the health costs of air pollution, incineration becomes a less attractive method of solid waste disposal. At one time it was thought desirable to pass as much material as possible through the smokestack; now we find it is necessary to reconvert gaseous wastes back into solids and liquids.

Although nearly all municipal solid waste is treated in one of the above three ways, these methods are generally not considered satisfactory. Other methods of disposal are increasingly being proposed, some of which require elaborate and unproven technology, and none of which is in widespread use. Some of the more seriously considered methods are mentioned below.[6]

1. *Composting.* As we have seen in table 2, municipal solid waste is mostly paper fiber and other organic matter. Regionally the paper fraction varies from perhaps 25 to 60 percent. In composting, the organic matter is separated from the metal, glass, rubber, and plastic, and then decomposed aerobically. (The process may be partially anaerobic, with little oxygen at the center of the pile.) The resulting product, however useful as a soil conditioner, lacks the elements of a fertilizer. According to Burke and Fisher, composting is not presently a viable solid waste management option because of the difficulty in separating inorganic material, lack of markets for the final compost product, and process costs that are substantially higher than alternative disposal methods.[7]

2. *Incineration with Energy Recovery.* With the recent increase in energy prices, energy recovery has become much more attractive. In this form of incineration, some of the incombustible material is likely to be removed before burning, although this is not always the case, and the waste matter is likely to be mixed with coal or some other fuel, although this is not always the case either. The resulting charge is burned to produce electricity or steam for space heating. The incinerator residue is often disposed of by landfill. Incineration with energy recovery has been used in Europe for many years. As with other forms of incineration, before such methods are widely adopted, close attention should be paid to the materials being incinerated and the resulting air pollution. Some of the toxic substances can be treated after they are burned and before they leave the stack; others may best be prevented from entering the waste stream. The tradeoff of prevention versus cure depends on the scale of use, among other things.

3. *Pyrolysis.* Again, in pyrolysis preprocessing is needed to remove incombustible, corrosive, and otherwise harmful substances. The waste is then heated at very high temperatures in the absence of oxygen. Paper, tires, and plastics, each with a high energy content, are converted into liquid and gaseous fuels.

4. *Anaerobic Digestion to Produce Methane.* If all the dry organic fraction of the annual production of municipal solid waste could be transformed into methane by microorganisms, this methane would amount to perhaps half our present annual consumption of natural gas. However, much of the waste material is dispersed and unavailable, so

that perhaps only 6 percent of any natural gas consumption could be replaced by methane from organic waste.[8] Still, this is an enormous quantity. To produce methane on a large scale, however, it would be necessary to speed up greatly the natural anaerobic processes, which are presently very slow. Moreover, anaerobic digestion may not be complete, leaving some sludge for disposal.

5. *Resource Recovery*. In the past several years it has been proposed, principally by the Bureau of Mines, but also by EPA, that materials should be recovered from municipal solid waste by techniques similar to those found in the extraction of virgin materials. To do this, large amounts of energy and capital are used to "mine urban ore," as the catch phrase has it, by crushing, grinding, separating by air streams, magnets, and wet gravity techniques, and by other processing.

One example of a "mineral industry" technique is the wet process developed by the Black Clawson Company to separate and recover paper fiber, metals, and glass. In an initial demonstration, the outputs were roughly: cellulose fiber, 18 percent by weight; iron, 6 percent; glass, 4 percent; aluminum, 0.5 percent; landfill material, 9.5 percent; and air emission, 62 percent.[9] The process is heavily capital- and energy-intensive. A pilot plant in Franklin, Ohio, uses about 23 gallons of oil per ton of waste processed, for example. Unfortunately, the wet process reduces the cellulose fiber to its lowest quality use. The process was originally designed to use the reclaimed fiber as roofing felt, which is already a cheap commodity. Presumably if there were many wet processes all producing roofing felt, the market would soon be saturated. Another use of the reclaimed paper fiber is to produce energy. The wet process leaves a homogeneous mass of cellulose fiber that can be dried and then burned. Drying of course requires energy.

It is often claimed that municipal solid waste is richer in metals and other valuable materials than virgin ores, but this certainly is not always the case.[10] Moreover, the components of the municipal solid wastes are contaminated in far more complicated and variable ways than virgin ores.

6. *Combination Methods*. An interesting combination of methods is being developed by Geoffrey Stanford.[11] As in the composting method, the organic matter is separated from the other material. The cellulose, garbage, leaves, and so forth, are then enriched with sewage sludge and plowed into impoverished soil and irrigated with treated sewage water. Instead of an inert soil conditioner, the resulting mixture becomes a topsoil material. Stanford's method goes a step further than the Muske-

gon method, which uses treated sewage water but not municipal solid waste for irrigation and fertilization. In Stanford's method, paper fiber is the principal resource. It is transformed by microorganisms into sugars which are available to plants as a high energy source. (In contrast, the burning of the dried fiber content for energy recovery is a low energy use of the fiber.) Metals and other inorganics can then be separated and reclaimed by mining techniques similar to those described.

Stanford's method is intended to ameliorate both the solid waste problem and a large part of the water pollution problem, but there are several potential difficulties in the method. First there is the concern that viruses and other pathogens will be transmitted from the sewage sludge and sewage water to the soil, contaminating crops grown on it. It may be, however, that pathogens are more effectively controlled on land in the presence of air and soil microbes than in the water environment they presently inhabit. In any case, the matter will have to be thoroughly investigated before this method is accepted. A second problem is the presence of heavy metals—cadmium and mercury, for example—and other toxic substances in the industrial waste that is mixed with municipal solid waste and municipal sewage. The solution to this problem may be the segregation of municipal sewage from industrial sewage, which could be very expensive, or the banning of certain substances from the traditional municipal waste streams, or both. Upon examination it may turn out that heavy metals and other toxic substances that occur in municipal solid waste and sewage sludge are as damaging in their present treatments as they would be under this alternative. One interesting aspect of this alternative is that it could change the emphasis in collection from trucks, which represent one of the high-cost components in municipal waste treatment, to a further reliance on garbage grinders and slurries fed to the central treatment plant.

With the rising costs of waste disposal, these and other methods of dealing with urban waste are receiving much attention. There are already demonstration programs in several areas, and in the next few years there are likely to be large-scale production programs using these or more exotic technologies of waste disposal, especially for energy recovery.

Financing Disposal

Collecting and processing solid waste is a sizable expenditure for local governments; perhaps it is now $2 billion for the entire country.[12] This amount represents an internal cost from the point of view of local governments, but this internal cost is different from the internal cost of waste disposal to the individual.

Consider a town of N people, where, for simplicity's sake, everyone pays the same amount in taxes, and imagine an individual disposing of an item of trash. The amount of $C_1 \phi$ is the marginal cost of collecting, processing, and disposing of this item; the amount of $C_2 \phi$ is the environmental cost associated with this item. The amount of $C_1 \phi$ is raised by taxes. Again for simplicity, assume that the environmental cost is distributed equally over the entire population. The internal cost from the point of view of the individual is $(C_1 + C_2)/N$, which for a large community is virtually zero. The internal cost from the point of view of the town is C_1. The total marginal cost from the social point of view is $C_1 + C_2$.

The allocational incentive is determined by the internal cost (or price) from the point of view of the agent acting. In terms of allocational incentive, each individual is operating as a "rational economic man" in believing and acting as though disposal of his own refuse were free. In this market inefficiency, each individual is able to externalize nearly all the costs of his own disposal activities to other taxpayers. The fact that others do the same to him does not remove the externality, it merely compounds it. To understand how this situation can lead to a severe allocational inefficiency, consider a less familiar example than free solid waste pickup. Suppose the government declared that its policy was to make copper a free good. It collected tax money, hired miners and refiners to process copper ore, and then placed copper at selected distribution points for free pickup. Copper would be substituted for many materials and find its way into nearly every product. We could enjoy the benefits of free copper through cheaper product prices and collectively we would pay the production costs through taxes. The main source of the allocative inefficiency associated with the use of copper is the zero price facing the user. The underpriced resource, priced at zero, would be enormously overused. The same is true for municipal solid waste. Free pickup encourages too much material throughput in the economy.

For municipal solid waste, the principal allocational distortion is caused by the near zero prices facing the potential generators of waste, although the general tax burden required to finance C_1 leads to additional inefficiencies, or deadweight social losses.[13] Moreover, the amount of the distortion cannot be simply calculated by the amount a municipality spends on solid waste disposal. The calculation of the total social cost of disposal is somewhat different from the municipalities' total expenditure, for several reasons.

1. A municipality's expenditure counts only the internal costs from the point of view of the municipality. This accounting leaves out the health costs from the air pollution of the incinerator and other environmental costs. As a first approximation of the total social cost of municipal solid waste disposal, we could estimate the residual environmental costs (air pollution from incinerators, leaching from landfills, and so forth) and add them to the $2 billion figure. This would be a measure of the existing costs, but it would overstate the costs if solid waste were managed efficiently.

The tendency for economic agents to externalize costs upon others can be characterized as a Gresham's law of external costs. Just as bad money drives out good money, external costs replace internal costs. There is a tendency for each economic agent to substitute external costs for internal costs up to the point where the effort in making the substitution equals the internal costs saved. Governments are subject to the same temptation of Gresham's law of external costs as are individuals. The health cost from the smoke of the city's incinerator is just as real a cash cost in the budget but it is less visible, and one cost is internal to the budget, the other external. Thus there is a second difficulty with the $2 billion beyond the fact that it represents only governments' internal costs (such as C_1): the accounting problem is more than the "simple" one of estimating external costs such as C_2 and adding them to the internal costs for the municipalities, because municipalities tend to have the wrong mix of external and internal costs. If the costs of disposal were internalized at the individual and the municipal levels, not only would the total costs of disposal over time become lower, but alternative methods of disposal such as recycling would become more "economic."

2. Municipalities tend to have a narrow view of the solid waste problem. Every minute or so, at the disposal site of even a small city, another truck will roll in, needing to be unloaded. The immediate goal of not being buried by the solid waste stream often preempts more systematic planning. The view is "Here it is, what do we do with it?" To a municipality, its expenditures may be a short-term evaluation of the internal costs.

But even if a municipality had time for comprehensive planning, it would be economically rational for it to have a narrow view of its objectives. What might be efficient from the viewpoint of the whole society may be a sacrifice to the individual town. A single city, for example, is unlikely to impose packaging restrictions on manufacturers in its jurisdiction if the products are sold to other towns, because the benefits of lightened waste load are not felt by the town inconveniencing its industry. This is a variation of the theme of externalities, discussed above.

3. Because municipalities carry out their activities within a tax-exempt sector of the economy, they finance their activities on a different basis than the private sector. Unlike private firms, they do not have to earn profits to satisfy shareholders, nor do they pay income taxes to the federal government. They can borrow money at a lower rate than the private sector because municipal bond interest payments are not taxed by the federal government. While private firms pay property and excise taxes, local governments do not. To the extent that municipalities contract out solid waste collection and processing to private firms, this difference becomes less important. However, most municipalities manage some portion of the solid wastes generated within their boundaries, and the value of the resources used in collection and processing is understated in comparison with their value in the private sector.

For these three reasons it is difficult to use municipal expenditures on solid waste as a measure of the distortion that occurs because the individual is not charged the full cost of disposal. Thus cautioned, we can take the average cost of municipal solid waste disposal, $26 per ton, as a rough indication of the distortion; it does not include the residual environmental costs and may be an underestimate by half. For some products this figure, something more than a penny a pound, is an insignificant fraction of the product's price, but for bulky cheap items such as newspapers, glass bottles, and other forms of packaging, it is as much as 10 percent. Again, this is not a particularly meaningful comparison because the *average cash* cost of municipal collection and processing does not equal the *marginal social* burden of disposal for each item thrown away. Some things are much more and some much less burdensome than others. This is especially true of dispersed litter, for which the aesthetic costs of noncollection and late collection, as well as the collection costs themselves, are much higher than for items "properly disposed" in the solid waste stream.[14] With the residual environmental costs taken into account, it is quite possible that the marginal social damage of some items in the solid waste stream might be on the order of 20 percent or more of their prices.

The market channels the vast bulk of material products into the solid waste stream after their use, but it does not channel them all. For over fifty years the beer and soft drink industries were conspicuous examples of industries actively channeling the solid residuals of their product away from the municipal waste stream. In the next section we look at the market forces underlying this anomaly to see how comparisons of internal cost first led to returnable containers and then to throwaways.

Beverage Container Deposits

The lowly soft drink or beer container, costing the manufacturer 5 or 10 cents, may seem an insignificant part of the economy's material and energy flows. But multiply it by an annual consumption of about 60 billion containers and the container industry emerges as a major, multi-billion-dollar industry, and a rapidly growing one (164 percent growth in containers from 1959 to 1969).[15] A large part of the growth in container volume in the past decade has been a result of the switch from refillables to nonreturnables.[16] If refillables had maintained the same share of the market in 1969 as they had in 1959, the growth in beverage containers would have been only about 30 percent.[17] Beverage containers comprise a growing fraction of litter and municipal solid waste, and by various estimates presently make up somewhere between 54 and 70 percent of the volume of roadside litter and about 7 percent of all municipal solid waste.[18]

Up until the 1950s, refillable bottles were by far the most used container, but since 1954 for beer containers and since 1960 for soft drinks, the decline of refillable bottles has been dramatic. The competition between refillables and throwaways is a paradigm of Gresham's law of external costs. By shifting to a throwaway system, the beverge industry externalizes the cost of disposal to be borne by government. Because the shift from refillable bottles to throwaways externalizes costs amounting to many millions of dollars, the question is not why the shift was made, but why it was not made much earlier.

Although beer is a very old product, until a century ago it was sold fresh, in draft form, because it would spoil when bottled. Pasteurization solved the spoilage problem, and the invention of bottle crowns made it possible to mass-distribute beer in bottles by 1900. The soft drink industry can be dated as beginning in 1886 when Coca-Cola was first sold as a headache cure. Containerized beer and soft drinks are both recent phenomena. In the early years of the two industries there quickly grew up thousands of local brewers, soft drink franchises, and bottlers. At this time the container for beer and soft drinks was the expensive glass bottle, blown individually by artisans.

Consider the case of a soft drink manufacturer as he decides how to merchandise his product in those early days. He could institute a simple throwaway system, as in panel A in figure 17. This would require an expensive new bottle for every filling. Or, alternatively, he could use his own distribution system to channel the used bottles back to the bottling plant, as in panel B in figure 17. His choice depends upon a comparison of the internal costs of the two systems. His forward-distribution costs are about the same in either case and his decision is determined by whether or not the cost of a new bottle is greater than the storage, transportation, and washing costs of the returned bottle; included in these internal costs is the inconvenience to the customer of storing and returning the bottle to the store. In the early days of expensive glass bottles, this comparison favored the returnable system.

There is, however, a small problem. For two locations on the material flow path, the value of the material dips to zero, from the point of view of the owner. To keep the material on track and out of the environment or the solid waste stream, the soft drink company instituted two deposits at the crucial places. The retailer paid a deposit upon receipt of the

Figure 17. Costs of throwaway and refillable beverage systems

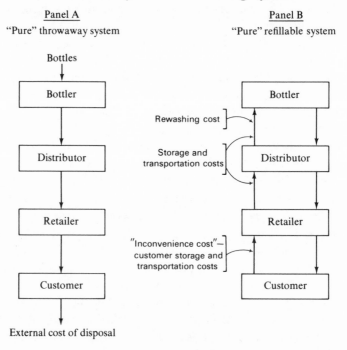

bottle, as did the customer. This was returned with the return of the bottle. The deposit is a device to keep a material along a desired flow path where the material's value to the owner at times dips to zero. Of course if the soft drink company had established a market for second-hand bottles, it could have accomplished much the same thing, but it would have not specified so narrowly and conveniently the material's flow path.

Having opted for a deposit system, the company must decide how large to make the deposit. This decision rests upon a comparison of internal costs and benefits. The higher the deposit, the greater the incentive to return the bottle, but also the higher the inconvenience of carrying the deposit for the customer and the more likely to discourage his demand for the beverage. The optimal deposit from the point of view of the beverage company is one where the marginal costs of discouraging demand from a slightly higher deposit just balance the marginal gains from encouraging a higher return rate for the container. The optimal deposit would not be high enough to get every bottle back, so that the optimal system would be a mixed system, composed of parts of panels A and B in figure 17. In the early part of the century the system was heavily weighted toward refillable bottles, with the return rate as high as twenty-five trips per bottle. For a 5-cent Coca-Cola, the 2-cent deposit was a substantial fraction of the product price.

In 1903 Michael Owens invented an automatic bottle machine that greatly reduced the cost of bottle manufacture and could have led to swift elimination of the refillable beverage system. However, the price of bottles did not come down to reflect the new lower cost of manufacture because Owens introduced a "live-and-let-live" pricing policy that set the price of machine-made bottles at the cost of hand manufacture.[19] With the cost of a throwaway system remaining higher than the cost of a refillable system, refillables continued to be the only type of beer and soft drink container.

The soft drink industry formalized the practice of refillables by adopting a "Code of Fair Competition," which made deposits mandatory after 1934 as well as specifying limits to price competition. The code was ruled an illegal constraint of trade but the deposit system remained intact. Some states passed legislation requiring deposits.

In the early 1930s the technical problems of canning beer were solved, and in 1935, after Prohibition, the American Can Company introduced metal containers for beer. While cans were expensive, they stacked more compactly and were lighter, saving transportation and storage costs.

They were also inherently nonrefillable but they were advertised as especially convenient to consumers, saving them the bother of a deposit and the return trip to the store. One might think that the Depression was a poor time to sell convenience to the consumer,[20] but cans were a marketing success and within a year most brewers offered beer in cans.[21]

Before the introduction of throwaway cans, Owens-Illinois, a glass manufacturer that dominated the beer and soft drink container industry, had not promoted throwaway glass containers. Compared with refillables, the throwaways might have required a lower price to make them sell to the bottling companies, but they might also have been sold in much higher volume. However, with throwaway cans penetrating the beverage container market, Owens-Illinois quickly responded with a throwaway glass "stubby."[22]

By this time there were several obstacles to the introduction of throwaway bottles. As reported by *Business Week* in 1939, the "campaign for the throwaway bottle is temporarily stymied in Michigan, Vermont, and New Hampshire by a refusal of authorities to revoke regulations requiring deposits for beer bottles. . . . Opponents to change say . . . that convivialists will clutter the highways and create tire hazards with empties."[23] Nonetheless these obstacles were overcome and the throwaway glass bottle also became a market success, though a much more limited one than cans. By 1950 cans held 26 percent of the packaged beer market, while throwaway bottles held only 2.4 percent.

The can industry finally solved the technical problems of containerizing soft drinks and introduced cans for soft drinks in 1953. (Soft drinks generated higher pressures and tended to corrode the cans.)[24] During the 1950s the volume of both throwaway bottles and cans grew rather slowly, but there was a sharp increase in production in the 1960s, a period of intense competition among container manufacturers.[25]

The story of how beer and soft drinks switched from refillable bottles to throwaways is considerably more complicated than that sketched above. It includes interindustry competition among the monopolistic glass, tinplate, and aluminum producers, all of whom were prosecuted for antitrust violations; the market structures of the beer and soft drink producers; and the roles of the retailers and bottlers, many of whom were tied to beverage producers through strict franchise agreements.[26] Yet the broad outline is clear; within a few years after sufficiently inexpensive throwaway containers became available, throwaway cans and bottles became the dominant form of packaging. Gresham's law of external costs was about to drive refillable bottles completely from the market when environmentalists began to stress the costs of solid waste and littering associated with throwaways. One of the first results was that in 1971 Oregon passed a law banning throwaway bottle containers.

Deposit legislation has several important effects. A principal purpose of the Oregon bottle bill, to reduce roadside litter, has been achieved. After the law went into effect, the littering rate for beverage containers fell by 83 percent and the total volume of litter fell by 47 percent.[27]

A second important purpose of container deposit legislation is to conserve energy and materials. Hannon has estimated that with an average of fifteen trips per bottle there would be an energy saving of 75 percent in a refillable system compared with a throwaway system.[28] There are few, if any, other industries with potential savings of this proportion. Savings in materials are substantial as well, mainly in the reduction of steel and aluminum consumption. Along with these material savings there are enormous savings in air and water pollutants generated in the processing of materials, as noted by the Environmental Protection Agency.[29]

Another effect of deposit legislation is to shift employment from the aluminum and steel industries (and the trash collection industry) to distribution and retail industries. One estimate is that 60,800 new jobs would be created and 60,500 would be lost.[30] In the past, before deposit legislation became a political controversy,[31] where refillable bottles and throwaways have been available side by side, the refillables have been about 20 percent cheaper, which is consistent with studies of the costs of the two systems. Comparing a total switch from throwaways to refillables, this would represent a saving to consumers of about $1.5 billion, which, except for the added inconvenience to consumers, represents a welfare gain to society. A large fraction of this $1.5 billion would be respent on other material goods, creating new jobs and offsetting some of the conservation gains in energy and materials. In the aggregate, however, this would tend toward a decline in the material intensity per unit of service and an increase in economic welfare per capita.

Waste Lubricating Oil

In the case of beverage containers we have seen a deposit system first established and then dismantled in response to internal cost comparisons by beverage industries. Deposit or depositlike systems can also be established by governments, as in the case of the Oregon bottle bill, and the practice need not be limited to beverage containers,[32] as can be seen in the treatment of waste lubricating oil.

In this country, waste lubricating oil is generated in automobile crankcases and many industrial machines. Some is filtered and rerefined into automobile and industrial lubricating oils, some is used for oiling roads in dust control, and some is used as a fuel. Most is dumped directly into the environment.[33]

In Germany, a greater density of industrial areas and almost total dependence on foreign sources for virgin oil have made the goals of pollution control and conservation of virgin oil more pressing. Beginning in the 1930s, Germany subsidized the reuse of its oil through its tax code. (After the 1956 Suez crisis France also subsidized its oil rerefiners.)[34] But to bring its tax system into harmony with other countries upon joining the Common Market, Germany eliminated its tax preferences to the rerefiners. In place of the tax preferences it established a depositlike system in which suppliers of virgin oil are taxed at a rate of about 6 cents a gallon. The revenue goes into a special federal fund that is used to contract with private companies for the collection and reprocessing of waste oil. The contracts are more generous for rerefined oil than for oil burned. Any generator of more than 200 liters of waste oil is assured free collection by the contractor in its region. To make the system work, there is provision for record keeping and disclosure.

This system is depositlike in the sense that money is collected from the virgin oil suppliers, and it is returned upon the flow of material to the scavenger and reprocessor. The material flow system has a price dip to zero at the filling station, which collects oil for the scavenger. Without the contracts, the filling station operator would have an incentive to dump surreptitiously. With the contracts, the waste oil is sufficiently desirable so that scavengers compete for waste oil, establishing a market for it. If the rerefiners were the same firms as the virgin oil producers, the system would look more like a deposit one, and if the internal costs of this returnable oil system were lower than the costs of the throwaway oil system, there would be an incentive for the virgin oil producers to institute the deposit system on their own.

Internalizing the Cost

Although not all products are channeled into the solid waste stream after use, most are. The failure to internalize the cost of solid waste disposal as part of a product's price is no different in principle from the failure to include the cost of liquid waste disposal (water pollution) or gaseous waste disposal (air pollution) in the price. For both air and water pollution, the solution favored in economic theory is effluent taxes imposed upon the emitters. If the administrative costs were manageable, this same solution could be recommended for the solid waste disposal problem. Unfortunately, for most cases of solid waste disposal, the administrative costs appear unmanageable. The major exception is the case of mandatory beverage container deposits. The Oregon bottle bill is probably the closest thing we have to an effluent tax functioning in wide use for any environmental problem, air pollution, water pollution, or solid waste. The difficulties in the administration of effluent taxes have to do with the following: (1) the number of polluters to be taxed, (2) identifiability of the polluter and his emissions, and (3) the size of the damage of the emission in comparison with the collection cost.

Administrative costs are an important consideration in any tax system, and not just in an effluent tax one, as can be seen in the case of developing countries. In the course of development, many countries faced the problem of how to finance much larger state budgets; should they concentrate on sales taxes, income taxes, or import tariffs? In the initial stages of urbanization, people and merchants are mobile and often anonymous, the wage per head is low, as is the sales value per transaction, so that the administrative burden of sales taxes and income taxes is a heavy one. Many countries begin with a concentration on import tariffs. There are relatively few ports, the goods are readily identifiable as they are unloaded, and the revenue per transaction is large because the value of the average transaction is large. In terms of the analogy, the number of "polluters" is small, they and their product stream are identifiable, and the product flow and, hence, the revenues are large for the average collection.

In the case of waste materials, considerations of administrative cost may dominate the design of an effluent tax system, much as they may dominate the design of a revenue tax system. The most important water polluters are relatively few in number; they are easily identified, being located along water bodies with fixed outflow pipes; and the quantity of pollutants per emitter is large, with an associated heavy environmental damage. In many cases, the administrative costs of monitoring and taxing water pollution effluents are small compared with the pollutant burdens taxed.

For some air pollution emitters the situation is rather different. Millions of cars and trucks are millions of individual small polluters.

These sources are mobile and vary over time in the volume of their emissions, depending on maintenance of the vehicles. Consequently, the measurement of emission volume by each polluter is difficult. Moreover, the environmental damage per polluter is small, so that the cost of collecting taxes per individual vehicle would be high relative to the damage. For these reasons, it is more effective to treat automotive pollution at the level of the manufacturer, rather than at the level of the emitter, the car or truck owner. At the manufacturing level there are only a handful of companies building pollution into vehicle design.

Compared with cars and trucks, the number of "emitters" of municipal solid waste is even larger. Each household is an emitter, each person is an emitter. There is no way of keeping track of each item of waste disposed of by each "emitter." And finally, the external damage associated with each solid waste emission is small compared with an average water or air polluter. In principle, if there were no administrative costs, a disposal tax equal to the marginal external cost of disposal could be levied on each item discarded into the municipal solid waste stream. The tax might be a penny or so for a person who disposed of a beverage container in a public trash can, and a dime for another who dropped the same container on a highway. Clearly, such fine tuning of the tax system is impossible because the administrative costs are too high to implement such a scheme.

As a particular case of solid waste disposed in public places, littering is usually handled by a simple prohibition. Beyond the prohibition against littering and requirements for disposing of solid waste in "proper" channels, the inefficiency arising from the market's inability to internalize disposal costs is usually accepted.[35] We can think of a prohibition against littering as a disposal tax tuned to the method of disposal. If a beverage container is disposed of in a trash can, the tax is zero; if the container is thrown on the highway, the tax is the chance of being caught, paying a fine, and perhaps being ordered to pick up a mile's worth of roadside litter. But this chance of enforcement is virtually zero, so that $50 or $100 fines for littering have very little effect. Littering is one of the nation's commonest crimes with one of the lowest conviction rates.

We can also think of a deposit system as a conditional disposal tax, but in this case the deposit is approached differently from the way in which it was used by beverage industries in the early part of the century. To illustrate, suppose for simplicity that the cost of disposal to society is 3 cents and a 3-cent deposit is being considered. The efficiency gain comes from the following comparison. The beverage consumer compares the convenience of throwing the container away with the forfeiture of the 3-cent deposit. If the convenience is worth less than the cost of disposal, measured by the 3 cents, it is to the advantage of the consumer to return the container. If the convenience is worth more than the 3 cents, disposal is more efficient than return. The fact that littering imposed higher social costs than proper disposal complicates the analysis but the principle is the same, and there still can be efficiency gains from mandating deposits.

Sometimes it is suggested that deposit systems should not be mandatory. A deposit system and a throwaway system should be equally available so that the consumer can choose between the two. With the interpretation of a deposit system as a conditional disposal tax, this is the wrong choice according to the efficiency criterion. The deposit should be mandatory and set equal to the external disposal cost. The correct choice, in terms of panel B in figure 17, is between the consumer's convenience associated with disposal and the forfeit of the deposit. In a mandatory deposit system the consumer has this choice. To generalize, under the efficiency criterion the choice should be whether to generate disposal costs while paying for them or whether to refrain from generating the disposal cost in order to save the internalized payment. The efficiency criterion does not provide for the choice of whether or not to impose an external cost in order to save an internal cost.

Deposit systems may be a solution in only a few solid waste problems: their application depends a great deal on administrative costs. In the case of beverage containers, deposits are a proven system and largely self-administering. Deposit systems are useful devices for moving materials down flow paths for which the material price dips at times to zero (without the deposit). An alternative, a straightforward disposal fee, has been proposed by Fred Smith at the Environmental Protection Agency. A fee, or tax, representing the cost of disposal, would be imposed upon new products' paper and packaging, perhaps at some bulk stage in their production. By making new materials more expensive, this incentive would increase recycling in the consumption sector, lengthen durability, and decrease material throughput, lightening the load on municipal solid waste facilities. If the tax were imposed on the basis of weight, and if the tax were not to be collected on too many items at too many points, its administration would not be difficult.

The tax would be no more complicated than other excises already in existence, if the tax were based on some easily measurable characteristic like weight. As solid waste disposal costs are in the range of a penny a pound it has been proposed to set the fee at this rate. At the manufacturer's level there is some efficiency loss in that the tax is "collected too early." That is, it is too early to tell which waste stream the product will eventually be thrown into and too early to have an incentive effect on the consumer's choice of waste stream. Still, the manufacturer has the incentive to economize on the material intensiveness of his products, which is an important reason for the tax. We have to weigh the gain in administrative ease in collecting the tax earlier with the loss of efficiency by not collecting the tax at the level of the final disposer. Because the tax is likely to be based on some simple characteristic in any case, such as weight, there will be some efficiency loss anyway from not being able to finely tune the tax to the social cost of disposal, so that the increase in the efficiency loss may be small when we move back a level in the tax's collection.

A disposal tax at the manufacturers' level would discourage all material flowing out of the manufacturing sector, recycled material as well as virgin material. But in principle a disposal tax should reflect disposal costs. Material that imposed no disposal cost because it was recycled before it reached the municipal dump should not be taxed; the disposal tax should allow for a rebate upon evidence of satisfactory salvage or recycling of the material. This would reverse the incentive so that recycling in the production sector is encouraged instead of discouraged. A rebate provision has, in principle, considerable merit as it fine tunes the tax to actual downstream disposal costs. A disposal tax without a rebate provision is like a litter tax on beverage containers, while a disposal tax with a rebate provision is like a deposit system on beverage containers. But unlike deposit systems, a disposal tax with a rebate provision on most materials would be difficult to administer, encouraging problems of definition and certification of "recycled." Depending on the rebate provision, there would be an incentive to relabel or sell home scrap to qualify for the rebate.

In choosing the most appropriate level for a disposal tax, a compromise must be struck among several factors. The further toward the final consumer, the more points of collection and items to keep track of. The further toward the mine's mouth, the fewer points of collection and the smaller the number of product types to keep track of, but the less finely tuned the tax to the final costs of disposal. The more coarsely tuned the tax—for example one based on weight—the simpler its administration and the less the loss from shifting its level of collection backward. It would simplify the tax if it were collected at a level where there were fewer recycling loops to contend with and hence less of a rebate problem.

At levels of the economy before the disposal tax is collected, unwanted materials are discarded as though their disposal cost were zero. For some bulky materials (such as tree slash) this may be nearly true, while for others (such as taconite mine refuse dumped into Lake Superior), this may be far from the case. In principle, social costs from dumped materials at earlier levels should be treated by specific effluent taxes or other controls, but such fine tuning is often lacking so that aggregate disposal charges may have to do some of the work of specific effluent taxes or other controls. And so the question remains, in a broadened form, where is the best level to impose a disposal tax?

At the level of the economy where the tax is collected there is the incentive to cheat by dumping surreptitiously. In a town which charges for each barrel of refuse picked up from each household, there is the incentive to use public trash barrels or even the roadside or street. Similarly, for a firm dumping smoke, but ostensibly under controls of either effluent taxes or standards, there is the incentive to emit more at night or when the inspectors are not around or the monitors somehow avoided. By collecting the disposal tax "too early" some of this problem is avoided. The tax is prepaid, for those after the tax's level of collection. Granted that although for those after the tax's level of collection the incentive to change their behavior toward less socially costly means of disposal is lost, still some of the proper incentive to economize on material is already felt and unavoidable.

It is likely that for different materials, the accounting of the various inefficiencies and administrative costs would indicate different levels of collection of the tax, different arrangements for rebates, and so forth. If the tax is to be based on some simple characteristic like weight, and if materials discarded at earlier levels of the economy impose social costs not too different from materials disposed of later, then there is a good case for collecting the disposal tax all the way back to the material's level of extraction. Here the number of collection points is the smallest and, like import tariffs, the administrative burdens of collecting the tax are modest. The problems of rebates for recycled content is solved automatically; there are no recycling loops that go back before the mine's mouth.

If based on weight, the "disposal cost prepayment" is no more than a specific severance tax. For some materials, such as wood, mercury, or cadmium, whose social costs of disposal are roughly proportionate to the product's own market value, the disposal charge might be set as a fraction of the product's market value, and in this case the disposal charge would be an ad valorem severance tax. As we shall see more clearly in the next chapter, an ad valorem severance tax is very nearly the same as a percentage depletion allowance, except that the payment flows to the government instead of away from it. Thus we could impose disposal charges at the mine's mouth at virtually no extra administrative cost; all that would be needed would be to change the sign on the percentage depletion allowance. Over the past fifty years the details concerning cutoff points and other administrative problems have been minutely litigated and defined. Of course, with the change in sign in the percentage depletion deduction, it would be in the interest of extractive industries to argue for cutoff points with less processing rather than more processing as they have argued for in the past.

Without a full accounting of the external costs of a material as it follows its flow path from one end of its life to the other, we cannot rely entirely on the market for efficient allocations. In this chapter we have considered one type of externality calculation, the external cost of disposal. In a world where all the externalities except those of solid waste disposal are internalized, it would make sense to set disposal fees equal to the external disposal costs, and let the market allocate materials over paths. But in a world where many external costs remain external, the situation cannot be remedied by a single disposal tax or a single deposit equal to disposal cost. In such cases it may sometimes be preferable to compare the total costs associated with materials over alternative paths, for paths yielding the same product service. If one path clearly dominates another, it may make sense to guide material down the better path. For example, a refillable beverage container system dominates a throwaway system—the savings in energy, materials, air and water pollution, and solid waste costs more than offset the loss in convenience of the throwaway. In such a case, the optimal deposit might be set to be more than the cost of solid waste disposal averaged over littering and "proper" disposal. It would be the amount required to induce the optimal amount of reuse, where optimal is defined as the least-cost balance of refilling and discarding, and where cost is the total cost, internal plus external.

In other cases, and perhaps more generally, a disposal fee may be preferable. How broad it should be, how far back from the consumer toward the point of extraction, and what provision for a recycling rebate there should be are in large part questions of administrative cost. The work done by Fred Smith of the Office of Solid Waste Management Programs suggests a concentration on paper and packaging products, which dominate the municipal solid waste stream. For paper, the tax would be collected at the paper mills, of which there are fewer than 800. In other cases, the administrative costs of remedy may be too high to be worth the cure and it may be preferable for us to live with the inefficiency arising from the market's inability to incorporate disposal costs into product price.

Notes

1. If the costs of disposal were internalized, the price to the disposer would be negative in the following sense mentioned in chapter 2: for valuable material objects one receives cash or something valuable for giving them up, but for waste materials one expends cash or effort in getting rid of them. In some economic models it is mathematically convenient to deal only in nonnegative prices, and in such cases it is customary to cast the problem as paying or not paying non-negative prices for waste removal services.

2. To the extent that mining wastes are long lived, they may affect the resource base for future generations and become an issue of intertemporal fairness.

3. For a comprehensive treatment of the costs of solid waste collection and processing in rural areas, see F. Lee Brown and A. O. Lebeck, *Cars, Cans, and Dumps: Solutions for Rural Residuals* (Baltimore, Md., Johns Hopkins University Press for Resources for the Future, 1976).

4. Environmental Protection Agency update of the 1971 figure cited in U.S. Environmental Protection Agency, *Second Report to Congress: Resource Recovery and Source Reduction* (Washington, D.C., 1974), table 1, p. 3.

5. This is an estimated national average, by the Office of Solid Waste Management Programs, U.S. Environmental Protection Agency, 1974. For Washington, D.C., for 1969–70, Quimby found the cost of collection to be $25 a ton, the cost of landfill $3 a ton, and the cost of incineration $8 a ton. Quimby, *Recycling*, table 11, pp. 104–105.

6. The first five methods are taken from Burke and Fisher. For more on this subject and for further references, see Jacquelin Burke and Weston Fisher, *Realities of Recycling* (Minneapolis, Minn., Minnesota Pollution Control Agency, 1973).

7. Burke and Fisher, *Realities*, p. 37.

8. Allen Hammond, William Metz, and Thomas Maugh II, *Energy and the Future* (Washington, D.C., American Association for the Advancement of Science, 1973) p. 73.

9. Burke and Fisher, *Realities*, p. 48.

10. The iron content of municipal solid waste is at best 5 percent, while the iron content of low grade iron ore is 35–40 percent; aluminum is 0.7 percent of municipal solid waste and is 15–25 percent of bauxite.

11. A presentation at the Engineering Foundation Conference "Recycle Implementation" (Asimolar Conference Grounds, Pacific Grove, Cal., Feb. 13–17, 1972).

12. The figure of $4 billion is often used but this appears too high. While it is often said that collection, processing, and disposal of solid waste constitute the third highest local expenditure, ranking just after schools and roads, Vaughan and the Bureau of the Census arrive at a figure of direct local expenditure of $1.7 billion. See Richard D. Vaughan, "National Solid Wastes Survey: Report, Sum-

mary and Interpretation," in *1968 National Survey of Community Solid Waste Practices: An Interim Report*, U.S. Department of Health, Education and Welfare, Oct. 1968 (presented at the 1968 Annual Meeting of the Institute for Solid Waste of the American Public Works Association, Miami Beach, Oct. 1968) p. 50; and U.S. Bureau of the Census, *Government Finances in 1972–73*, GF 73, no. 5 (Washington, D.C., Oct. 1974) table 7, p. 23. This $1.7 billion figure can be compared with the figure of $114 billion of total direct spending by local governments (same table). We cannot simply multiply the EPA estimate of average solid waste cost of $26 per ton times the EPA estimate of total municipal waste, 135 million tons, because much of this waste cost is borne by the private sector and not local governments.

13. This argument does not necessarily mean that there should be charges, per barrel of trash pickup, as is mentioned below.

14. Estimates for dispersed litter range from a low of 4.4 cents per pound (Council on Environmental Quality, *The First Annual Report* [Washington, D.C., U.S. Government Printing Office, 1970] p. 109) to a high of 32 cents per item, by Arsen Darnay and William Franklin in *Proceedings of the First National Conference on Packaging Wastes* (Davis, Cal., University of California 1969) p. 16. This latter cost is cited by Darnay and Franklin from Solid Waste Management's estimate of the cost of bottle pickup in New York City. For a discussion of litter collection costs, see Brown and Lebeck, *Cars, Cans, and Dumps*.

15. Statement of Eileen Claussen, Office of Solid Waste Management Programs (OSWMP), U.S. Environmental Protection Agency, before the California Legislative Assembly Committee on Natural Resources and Conservation, January 1974, p. 1.

16. Refillables are glass bottles that are washed and refilled; "recycled" bottles are usually smashed and remelted; in this context "recycled" cans are remelted and milled into new cans in the case of aluminum, and perhaps into other products in the case of steel; returnables may be either refillables or "recyclables" or may be collected by the retailer and thrown away.

17. Research Triangle Institute figures quoted by Claussen.

18. Claussen, "Statement," p. 2.

19. Kenneth Fraundorf, "Social Costs Imposed by Containers for Beer and Soft Drinks," (Ph.D. dissertation, Cornell University, 1971) chapter 4, pp. 2, 5.

20. Linder suggests that leisure and hence "convenience" increases in value with higher productivity, which makes the growth of more expensive throwaways during the Depression seem anomalous. According to Linder's thesis, we should expect to see more throwaways and other forms of convenience packaging with higher wealth, as people try to economize on scarce time. Thus Linder's thesis is an important explanation for the growth of the "throwaway society," in general, but not for the growth of throwaway beverage containers during the Depression. See Staffan B. Linder, *The Harried Leisure Class* (New York, Columbia University Press, 1970).

21. Fraundorf, "Containers," chapter 2, pp. 8–9.

22. Fraundorf, "Containers," chapter 2, p. 9.

23. Cited from John Lesow, "Litter and the Nonreturnable Beverage Container: A Comparative Analysis," *Environmental Law* vol. 2 (Winter 1971) pp. 197–202.

24. Fraundorf, "Containers," chapter 3, pp. 11–12.

25. Fraundorf, "Containers," chapter 4, p. 20.

26. As the reader may have guessed, Fraundorf is a good source for more details.

27. These figures are from the Oregon State Highway Department surveys of thirty randomly selected sites on state highways. Collections were made monthly. Cited from Don Waggoner, *Oregon's Bottle V Bill Two Years Later* (Portland, Ore., Columbia Group Press, 1975) pp. 6, 14.

28. Bruce Hannon, "System Energy and Recycling" (document no. 23) (Urbana, Ill. Center for Advanced Computation, University of Illinois, Jan. 5, 1972) p. 43.

29. In a study done by Midwest Research Institute for the Environmental Protection Agency, "Resource and Environmental Profile Analysis of Nine Beverage Container Alternatives, Final Report," it is estimated that a ten-trip refillable glass bottle generates 82 percent less waterborne wastes and 71 percent less atmospheric emissions than an aluminum can. Cited from Diana Wahl, *Reduce* (Washington, D.C., League of Women Voters Education Fund, 1975) p. 15.

30. Taylor Bingham and Paul Mulligan, *The Beverage Container Problem: Analysis and Recommendations,* a study prepared for the U.S. Environmental Protection Agency, Research Triangle Institute (Washington, D.C., U.S. Government Printing Office, September 1972) pp. 83–84.

31. Beverage container deposits have become an intense political issue, with hundreds of bills introduced requiring deposits. William Coors, a chairman of the board of Adolph Coors Co., estimated that $20 million is being spent annually to oppose deposit legislation. (*The Washington Post,* June 30, 1975, p. A1.) For a discussion of the inefficiences attendant on imbalance of resources and industry participation in environmental, legislative decision making, see Mark Sharefkin and Talbot Page, "Industry Influence on Environmental Decision Making," in Edwin Haefele, ed., *The Governance of Common Property Resources* (Baltimore, Md., Johns Hopkins University Press for Resources for the Future, 1974).

32. In some countries, such as Israel, deposits are common for many glass containers other than beer and soft drink bottles.

33. It is estimated but probably greatly overestimated that automobile crankcase oil is responsible for 30 percent of the ocean oil pollution, an amount that is more than the discharge of ocean tankers. National Commission on Materials Policy, *Material Needs and the Environment Today and Tomorrow* (Washington, D.C., U.S. Government Printing Office, June 1973) pp. 2–30.

34. William Irwin and Wolfgang Burhenne, "A Model Waste Oil Disposal Program in the Federal Republic of Germany," *Ecology Law Quarterly* vol. 1, no. 3 (Summer 1971) p. 475. Pages 471–494 of this article are used for many other details about the treatment of waste oil in Germany.

35. There are a few schemes to internalize the cost by charging households by the number of trash barrels collected. With such schemes there is the temptation for people to become litterers (where littering is taken to mean any illegal dumping of solid waste). Disposal fees levied upon industrial users of the municipal facilities are more successful, the industrial generators being larger, fewer in number, more identifiable, and less able to dump surreptitiously.

6
Taxes on Virgin Materials

I see no justification for the mining industry to continue to operate under outmoded laws that do not provide for payment to the acknowledged owners—the public—for minerals extracted.
—Congressman Wayne Aspinall, on federal, public land, shortly after his retirement.

THE THIRD and final source of market inefficiency to be discussed here is that relating to taxation of virgin materials. Special provisions have lightened the tax load on mineral industries since the enactment of the income tax in 1913. At first the federal tax rate was low and the special provisions for mineral industries were minor. But over the past sixty years the provisions favoring mineral and other extractive industries have greatly expanded. Since the federal tax rates have substantially increased as well, the provisions favoring virgin materials have also increased relatively. To some extent it has been the intention of Congress to favor the extractive industries, and to some extent the extractive industries' lightened tax load has been fortuitous (from the point of view of the extractive industries); some tax provisions, available to all industries, have been most advantageous to the extractive industries.

The lightened tax load may result in lower prices for virgin materials, higher profits in the extractive industries, more investment and exploration for extractive resources, and higher rents for landowners of mineral and timber property. Our concern is focused on the impact of tax advantages upon the prices of virgin materials, because these prices affect material flows and the market for scrap materials. In their taxation, secondary firms are treated like manufacturing firms, so that much of what we need to know about the effects of taxation on the balance of material flows can be learned by focusing on the tax treatment of virgin material producers in comparison with taxation of other firms. We will find in this chapter that there is little agreement on just how much of the tax advantage accorded virgin materials goes into prices, rents, exploration and other investment, and profits. The extractive industries assure us that their special tax treatment increases exploration, adds new reserves, and lowers prices to the consumer. Some consumer advocates fear the tax preferences mainly inflate the profits of the favored industries. Economists tend to think that the tax preferences initially raised profits, but that this effect has long since disappeared in competition as additional firms have been attracted into the extractive industries; that the long-term effects are lowered prices, increased rents, and more exploration and other investment in the extractive industries. Unfortunately, there have been few studies to estimate the strengths of the various effects. And most of what little research has been done has concentrated on the petroleum industry.

This chapter briefly outlines what these tax preferences are and how they came into being. An effort is made to translate them into effects on prices. A more careful look is taken at the efficiency question, first on the capital allocation side, then on the product allocation side.

The Tax Advantages

A favored tax position is equivalent to a situation in which there is a direct subsidy from the U.S. Treasury and no tax advantages. In this sense, favored tax provisions constitute an indirect subsidy to the extractive industries. Estimates of some of these indirect subsidies are shown in table 3.

Table 3. Indirect Tax Subsidies to Extractive Industries, 1969, 1972, 1974
(millions of dollars)

	Domestic			Foreign		
Provisions	1969	1972	1974	1969	1972	1974
Excess of percentage over cost depletion	1,470	1,400	n.a.	n.a.	n.a.	50
Expensing of mineral development costs	340	650	n.a.	n.a.	150	n.a.
Capital gains treatment:						
For cutting timber	140	175	n.a.			
On coal and iron royalties	n.a.	n.a.	5			
Foreign tax credit				n.a.	1,500	n.a.

Sources: *The Economics of Federal Subsidy Programs*, a Staff Study prepared for the use of the Joint Economic Committee of the U.S. Congress, Jan. 11, 1972, p. 167, for 1969 data; other estimates from personal communications, except the 1974 estimate of foreign excess depletion, which is from a statement of G. B. Schultz, Feb. 4, 1974, to the House Ways and Means Committee.

Note: n.a. indicates data not available; blank spaces indicate absence of data in original tables.

Of the four provisions listed in table 3, only one, percentage depletion or the depletion allowance, is unique to the extractive industries. The expensing of exploration and development costs ("intangibles" for the petroleum industry) is nearly unique, but this preference has its counterpart, to a limited degree, in the expensing of research and development allowed in other industries. Capital gains rates are applied to many types of assets and are certainly not limited to mineral and timber assets, although they are especially important there. And perhaps the most important provision, the foreign tax credit, is definitely a uniform provision extending to foreign income generated by any U.S. corporation. But again it happens that the advantages of the foreign tax credit fall mainly on the extractive industries.

These provisions should be considered together as a group. They interact, and to some extent one may substitute for another. For this reason the total effect of the combined provisions cannot be found by simply adding up the individual tax losses taken one at a time. Setting this sort of problem aside for the moment, we can crudely add the tax losses of a particular industry and compare them with the gross income of that industry. Four-fifths of depletion claimed in 1960 was for petroleum, of which 95 percent was classed as excess by the U.S. Treasury. For the same year, the treasury estimated that 98 percent of the claimed deductions for exploration and development were made by the petroleum industry.[1] Assuming that these patterns have roughly remained the same, about 80 percent of the excess depletion ($0.80 \times 1,400 = 1,120$) and 98 percent of the expensing subsidy ($0.98 \times 650 = 638$) can be allocated to the petroleum industry. With a gross income of crude oil and gas that was about $16.1 billion in 1972,[2] we can calculate the effect of eliminating the tax subsidies if the total effect were shifted forward into prices. Petroleum prices would be expected to increase by $1.76/16.1$, or 11 percent.

Obviously this method is very crude and depends heavily on aggregate estimates of "legitimate" and "excess" tax preferences. The treasury estimates depend upon asking firms what would be the tax payment with and without the special provisions. If this difference is understated, as indeed we shall see it is with respect to the excess of percentage depletion over cost depletion because of the capitalization of lease acquisition costs, the impact of the indirect subsidies will be understated. On the other hand, only part of the tax advantage will be shifted into lower prices. These two qualifications work in opposite directions, and without knowing the strengths of the two factors, it is impossible to tell whether

11 percent is too high or too low for the petroleum industry. Thus cautioned, we can move on to consider the provisions in somewhat more detail.

1. Depletion

Over the years there have been three forms of the depletion allowance. Here we consider percentage depletion and cost depletion. In a later section we see how discovery depletion, which now no longer exists, gave rise to the concept of percentage depletion.

PERCENTAGE DEPLETION. The percentage depletion allowance—percentage depletion for short—is a deduction from taxable income. In 1975, Congress removed the percentage depletion allowance from the seven largest oil corporations. The provision remains intact, however, for the rest of the oil industry and for virtually all other extractive industries.[3] Of the four provisions, percentage depletion is the easiest to translate directly into an equivalent price subsidy. The reason is that, unlike other deductions in the federal income tax, percentage depletion is calculated on the basis of *gross* income. For the mineral industries, gross income is basically the sales value of the mineral output at the stage of concentration. The value at this stage may include 50 miles of transportation and some processing. Thus the deduction varies in direct proportion to the value of the mineral output and functions as a negative sales tax.[4] If such a "tax" existed, a negative sales tax would be a transfer of money per unit value of a product *from* the government instead of *to* the government. A 22 percent depletion deduction, for example, might be equivalent to an 18 percent negative sales tax; then this depletion deduction acts as though the U.S. Treasury were giving 18 cents for every dollar's worth of output to the mineral firm.

Although most of the discussion of percentage depletion has been limited to its effects on oil and gas, relatively, the subsidy of percentage depletion is about as important to other extractive industries as it is to the petroleum industry. Although it is true that 80 percent of the percentage depletion allowance goes into the petroleum industry, this single industry is about three times bigger than all the other mineral industries combined. The deduction extends to seashells and clay, at a 5 percent rate, and the allowance encourages the extraction of such toxic materials as mercury and cadmium at a rate of 22 percent, which is now the present rate for oil and gas as well. Thus it is misleading to think that just because the tax losses are greater for the petroleum industry, the price effects must be greater in the petroleum industry than in other industries.

The basic equivalence between percentage depletion and a negative sales tax is very simple; complications will be discussed later. Imagine a mineral corporation with

> Y gross income from the mine (sales value)
> C costs of production
> t tax rate (48 percent)
> p percentage depletion deduction (the statutory rate that varies from mineral to mineral)

The corporate federal income tax is the tax rate times taxable income. To arrive at taxable income not only are the costs of production subtracted from gross income, but also the depletion deduction rate (p) times gross income (Y). Thus the mineral corporation's tax payment is (tax rate) times (taxable income):

$$t\,(Y - pY - C) = \text{tax payment}$$

and hence its after-tax profits are net income − tax paid:

$$(Y - C) - t\,(Y - pY - C)$$

Now imagine that the depletion allowance is eliminated and in its place a subsidy on sales is offered. Let s be the per unit subsidy on sales. How large must this subsidy be to be equivalent to the depletion allowance? To answer this question, we first write down the income tax payment with the sales subsidy but no depletion deduction. This is the tax rate times taxable income:

$$t\,(Y + sY - C),$$

which equals the tax payment with the sales subsidy. Second, we write the after-tax profits; that is, net income − tax paid.

$$(Y + sY - C) - t\,(Y + sY - C)$$

which equals after-tax profits with the sales subsidy. Then we equate the two after-tax profits and solve for s:

$$Y - C - tY + tpY + tC = Y + sY - C - tY - tsY + tC$$

$$tpY = (1 - t)\,sY$$

$$s = \frac{t}{1 - t}\,p \tag{6.1}$$

When s equals $tp/(1 - t)$, s is just large enough to make the direct sales subsidy exactly equivalent to the percentage depletion. If the tax rate were 0.5 instead of 0.48, the depletion allowance would be equivalent to a subsidy on sales of the same nominal rate. That is, a 22 percent depletion allowance would be equivalent to a 22 percent negative sales tax. The mining corporation would be just as well off if the allowance were eliminated and replaced by a subsidy of 22 cents for each dollar's worth of sales.

There are several qualifications which make the algebra more complicated but which leave the result above essentially correct. First, of course, the corporate tax rate is not 50 percent. With a 48 percent tax rate, s becomes equivalent to 92 percent of p [92 percent $= 48/(1 - 48)$]. Second, there is a 50 percent of net income limitation to percentage depletion. By this limitation, if one-half net income is less than the depletion rate times gross income or, in other words, if $(Y - C)/2 < pY$, then the law requires that the allowable percentage depletion is not pY but half of net income, or $(Y - C)/2$. The purpose of the limitation is to prevent the depletion allowance from exempting or sheltering more than half of net income from the income tax. Because of this limitation, the depletion allowance, in the absence of other provisions that make it more favorable, can do no more than halve the effective tax rate.[5]

In the depletion study of 1963,[6] the U.S. Treasury found, for domestic properties, that about three-quarters of the depletion taken by all minerals produced was based on percentage depletion, one-fifth on the 50 percent of net income limitation, and the rest on cost depletion.[7] Table 4 shows the relation between depletion actually taken and the statutory rate (p) that the treasury established by using 1960 tax data.

In some cases (for example, coal, lead, and zinc), the effective rate of the depletion allowance is considerably below the statutory rate; however, for most of the minerals important for recycling, the two rates are rather close. The 50 percent of net income limit explains part of the divergencies, though not the cases (such as sulfur), where actual depletion taken is greater than the statutory rate of percentage depletion. Timing and cost depletion help explain such cases as these. In 1969 the percentage depletion rate for oil and gas was decreased from 27½ percent to 22 percent; the rates for a few other minerals were decreased by a percentage point, and many stayed the same (molybdenum went up from 15 to 22 percent). The reductions in p decrease the frequency with which the 50 percent of net income limitation becomes operative.

Table 4. Depletion Allowance Rates

(percentage)

Mineral products	Statutory rate (p)	Computed price subsidy, 92% of statutory rate	Effective rate of depletion: depletion as a percentage of gross income
Oil and gas	27½	25.2	26.6
Sulfur	23	21.2	24.3
Bauxite	23	21.2	22.7
Lead and zinc	23	21.2	11.4
Iron	15	13.8	13.8
Copper	15	13.8	12.6
Limestone rock	15	13.8	13.2
Phosphate rock	15	13.8	14.4
Bituminous coal	10	9.2	6
Anthracite coal	10	9.2	2.7
Sand and gravel	5	4.6	4.9
Stone	5	4.6	4.7
All mineral products			20.7

Source: President's 1963 Tax Message, Part I (revised Mar. 27, 1963) Committee on Ways and Means, 88 Cong. 1 sess. (1963) p. 309.

For this reason one would expect that a survey after 1969 would find that the effect of the present depletion allowance for most minerals is more like that of a negative sales tax than the pre-1969 depletion allowance.

So far we have seen that percentage depletion, being based on the sales value of the mineral product, is nearly equivalent to a negative sales tax on the product. Normal sales taxes, which are positive transfers to the government, are levied independently of the election of the taxpayer for other tax provisions. But the depletion deduction is not independent of other tax provisions. In order to use percentage depletion, a mineral firm must give up some of the advantages of other tax provisions, of which cost depletion is the most important. And if percentage depletion were eliminated, it is likely that other provisions besides cost depletion—capital gains, expensing, and foreign tax credits—would be used more intensively than at present and would to some extent substitute for the loss of percentage depletion.

COST DEPLETION. A mineral firm must choose between percentage depletion and another deduction, cost depletion. In choosing one, the firm must give up the other. (In practice there are rules that prescribe the choice of deduction.) Cost depletion is analogous to depreciation.

In the process of establishing a mine, there are expenditures for geological surveys, the acquisition of a lease, for shafts, drilling rigs, and other structures. Some of these expenditures are added together into an account called the adjusted basis. The adjusted basis is the same account used to determine the capital gain or loss at the time of sale. If all the acquisition, exploration, and development costs were included in this account, the adjusted basis would measure the cost of creating a capital instrument (the mine). An estimate is made of total minerals to be produced by the mine during its lifetime. When the mine begins to produce, it is allowed a cost depletion deduction which is the same fraction of the adjusted basis as the first-year's production is of the total mineral stock to be eventually mined. The adjusted basis is then decreased by whichever amount is larger, percentage depletion or cost depletion. For the next year the allowable cost depletion deduction is the same fraction of the new adjusted basis as that year's production is of the remaining amount of mineral to be eventually mined. Thus in the final year of production, just when the mine is being closed down, the last year's production is 100 percent of the mineral remaining to be mined, and the cost depletion deduction is equal to whatever adjusted basis is left. If all the expenditures in creating the mine were included in the adjusted basis, and if there were no percentage depletion, cost depletion would satisfy two principles of depreciation: (1) the sum of cost depletion deductions would equal the cost of producing the capital asset, and (2) the deductions would be spread over time to match the flow of income from the asset. This, in principle, is the case in depreciating the cost of a machine for a manufacturing firm.

The existence of percentage depletion complicates the picture, however. In the first few years of production the adjusted basis is likely to be high and the net income low. The 50 percent of net income limitation for percentage depletion may make cost depletion more generous than percentage depletion. But after a few years, when the adjusted basis is lower and production is at a larger rate, both gross and net incomes become larger. The adjusted basis will be smaller because of previous depletion deductions and percentage depletion is likely to be more generous than cost depletion.

If there were only cost depletion, the adjusted basis would reach zero only when the mine was exhausted. A percentage depletion deduction lowers the adjusted basis by the amount of the deduction, as long as the basis is greater than zero. But with percentage depletion available, the adjusted basis can be reduced to zero while the mine is still young. Once the adjusted basis is reduced to zero, the original capital cost of the mine is recovered—at least for the exploration, development, and acquisition expenditures that went into the adjusted basis account. There is no more cost depletion, but there is no such limitation to percentage depletion. As long as there are gross income and net income, percentage depletion is allowable even though the original cost of creating the asset has been recovered. Deductions for percentage depletion do not make the basis negative; once zero, the basis remains zero even though percentage depletion deductions are still being taken. Because of this non-limitation to percentage depletion, the total depletion deductions, cost, and percentage—over the entire life of the mine—can be many times the cost of original investment, measured by the original adjusted cost basis. The petroleum industry has been able to deduct through depletion nineteen times the original adjusted basis and the sulfur industry, because of the low initial cost of investment, two hundred times.[8]

From the point of view of a mineral firm trying to minimize its tax payment, the adjusted basis is wasted in the years the firm elects the percentage depletion option. The same percentage depletion is allowable no matter what expenditures go into the adjusted basis account. If exploration and development expenditures could be shifted to other accounts, which are also deducted from income, for tax purposes the mineral firm's total deductions could be increased. By shifting expenditures from the adjusted basis account to other accounts, a mineral firm can take both percentage depletion and deductions based on these other accounts at the same time.

2. *Exploration and Development Costs, and Other Accounts*

Over the years, more and more exploration and development expenditures have been taken from the depletion account (adjusted basis) and placed into other accounts. These changes have been accomplished by congressional action and by administrative ruling.

In the original income tax, the intention was to treat the capital costs of establishing a mine analogously with capital costs in other industries: the amount of deductions should equal the total capital expenditures of exploration, acquisition, and development, and these deductions should be spread in time against the income flowing from the mine. This concept of depreciation for mining gradually changed in a fundamental way. The success of the mineral industries in breaking away from the original concept of depreciation is shown in table 5. In the first three rows are

Table 5. **Deductions for Capital Expenditures, by Percentage Depletion Rates**
(dollar figures in millions)

	All rates (all mineral products)	27½% (petroleum)	23% (mineral products)[a]	15% (metals)[b]	15% (non-metals)[c]	10% (mineral products)[d]	5% (mineral products)[e]
Actual capital expenditures							
1. Acquisition	783	754	11	2	9	6	1.4
2. Exploration	1,207	1,189	4	10	2	0.9	0.5
3. Development	2,087	1,907	39	108	17	13	2.5
4. Total	4,077	3,850	54	120	29	20	4.4
Capital recovery through depletion account							
5. Depletion (domestic)	2,050	1,613	97	144	118	70	9
6. Depletion (foreign)	765	655	4	105	n.a.	1	n.a.
7. Total	2,815	2,268	101	249	118	71	9
Capital recovery from accounts other than depletion							
8. Exploration expensed	925	917	2.1	3.8	1.0	0.5	0.5
9. Exploration deferred expense	68	61	0.9	4.9	0.9	0.1	n.a.
10. Exploration charged to depreciation	48	48	n.a.	n.a.	n.a.	n.a.	n.a.
11. Development expensed	1,290	1,151	23	90	13.4	11.6	0.9
12. Development deferred expense	25	1.5	2.7	17	3.2	0.6	n.a.
13. Development charged to depreciation	701	688	10	0.5	0.1	0.9	1.6
14. Abandonment losses	495	484	2.3	1.6	2.4	5.1	n.a.
15. Total	3,552	3,351	42	118	21	19	3.0
16. Percent capital recovered other than through depletion account (line 15/line 4)	87	87	78	98	72	95	68
17. "Legitimate" depletion (line 4 minus line 15)	525	499	12	2	8	1	1.4
18. Percent depletion legitimate (line 17/line 7)	19	22	12	0.8	6.8	1.4	16

Source: Compiled from information in the *President's 1963 Tax Message*, Part I (revised Mar. 27, 1963) Committee on Ways and Means, 88 Cong. 1 sess. (1963).

Note: n.a. indicates data not available.

[a] Sulfur, uranium, bauxite, lead, and zinc.
[b] Iron, copper, gold, and silver.
[c] Refractory clay and quartzite, fire clay, other clay, calcium carbonates, dimension and ornamental stone, limestone, phosphate rock.
[d] Bituminous coal and lignite, anthracite, sodium chloride.
[e] Sand and gravel, stone, clay, and shale.

the capital costs of establishing the mineral asset, the mine, for mineral industries categorized by the various statutory percentage depletion rates (p). Rows 5 and 6 show the actual depletion deductions taken, including both percentage and cost depletion. Rows 8 to 15 show deductions, for the same original capital outlays, taken on the basis of other accounts. Row 16 shows the percentage of capital recovered other than through depletion. In row 17 are the "legitimate" residual capital expenditures to be recovered through depletion deductions. A "legitimate" depletion deduction is the difference between total capital expenditures and deductions taken through accounts listed on rows 8 to 14. And finally, in row 18 is the percentage of total depletion taken that is "legitimate."

One can see from row 18 that the petroleum industry has been less successful in shifting expenditures from the adjusted basis account to other accounts than industries with more modest rates of percentage depletion. If an industry were successful in shifting all its capital expenditures to other accounts, the percentage depletion deduction would be equivalent to a pure negative sales tax. Under the original concept of depreciation, this would be a pure subsidy. At the time of the depletion study, percentage depletion was about 80 percent a pure negative sales tax subsidy for the petroleum industry and nearly 100 percent pure for many of the other minerals.

So far we have considered only one of the two principles of depreciation—the total deductions for capital expenditures should equal the expenditures actually taken. In the second principle (timing of deductions for capital expenditures), mineral industries have been favored a second time. The present situation, which is somewhat more favorable to the mineral industries than when the data were collected for table 5, is as follows. For hard minerals (ones other than petroleum), all domestic exploration and development expenditures can be deducted immediately from income from any source (immediate deduction is called expensing). For unsuccessful ventures, this is the end of the matter for these expenditures. For successful ventures, exploration but not development expenditures are "recaptured." The amount of the exploration expenditure expensed is either subtracted from future depletion deductions or added onto taxable income. And the expenditure is added to the adjusted basis.

To see the basic differences between tax treatment of mineral industries and other industries, imagine that percentage depletion did not exist and that recapture occurred in the same year of both discovery and expensing. With expensing and recapture simultaneous, the situation would be as though neither provision existed. The exploration expenditure would be capitalized by adding it to the adjusted basis, and without percentage depletion, the exploration expenditure would be recovered through cost depletion. The situation would be analogous to other industries where capital expenditures lead to deductions spread out over time to match the income stream generated by the capital expenditures. With recapture taking place after the expensing, there is the advantage of timing: immediate expensing lowers present taxes, recapture increases future taxes by the same amount. Development expenditures, which are much greater for most extractive firms, are treated still more favorably. One might think of recapture as infinitely far off. There is immediate expensing but no recapture; but there is no adding to the adjusted basis either. The situation is analogous to very rapid depreciation in other industries: the entire asset is written off in the first year. Thus exploration expenditures are treated less favorably than development ones, which allow for immediate expensing without later recapture. This situation is a little strange. One would think that if the mineral industries are to be subsidized, exploration should be given more favorable treatment than development.[9]

The privilege of expensing allows a hard mineral firm to take deductions earlier than would be the case under the concept of depreciation, a concept that would match the deductions against the flow of income. Taking deductions sooner has the effect of pushing tax payments off into the future. This is equivalent to an interest-free loan from the U.S. Treasury for the amount of the tax deferred and for the same length of time that the deduction would have been taken in the absence of the expensing privilege. If, for example, a corporation's discount rate were 14 percent, postponement of a tax for five years would effectively halve the burden of the tax. And with inflation, an interest-free loan is made more attractive by the amount of the rate of inflation. The privilege of immediate expensing of exploration and development expenditures is even more advantageous to some individual mineral firms, especially smaller ones, than percentage depletion.

For petroleum, many of the exploration and development expenditures are lumped together in the term "intangibles." Intangibles do not divide the visible and the invisible, but the salvageable from the nonsalvageable. Thus drilling rigs, pipe, and tanks, which can be moved from one site to another, are tangible, while the "expenditures for labor, fuel, power, materials, supplies, tool rental, and repairs of drilling equipment in connection with drilling and equipping productive wells"[10] are intangible. Lease acquisition costs and some exploratory expenditures such as geophysical and geological surveys (where there is likely to be further exploratory work) are placed in the adjusted basis account to be recovered through depletion; these two latter costs can be written off whenever the effort is abandoned. About 75–80 percent of the total cost of establishing a producing property is classed as intangible, to be expensed immediately. Just as in the case of hard minerals, those expenses to be deducted immediately can be used to offset income from any source, and not only income from petroleum output.

In summary, it can be said that both petroleum and hard mineral industries have been successful in two respects: (1) Most of the exploration and development expenditures have been shifted from the adjusted basis account to other accounts so that deductions for exploration and development can be taken in addition to percentage depletion. (The ability to take two deductions for the same cost is called the "double dip.") (2) The timing of exploration and development expenditures has been made more advantageous by the privilege of expensing, even with eventual recapture.

3. Capital Gains

The capital gains provision was designed to lower the tax rate on long-term appreciation of value of any asset. But capital gains provisions are especially advantageous to the extractive industries in two ways.

TAXING INCOME AT CAPITAL GAINS RATES. For timber and, to a lesser extent, iron and coal, income that would normally be considered ordinary and taxed at the usual corporate rate of 48 percent is called capital gains and taxed at the more favorable capital gains rate of 30 percent. For timber, the increase in stumpage value (the value of the tree before cutting, a value which grows as the tree grows) is classified as capital gains. It may seem as if only a small fraction of a timber corporation's income would fall into the category of increase in stumpage value and thus be classed as capital gains. However, it appears that timber corporations are successful in classifying nearly all their taxable income as capital gains. Table 6 shows composite figures from four large corporations. One method of converting ordinary income into capital gains income is illustrated below. For a more thorough analysis the reader is referred to Sunley's "The Federal Tax Subsidy of the Timber Industry."[11]

Table 6. Percentage of Taxable Income, Long-term Capital Gains, for an
Average Large Firm

(dollar amounts in millions)

Year	Taxable income	Capital gain[1]	Capital gain as percentage of taxable income
1964	50.0	45.9	91.8
1965	50.4	49.6	98.4
1966	47.5	48.9	102.9
1967	42.2	50.2	118.9
1968	89.5	75.7	84.5
1969	96.1	101.4	105.5

Source: Emil Sunley, "The Federal Tax Subsidy of the Timber Industry," *The Economics of Federal Subsidy Programs,* a compendium of papers submitted to the Joint Economic Committee, 92 Cong. 2 sess. (1972) pt. 3, p. 331.

[1] Net long-term capital gains taxed at the 25 percent alternative tax rate.

Suppose that a timber firm buys a tract of forest land for $1,000. The acquisition cost is divided into two parts: $600 is considered to be the intrinsic value of the land and $400 the value of the timber already standing on the land. The $400 is the adjusted cost basis upon which capital gains will be computed (the same adjusted cost basis upon which cost depletion is computed for minerals). In fifteen years the timber grows in stumpage value to $1,400, with the basis value of the land still $600. When the trees are cut, $1,000 of the firm's income is taxed at the capital gains rate (the stumpage value minus the adjusted basis of the timber).

The adjusted basis, upon which capital gains will be computed for most industries, is adjusted by "capital" expenditures. A capital expenditure is one that increases the value of the capital asset (for timber the capital asset is the forest), and normally the adjusted basis is increased by the amount of these expenditures. But for timber, many capital expenditures are deducted directly (expensed) from income from other sources and are not added onto the adjusted basis. Suppose, to continue the example, $200 had been spent thinning and spraying in order to improve the forest to its final $1,400 stumpage value. These are not operating costs, for the benefits will be felt fifteen years later when the trees are cut. If this expenditure is treated as a capital cost and added onto the adjusted basis, the capital gain will be $200 less than otherwise [$1,400 − ($400 + $200) = $800 instead of $1,000]. The smaller capital gain means a smaller capital gain tax, and so by this calculation the firm saves $60 in taxes in fifteen years when the gain is realized ($200 × 0.30).

But it is considerably more favorable to the firm if instead of adding the forest improvement costs to the adjusted basis, the firm expenses these costs against current income generated by manufacturing or some other part of its activities. The current income is lowered by $200 and since this income is ordinary, the firm saves $96 ($200 × 0.48). In effect, by treating the forest improvement costs as current business expenses, the timber firm converts ordinary income into capital gains income. Compared with the situation in which these costs are treated as capital costs and added to the adjusted basis, income to be taxed at capital gains rates is $200 higher and income to be taxed at ordinary rates is $200 lower.

Besides converting ordinary income into capital gains income, expensing of forest improvement costs advances the timing of the deduction. If these costs are added to the adjusted basis, the $60 saving in taxes is felt fifteen years from now, but if these costs are expensed, the saving in taxes of $96 is felt immediately. Not only is the saving larger but it is sooner. In the mineral industries, expensing is like a zero interest loan, but in the timber industry expensing along with capital gains treatment is like a negative interest loan. Compared with other industries that must depreciate capital costs, the timber firm in the example is receiving $96 in benefit today and will give up only $60 in fifteen years. All told, Sunley estimated that capital gains treatment, the mismatching of income and expenses and resultant conversion of ordinary income into capital gains, could conceivably lower the effective tax rate from the nominal 48 percent to 7 percent.[12] The average timber firm does not do as well as the most successful hypothetical firm: the average firm's effective tax rate is somewhere near the capital gains rate of 30 percent and perhaps somewhat lower when the advantages in timing are taken into account.[13]

Unlike the timber industry, nowhere near the total income for coal and iron is taxed at capital gains rates. However, income going to the holders of coal and iron leases is subject to capital gains rates. While a much smaller fraction of coal and iron income is subject to capital gains rates, these two industries receive percentage depletion that is unavailable to the timber industry.

CAPITAL GAINS AND RISK. So far, the advantages of capital gains described accrue mainly to the timber industry. But to the extent that each of the mineral industries is risky, each benefits from capital gains provisions. In fact, for a given average return on exploration ventures, the lower the probability of success on any one venture, the greater is the advantage of capital gains to a mineral firm. This is contrary to the oft-accepted proposition that because mineral industries are risky they are less favored and should be accorded the special provisions of percentage depletion.

Suppose that there are two corporations, Long Shot and Sure Bet, prospecting for minerals. Corporation Long Shot concentrates on high payoff minerals with a large risk of failure. It acquires eleven leases, each costing $5. The first ten prove to be busts, but the last is a bonanza, which Long Shot sells off for $105. The difference between the investment cost of the successful venture ($5) and its market value ($105) is the project's *discovery value*. For the whole series of ventures, total costs are $55, total gains $105, gain $50, and average gain on investment 91 percent (50/55). Sure Bet concentrates on less risky minerals. It acquires two leases, each costing $27.50. The first is a failure but the second is successful and Sure Bet sells it off for $105. The total costs, gains, net gain, and average gain are the same as for Long Shot, but Long Shot receives more favorable tax treatment because it carries more risk for the same average return. For each of its ten failures, Long Shot offsets $5 (abandonment of lease) against income from other sources. These $50 of deductions save it $24 in taxes ($50 × 0.48) that it would otherwise have paid on ordinary income. Its adjusted basis for its successful venture is $5 so that its capital gain is $100 ($100 = $105 − $5). The tax on this gain is $30 and the net change in its tax bill from all its eleven exploratory efforts is $6.

Sure Bet does not fare as well with its tax bill. It, too, can offset its unsuccessful venture against ordinary income. Thus, for its unsuccessful venture it saves $13.20 in taxes ($27.50 × 0.48) from other sources of income. For its successful venture its adjusted basis is $27.50, so that its capital gain is $77.50 ($77.50 = $105 − $27.50). The tax on this gain is $23.25 ($77.50 × 0.30). The net change in Sure Bet's tax bill from its two exploratory efforts is $10.05. Sure Bet is taxed almost twice as heavily as Long Shot for minerals of the same value and for the same long-run expected net return on the same net cost of investment. The reason of course is that the more risky explorations increase the opportunity to match expenses against ordinary income, decreasing ordinary income to be taxed. And with the greater separation between successful and unsuccessful ventures, the adjusted basis of the successful venture is smaller, permitting more of the proceeds to be taxed at capital gains rates. Such calculations can make big differences in the aggregation of properties for tax purposes. The more risky the mineral industry, the more ordinary income can be effectively converted into capital gains income.

The situation is as if the government were a generous silent partner sharing 48 percent of the losses and only 30 percent of the wins as long as the losses and wins are on separate bets. Thus, for the same average return it pays the mineral gambler to take long shots in order to spread out his costs on unsuccessful bets. The government is an even more generous silent partner to a wealthy private individual, as in this case the difference between tax rates for ordinary income and capital gains income is larger.[14]

4. The Foreign Tax Credit

Foreign tax credits were established a long time ago (1918) with the idea of preventing double taxation. Basically the credit allows companies to subtract the tax paid to foreign governments from the U.S. federal tax liability.[15]

While foreign tax credits are available to all, they are especially important to the extractive industries. One of the important costs to an extractive firm is the payment to the owner of the land or mineral right. The payment is normally in the form of a lease purchase, sometimes called a "bonus payment," or in the form of a royalty, which is a payment per unit, or per unit value, of the mineral extracted. For foreign operations, the landowner is often a foreign government, and what would be a royalty payment in this country is often called a foreign income tax. Royalty payments are considered costs of doing business and are deducted from income for tax purposes. The same payment, treated as a royalty, lowers the federal tax by 48 percent of the payment, but treated as a foreign tax lowers the federal tax by 100 percent of the payment. Thus there is a natural tendency among mineral firms to encourage foreign governments to relabel royalty payments as foreign taxes. Of the $4 billion claimed in foreign tax credits in 1969, 1.8 billion went to the petroleum industry.[16]

While the logic of the foreign tax credit is to avoid double taxation, this logic is not applied to domestic state and local taxes. These taxes are deducted from income as normal expenses of doing business and are not subtracted dollar for dollar from the federal tax liability—not treated as a credit. If they were, there would be a strong incentive for state and local governments to increase their taxes to the point where all the federal tax payment is diverted into the state and local treasuries. Such increases in state and local taxes would have no effect on tax-paying companies.

The foreign tax credit, along with the federal income tax, creates a floor of 48 percent of net income under which tax payments to the foreign government are entirely painless to the U.S. firm. Up to this floor, the interests of the foreign government and the U.S. corporation are not in conflict: it is to the advantage of the foreign government, and it costs nothing to the U.S. firm (while generating the good will of the foreign government) to divert tax money up to this floor from the U.S. Treasury to the foreign treasury. In this sense, U.S. corporations become tax collectors for foreign governments.[17]

The foreign tax credit can be both defended and attacked under the efficiency criterion, as will be shown in a later section on efficiency. Foreign tax credits are a complicated subject, having to do with the desirability of U.S. investment abroad and foreign competition to U.S. companies in foreign lands, multinational corporations, producer cartels, and balance-of-payments effects. No more will be said here about foreign tax credits, except that they are a very large subsidy and whatever the gains from them in terms of these other factors, these gains should be weighed against a major tax loss, which is the cost of the subsidy. This subsidy is important to the extractive industries. Percentage depletion, by itself, can only halve the federal tax rate, due to the 50 percent of net income limitation. Foreign tax credits, in addition to depletion allowances, permit many extractive companies to pay little or no federal tax.

Taken together, percentage depletion and cost depletion, expensing and other timing provisions, capital gains and the foreign tax credit form a package leading to low effective federal income tax rates for firms in extractive industries. It is important to realize that the various provisions are not independent. If percentage depletion were eliminated, the amount of income to be taxed at capital gains rates would almost certainly increase as would the amount of cost depletion taken—there would be a larger incentive for "discovery companies" to sell out at capital gains rates, leading to a new higher adjusted basis for the buyers that could be used to their advantage for cost depletion. The same sort of interaction makes the percentage depletion worth more than what appears by a comparison of percentage depletion and cost depletion (and by the U.S. Treasury's definition of "excess" depletion, which measures the difference between the depletion deduction calculated by each method for a given company for a given year). The existence of percentage depletion makes mineral properties more valuable; mineral land values are bid up accordingly so that the percentage depletion tax provision leads to higher lease acquisition costs, higher adjusted basis, and more cost depletion allowable. Thus part of the effect of percentage depletion spreads over to make the cost depletion provision more valuable. A simple calculation of "excess" depletion as the difference between the two options for a given year understates the true worth of the percentage depletion for a mineral company.

As we shall see in a later section, the complicated tax package for extractive industries leads to many types of inefficiencies. One may ask how this structure of taxation came about and what the intentions of the legislators were. Were the legislators generally aware of the inefficiencies and were they explicitly accepted in order to achieve other goals? The answer appears to be, no. In the next section, we trace the history of percentage depletion. This story gives an idea of how the development of discovery value is related to the question of ownership and the use of the resource base over time.

A Brief Chronicle of the Depletion Deduction

The story begins with the 1913 Internal Revenue Act, which in a single sentence permitted "a reasonable allowance [deduction] for the exhaustion, wear and tear of property arising out of its use in the employment in the business, not to exceed, in the case of mines, 5 percentum of the gross value at the mine of the output for the year . . ."[18] The statute did not use the term depletion. The wear and tear of mineral capital (the ore in the ground), both the man-made structures and the mineral *in situ,* were lumped together and treated the same as other kinds of capital in other industries. Both mineral capital and man-made capital were to be subject to deductions for depreciation. The total sum of deductions was to equal the original investment, and the deductions were to be spread out over time and matched against income. The difference between mineral industries and other industries was the extra limitation on mineral industries that the deduction each year must be less than 5 percent of the gross income that year. Instead of being favored, the mineral industries were placed slightly at a disadvantage compared with other industries.

Soon after the Revenue Act came into effect, there were complaints that some income generated before 1913 was being unfairly taxed. Some capital assets (mines) were established before 1913 and had appreciated in value by this date. For these assets, the market value in 1913 was considerably greater than the cost of investment. During this time of appreciation, income was accruing in these assets, later to be realized as streams of income by the sale of minerals. Those who had been lucky enough to realize the accrued income before 1913 paid no tax and those unlucky enough not to have realized the same income by 1913 had to pay a tax on the accrued income when it was eventually realized. Clearly, it was argued, the intention of Congress was to tax income *accrued and realized* after 1913. Income accrued before 1913 should be tax free, just as income realized before 1913.

The remedy, which became law in the Revenue Act of 1916, was to allow deductions up to the original investment or the fair market value as of 1913, whichever was larger. It was considered a temporary adjustment which would become obsolete in a few years. While apparently it applied generally to depreciable capital assets in all industries, it was particularly important to mineral industries.[19] For them there often was a great difference between the original investment and the fair market value, the difference being attributable to the value of successful discoveries. A successful venture might take $1,000 of original investment in lease acquisition, exploration, and development to establish a property worth $1 million. The 1913 law would allow deductions totaling the original investment, $1,000, while the 1916 law would allow deductions totaling the fair market value, which was equal to the original investment plus the increase in value due to the successful discovery (the whole million dollars). At the same time, the 1916 law eliminated the 5 percent of gross income annual limitation, substituting the requirement that the annual deduction, now called a depletion deduction, be no more than the market value of the mineral at the point of extraction. In terms of the example, the 1916 law allowed new deductions of $999,000 (for the discovery value) to be subtracted from income earned after 1913, as long as the $1 million was the fair market value at the time of the imposition of the income tax.

The worth of the deduction, to the firm, is the amount of taxes saved by having a lower taxable income. An equivalent way of thinking, but from the opposite perspective, is to look at the amount of income the deduction exempts or shelters from the income tax. In this view, the deduction for discovery value shelters $999,000 of later income from taxation. The worth of the shelter is the amount of tax that would have to be paid on the sheltered income if the shelter disappeared. The 1916 law introduced a new tax shelter, exempting income from taxation equal in amount to the discovery value. One can think of the 1916 law as exempting from taxation the increase in value of a mineral holding due to discoveries made before the imposition of the income tax.

In the process of discovery and appropriation, new value is introduced into the economy. In terms of figure 2 (Schematic of Material Flows) in chapter 2, the process of discovery and appropriation brings material across the boundary from the environment into the economy. The 1916 law said, in effect, that such introductions of valuable material should go tax free as long as they occurred before 1913, even though they meant an increase in income to the mineral firm and they are not matched by investment expenditures. The intention does not appear to have been to introduce a new principle into the tax code but to repair a temporary inequity resulting from the introduction of the income tax and a peculiarity of mineral firms. The peculiarity is that for mineral firms the accrual of income and its realization can be separated by several years during the time it takes to develop a mine and put it into the production stage.

Only a year after the 1916 Revenue Act the United States became involved in World War I. It was argued that new mineral discoveries would aid the war effort and hence should be encouraged through tax incentives. One incentive proposed was to accelerate the timing of deductions for extractive industries. Another was to remove the limitation on discovery depletion which required that it be applied to discoveries before 1913. It was inequitable, it was argued, that mines opened up for the war effort in 1917 should receive less favorable tax treatment than mines discovered before 1913. Tax equity, remarked Louis Eisenstein, "is the privilege of paying as little as somebody else."[20] In this case "equity" was mixed with patriotism, and the proposal to extend discovery depletion was adopted by the Senate Finance Committee, with the proviso that the discovery valuation had to be determined within thirty days after the discovery. Mark Requa, a petroleum engineer and entrepreneur who was a prime advocate of discovery depletion and perhaps the most important witness, testified that with statistical and geological techniques, evaluation of the discovery value would be a relatively routine matter.[21] While the extension was popular in Congress, the armistice ending the war was signed before the bill extending discovery depletion could pass both houses. However, even though its intended purpose to aid the war effort was no longer relevant, the bill passed and became law in 1919.

Perhaps the bill's success was due to its momentum as a popular war measure, or perhaps it carried on the basis of its "equity" appeal— "mines opened up after 1913 should not receive less favorable tax treatment than mines discovered before 1913." Whatever the reason, the 1919 law introduced a new and enduring concept into the tax code: discovery value should be tax exempt.

In 1919 and 1920, mineral values were very high and valuations of discoveries made in those first two years of the law were correspondingly high. When the market for minerals fell sharply in 1921, many mineral firms found that deductions for discovery depletion, which were not recomputed in the face of changed market prices, were far in excess of their reduced incomes. Deductions for discovery values were sufficient to shelter not only all the mineral income for many firms, but income from other sources as well. It was embarrassing to see manufacturing firms with mineral operations paying no tax at all; to prevent this unintended result, Congress limited the discovery depletion deduction taken any one year to no more than the income from the mineral operation. This remedy still allowed mineral firms, whose entire income was from mineral output, to pay no tax. Apparently still embarrassed, Congress three years later tightened the limitation so that the deduction for discovery depletion taken in any one year could be no more than half the net income from the mineral property. By this amendment, discovery depletion could only halve the effective tax rate for any given year.

It soon became clear, contrary to Requa's assurances, that it was extraordinarily difficult to compute the value of a newly discovered mineral deposit buried in the ground. There were complaints that the U.S. Treasury was much too generous in its valuations of discovery value. At the time the secretary of the treasury was Andrew Mellon, who had extensive interests in petroleum and sulfur. Partly because of certain senators' mistrust of Mellon, a committee was established under Senator Couzens to investigate how discovery evaluations were determined. According to Lerner, "the investigation clearly established that the valuation of mineral deposits, the definition of discovery, and all other facets of discovery depletion were highly arbitrary and extremely difficult to administer."[22] In the hearings for the Revenue Act of 1926 the counsel to the Couzens' Committee proposed that the uncertainty and discrimination of discovery depletion could be eliminated by the substitution of an explicit rule of thumb for what had proved to be an unworkable process of evaluation of minerals underground. The rule of thumb was percentage depletion, which he recommended in place of discovery evaluation for all minerals. The idea was to set a percentage of gross income for each mineral so that the total of deductions based on percentage depletion would sum up, on average, to the value of discoveries of that mineral class.

The Senate accepted the idea of percentage depletion, but only for petroleum, and estimated that a 30 percent depletion allowance would be about the same, on average, as discovery depletion. The House estimated that 25 percent would be about equivalent to discovery value, and the difference was split in conference to 27½ percent, which remained in effect until 1969. Thus, percentage depletion came into effect, not as a new tax concession, but as a rule of thumb to make the old concept of discovery depletion workable. The 50 percent of net income limitation carried over to this new rule of computation.

Once percentage depletion was granted to the petroleum industry, its advantages became apparent to the other mineral industries. The American Mining Congress argued that the high cost of determining discovery value prevented small mining companies from applying for discovery depletion. This trade association suggested that a 15 percent depletion allowance would average out to the discovery value of hard minerals. The National Coal Association proposed 6 percent percentage depletion allowance on the grounds that reserves were uncertain, but because there were few discoveries of coal, the industry received little benefit from discovery depletion.[23] According to L. C. Graton, a mining geologist testifying for the industry, deductions up to the discovery value were a constitutional right, the right of property. The problem lay in the "clumsy wording" by which

the mining industry has suffered, and still in substantial measure suffers hardship, discrimination, and unnecessary expense, as well as uncertainty and embarrassment in its proper undertakings. . . . [The] simple solution of a long-standing vexatious difficulty . . . [is] the percentage method for determining depletion, a method simple in its conception and application, but indeed almost magical in its effects. . . . In fact, the percentage method may be described as the purified essence of the analytic appraisal method whereby all the crudities and uncertainties, all the assumptions and the differences of judgment are mainly, if not entirely, eliminated, and the true answer, or a close approximation to it, automatically furnished in every instance. . . . Like a spring balance, it weighs whatever is placed in its scale pan and automatically returns the correct answer. It is always right, it is never wrong. It is the essence of fairness and justice.[24]

Over the years from 1926 to 1954, extractive industries were largely successful in their attempts to gain percentage depletion. All the original minerals that were once subject to discovery depletion are now subject to percentage depletion, and a large number of extractive materials, which have virtually no discovery value, such as clay, have been added to the list of materials receiving percentage depletion.

The Tax Disadvantages

Not all of the special tax treatment accorded to the extractive industries is preferential. Although the property tax is in concept a uniform tax, it may appear that extractive firms, because of their large land holdings, may be burdened more heavily by the property tax than firms in other industries. A second circumstance may lead one to think that extractive firms are relatively more burdened by the property tax: the property tax is less than uniform in practice because firms bargain with localities for lower effective tax rates, and localities compete against each other by using lower effective rates to lure industry. Most firms gain bargaining power by threatening to locate elsewhere. But extractive firms cannot move their forests and mineral reserves, except by giving them up and acquiring new ones. Thus, extractive firms may be twice vulnerable to the property tax: by being relatively property-intensive they are more burdened by a uniform property tax, and to the extent that the uniformity of the property tax has been eroded, the less mobile extractive firms may have gained less by the erosion.

The possibilities of extraordinary burden upon the extractive industries do not seem borne out in practice, however. For a sample of extractive firms compared with a sample of manufacturing firms, Robert Anderson found that extractive firms pay less property tax per dollar of assets (property, plant, and equipment): the average of the sample of mining firms paid at a rate 63 percent of the rate for manufacturing; paper producers, 79 percent; timber producers, 88 percent; and petroleum firms, 47 percent.[25] But these figures tell only part of the story. Some extractive resources are strikingly underassessed compared with other assets. Consider the case of coal.

In this country, coal deposits are among the most valuable of assets. Even if coal companies paid a property tax at only half the rate paid by manufacturing companies, as long as the assessments were in proportion to the market value of the assets, one would expect people living in coal-bearing lands to be well off indeed (or at least the local governments). Such is not the case. Seventy percent of the coal consumed in the United States comes from Appalachia, and its residents (and local governments) are among the poorest in the country. Why?

Four-fifths of the coal in Tennessee lies in the five northeastern counties. In these counties nine corporations own 34 percent of the land and 80 percent of the coal. Because these lands are by far the most economically productive in the five-county area, one would expect their assessed value to be in excess of 34 percent of the total property assessment for the area. In fact, in 1970 the property assessments of the nine coal corporations was less than 4 percent of the total assessed property value of the area. It turns out that at the time, the mineral value of the coal was left entirely off the tax rolls—in effect, the property value of coal was assessed at zero. As for the surface land, it was assessed at $25 to $30 an acre, less than the cheapest farm land in the area. This was true, and remains substantially true, even though state law (not to mention economic theory) requires mineral assets to be included in the property tax base.[26]

Much the same pattern of underassessment prevails in the other central Appalachian coal states—Kentucky, West Virginia, and Virginia. In West Virginia there is the same sort of concentration in ownership of the best coal land, and there an average acre of coal land in 1970 was assessed at $40.[27]

While clearly there is a pattern of wide assessment, it is difficult to be certain of the fair market value of mineral property because many mineral properties remain out of the market for many years.

Severance taxes for many minerals, in many states, are correspondingly low. One more piece of information completes the explanation of how people can remain so poor living in such richly endowed land in Appalachia. Much of the coal land is owned by out-of-state companies. With the decrease in employment resulting from the increase in strip mining, much of the wealth that is not taxed by property and severance taxes flows out of state.[28] Appalachia, fortunately, appears to be something of a special case in the United States. While mineral firms may gradually impoverish communities that are outside Appalachia, as well as communities inside Appalachia, other localities appear less dualistic, in the colonial sense. In the West the property tax assessments seem to be closer to the fair market value of the properties.

In principle, the property tax can be levied on the entire value of a mine. The value includes the value of the ore in place as well as the man-made capital. In some states such a property tax on mineral value is required by statute or by state constitution. But the amount of ore in place can be thought of as a random variable that is only gradually observed over time. Perhaps for this reason assessments and collections of the property tax for ore in place are often low or even neglected entirely (as they have been in Tennessee). It is the same problem encountered in determining discovery value for discovery depletion, and we have seen that the attempt to determine discovery value was abandoned.

A government has at least two practical alternatives in dealing with the unknowns associated with ore in place. A government can make a guess about the amount of ore and add this expected value to the adjusted cost basis in order to obtain an assessment for the property tax. In doing so, the government would enter into a gamble with the firm. If the government overestimated, the firm would lose and vice versa if the government underestimated. Much of the risk of mis-estimation would be borne by the firm. Of course, the stakes could be lowered by provision for later readjustment, but the situation, analogous to discovery depletion, rapidly becomes complicated and subject to manipulation for private benefit.

As a second alternative, a government could avoid trying to guess the amount of mineral in place by simply taking a share of the ore as it is extracted (a severance tax). The change from guessing the value in place to sharing the extracted value is directly analogous to the change from discovery value depletion to percentage depletion. With a severance tax, the government shares the risk with the firm that the discovery will be large or small, and in doing so, the government lowers some of the burden of the gamble to the firm and avoids later bargaining and litigation between government and firm.

This view of the severance tax is symmetrically opposite to the idea of the depletion deduction, which on the federal level was designed to exempt from taxation the increase in capital value due to discovery; in this view of the severance tax the idea is to tax the capital value of the ore in place. To some extent the severance tax, as a risk-sharing form of the property tax, substitutes for it. Extractive firms bargain for a severance tax in place of a lower property tax. Besides its risk-sharing aspect, the severance tax defers the tax until production. Not only may the firm be better able to pay the tax when it is matched in time against production, but as we have seen, there are advantages to the firm in the postponement of tax. Generally severance taxes are more popular with extractive firms than property taxes. They should also be more popular with conservationists, because severance taxes tend to postpone production as well as the tax, compared with a property tax. Under the property tax, a firm may want to cut (or mine) and get out quickly in order to lessen the number of years and times the property tax is collected.

To whatever extent the severance tax substitutes for the property tax, the above remarks on the relative burden of the property tax should be amended to take into account both the property tax and the severance tax. However, as suggested by estimates of the impact of the severance tax, this tax is relatively small for most extractive firms, so that its inclusion would not significantly change the discussion.[29] It also appears, though, that the severance tax has been growing in importance and will be an increasingly important tax in the future. In 1972, Louisiana increased its severance tax on gas and oil by about 33 percent as an alternative to an increase in local property tax rates. Increasing the property tax rate increases the tax on local residential property owners as well as on out-of-state owners. An increase in the severance tax is often a way of "exporting" the tax. For a mineral extracted from one state and destined for other states, and for minerals with out-of-state owners, the severance tax provides a way of shifting a tax burden out of state without raising local property tax rates. Because the extractive activities eventually impoverish a locality's natural assets, some compensation, whether through property tax assessments or severance taxes, is appropriate.

In the 1969 Tax Reform Act, Congress established a minimum tax so that corporations and other taxpayers favored with tax preferences would at least pay some income tax.[30] Basically it is a tax on the income sheltered by special provisions. Suppose, for example, a mineral firm is able to shelter $140,000 of its net income from federal tax by means of percentage depletion, expensing, and capital gains. From this shelter, $30,000 is subtracted as an exemption, and from what is left the income tax plus the foreign tax credit is subtracted. The minimum tax is defined as 10 percent of what is left after the second subtraction. Suppose that the firm's regular income tax (without the minimum tax) is $45,000 and its foreign tax credit is $5,000. The computation is shown below.

1. Income sheltered from tax preferences $140,000
2. Exemption   30,000
3. Sum of the federal tax plus the foreign tax credit   50,000

4. Amount subject to minimum tax (line 1 minus line
   2 minus line 3) $60,000
5. Minimum tax (10 percent of line 4)   6,000
6. Total tax equals regular tax plus line 5
   ($45,000 plus $6,000)   51,000

As we can see, the minimum tax takes away less than 10 percent of the shelter; how much less depends on the regular tax already paid. If the firm is already paying some tax, the minimum tax may be very small or even nothing. For most extractive firms, the minimum tax seems to have had little effect.

Taxes and Inefficiencies

Special provisions of the tax code may lead to special inefficiencies, as may unusual abilities to take advantage of uniform provisions, such as capital gains and the foreign tax credit. The resulting misallocations of resources appear on two levels. First, on the product level, prices are distorted. The effects of percentage depletion happen primarily on the price level because the deduction is based on gross income, which is closely related to price.

Second, misallocation appears at the level of production, as a distortion in the use of capital. To the extent that profits are a payment to one factor of production, capital, differences in tax treatment, and hence differences in the return to capital taxed away, lead to (1) misallocations between capital used in the favored industry and capital used in other industries, and (2) misallocation between capital and other factors of production, such as labor, in the favored industries. Over time, the impact of a lightened burden of tax on capital spills over to affect product prices as well, lowering them, and affecting the competition of one material against another. In appendix D there are rough estimates of the effects of these two types of distortions, one on the product level and the other beginning on the factor level and spilling over into the product level. The combined price effect resulting from the differential tax treatment of primary industries and other industries may be to make virgin materials too cheap by about 10 percent, under the efficiency criterion.

Along with the effects of the depletion allowance, which have already been calculated for the simple case of a "pure" subsidy, there are also the effects of expensing and timing, capital gains, and foreign tax credits, along with the differential effects of the property tax and the offsetting effect of the severance tax. In general, the provisions of the federal income tax (excluding property taxes and severance taxes) lower the effective tax rate. Suppose that extractive industries pay an effective tax rate of 10 percent while other manufacturing firms pay an effective rate of 40 percent. Market forces will tend to equalize after-tax rates of return. This means that the before-tax rates of return in manufacturing will be considerably higher than in extractive industries. Consequently, there is an inefficiency between industries. Resources can be shifted from the extractive industries to other industries, raising the rate of productivity on the resources transferred. While this is true in general, some of the provisions can be related to specific distortions.

Exempting discovery value from taxation (through discovery and percentage depletion) leads toward an inefficiency distortion. For efficiency, discovery value should be taxed just like other productivities in the economy unless there are important nonmarket (externality) benefits associated with discovery effort. On average, the discovery of new deposits is part of the mineral industries' productivity just as new corn is a part of the agricultural industries' productivity. In order to achieve efficiency in the allocation of resources between the mining industries and the agricultural ones, unsuccessful discovery ventures can be expensed against ordinary income, and the discovery value of successful ventures can be taxed at ordinary income tax rates (this is for corporate income—problems arise for personal income, with increasing marginal rates for big discoveries which income averaging does not entirely solve). This policy would be neutral with respect to the extra riskiness of the extractive industries, at least for corporations large enough to be neither risk preferrers nor risk averters and which have other sources of ordinary income to offset the losses of unsuccessful ventures. However, to the extent that knowledge of new discoveries benefits everyone and these benefits are not captured by the discoverer, there is a valid argument for special incentives for discovery effort, under the efficiency criterion.

The special feature of capital gains taxation that permits losses to be offset against ordinary income and wins to be taxed at capital gains rates compounds the misallocation related to discovery value. Elimination of the depletion allowance would still permit misallocation through the asymmetrical treatment of discovery value at capital gains rates; thus, elimination of the depletion allowance would remove only part of the misallocation associated with the treatment of discovery value.

One interpretation of efficiency suggests that the rate of return before taxes should be the same for all firms, in the United States or abroad.

This is efficiency in a worldwide sense. Allowing the credit tends to equalize the before-tax rate of return. (Of course we cannot equalize the before-tax rate of all the firms in the world and not even all U.S. firms operating abroad, because some are being taxed at a rate higher than the 48 percent in the example.) On the other hand, foreign tax credits are inefficient from the point of view of *national efficiency*. From the national point of view, foreign taxes are real costs just as much as payments for labor and materials. The dollars that go into foreign tax payments will be redeemed in U.S. goods and services just the same way that dollars spent for labor and materials will. From the national efficiency point of view, the rates of return after foreign taxes but before U.S. taxes should be equalized. From this point of view foreign tax credits are doubly bad: they distort investment inefficiently toward foreign investment and at the same time constitute free gifts to foreign governments. We may want to give gifts to foreign governments, but using foreign tax credits is an unintentional and haphazard way of doing so. To achieve efficiency from a national point of view, foreign taxes should be treated as deductions from income rather than as tax credits.

It would appear that the effective rate of the property tax, even including the severance tax, is much lower for extractive industries than for other users of land. From the standpoint of the efficiency criterion, this would lead to two misallocations with respect to the extractive industries. The relative smallness of their effective property tax rate, compared with the rate for other users of land, would lead to too much land associated with the extractive industries compared with other uses. As a second inefficiency, the severance tax would lead to too slow a rate of extraction from the point of view of the present distribution of wealth and resource ownership.

Ownership

There is a wide range of alternatives in the taxation of discovery and appropriation of new materials. At one extreme, the discovery value may be considered tax exempt. The concept of tax exemption for discovery value survives in the successor to discovery depletion, percentage depletion. One alternative, and a change from the present concept, would be to tax the appreciation in capital value due to discovery at capital gains rates. Treating the appreciation in capital value from discovery equally with capital appreciation in other parts of the economy would take us about halfway from the present concept of a zero burden in discovery depletion and its practical rule of thumb, percentage depletion, to the concept of the normal burden incorporated in the ordinary income tax rates. A second alternative would go further to treat the increase in value resulting from new discoveries in the same way as the increase in value in crops to a farmer; in this alternative, discovery value would be taxed as ordinary income. A third alternative is at the other extreme from exemption embodied in percentage depletion and would attempt to tax away the entire discovery value by having the government retain property rights to minerals and by leasing extraction permits to the highest bidder.[31]

Which alternative is the most appropriate depends in part on concepts of ownership of the resource base. As we have seen, Graton believed that free appropriation of mineral value into private ownership through discovery depletion was a constitutional right. We can identify two polar views. In one view, the resource base belongs in its entirety to the present. It can be parceled out into private ownership, and the present owners may do with it what they please. In the second view, the resource base belongs jointly to all generations. In this view, the concept of private ownership of material resources is an instrumental concept and not a concept of rights. Private ownership by the present of material resource stocks may still be justifiable, insofar as it provides efficient and fair use of the resource base over time. Subscribers to the second view often recommend government management and ownership of resources if private management proves wasteful or neglectful of the future.

To a large extent, the first view describes the prevailing view as it is incorporated into law and economic thought, and it underlies much of the next chapter. There may be some shift occurring, however, toward the second view, which underlies the chapter after that. A related opinion, that ultimate ownership resides in the community and not in the individual or firm, definitely appears to be strengthening. The quotation at the head of this chapter by former Congressman Wayne Aspinall, defender of the mineral industries until his defeat in 1972, may be a sign of the change.[32] Regarded as a compensation to the community or as a method of changing the control of materials intertemporally, severance taxes may not be inefficient after all.

In this and the two preceding chapters we have looked at material flows and uses mainly from the perspective of economic efficiency. We have seen some of the implications of efficiency analysis in the evaluation of these flows and uses. But it is beyond the power of efficiency analysis to probe alternative concepts of ownership, just as it is beyond the power of efficiency analysis to decide what is a proper distribution of risk—the risk that substitutes will not be found in a timely fashion and the risk that certain long-lived wastes may impose upon the future. These are questions of intertemporal fairness, and we turn to them in the next three chapters.

Notes

1. *President's 1963 Tax Message*, Part I (revised Mar. 27, 1963) Committee on Ways and Means, 88 Cong. 1 sess. (1963) table 5C, p. 308 and table 8C, p. 317.
2. U.S. Department of Commerce, *Statistical Abstract of the United States, 1973* (94th edition, Washington, D.C., 1973) no. 1107, p. 658 and no. 1111, p. 660; U.S. Department of Interior, *Minerals Yearbook 1972* vol. I (Washington, D.C., 1974) table 1, p. 910; and assuming a wellhead price of natural gas of 20 cents per thousand cubic feet.
3. According to Oppenheimer, percentage depletion is more important to the major oil companies than it is to the smaller independents. See Bruce Oppenheimer, *Oil and the Congressional Process* (Lexington, Mass., Lexington Books, 1974) pp. 108–109. Oppenheimer discusses at length the political process relating to percentage depletion.
4. This is the circumstance that makes percentage depletion easy to analyze. Unlike other tax provisions, which fall directly on the use of capital, percentage depletion does not affect the tradeoff between capital and labor except for certain complications, which are discussed below.
5. Mancke draws supply and demand curves showing the percentage depletion allowance having no effect on either price or quantity, presumably because of the 50 percent of net income limitation. However, the marginal firm earning zero economic profit is still earning a normal profit of perhaps 10–12 percent, which may be sufficiently high to keep the 50 percent of net income limitation from binding. See Richard Mancke, *The Failure of U.S. Energy Policy* (New York, Columbia University Press, 1974) p. 86.
6. *President's 1963 Tax Message.*
7. Cost depletion, which is analogous to depreciation for other property, is an alternative to percentage depletion; cost depletion is defined in the following section.
8. Phillip Stern, *The Rape of the Taxpayer* (New York, Random House, 1973) p. 237.
9. For more detail and complication, see *General Explanation of the Tax Reform Act of 1969*, prepared by the staff of the Joint Committee on Internal Revenue Taxation, H. Rept. 13270, 91 Cong. (1970) PL 91-172, pp. 161–164.
10. Stephen McDonald, *Federal Tax Treatment of Income from Oil and Gas* (Washington, D.C., The Brookings Institution, 1963) p. 10.
11. Emil Sunley, "The Federal Tax Subsidy of the Timber Industry," in *The Economics of Federal Subsidy Programs,* a compendium of papers submitted to the Joint Economic Committee, 92 Cong. 2 sess. (1972) Part 3, July 1972, pp. 317–342.
12. Sunley, "Tax Subsidy," p. 323.
13. Another way of thinking about the capital gains treatment of the timber industry is to think in terms of *transfer prices.* Sunley quotes a 1971 price for Louisiana southern pine stumpage to be about $7.60 per ton (or $4.70 per cord). With the value of bleached kraft pulp per ton of pulpwood about $170, it is a little hard to imagine that all the profits appear at the lowly state of stumpage. Yet if the total profit is only a few percent of sales value, the unit profit might be just a couple of dollars per ton of wood. By counting the value of stumpage a couple of dollars more and the costs of other operations a couple of dollars less,

the total profits can be transferred to the stumpage stage and subjected to favorable capital gains rates. For an integrated firm, the stumpage price is an internal accounting price (subject to bargaining with the Internal Revenue Service). It can also be considered a transfer price, because by raising it, ordinary income can be transferred into capital gains income. Paper industry profits, however, are more than just a couple of percentage points of sales value of the pulp, and probably more is going on than simply the use of transfer prices. (The treatment of planting, thinning, and spraying expenses is a way of adjusting the transfer price of stumpage value.) (See Sunley, "Tax Subsidy," p. 328.)

A preliminary estimate in an Environmental Law Institute study of the effective federal income tax rate is 34 percent, from an average of nine firms in the pulp and paper industry. See Robert Anderson, "The Extent of Preferential Taxation in Mining and Timber Industries," in Environmental Law Institute, "Federal Tax Policy and Depletable Resources: Impacts and Alternatives for Recycling and Conservation," a study for the Environmental Protection Agency (Washington, D.C., forthcoming).

14. If the two corporations in the example were instead partnerships held by wealthy individuals in 70 percent marginal tax brackets (with a maximum 35 percent personal income capital gains rate), the government would be sharing 70 percent of the losses and 35 percent of the wins. The greater gap between the rates of sharing of losses and wins increases the tax advantage of risky ventures, for the same average return. Moreover, the greater the risk, again for the same average return, the greater the advantage of partnerships over corporations. These considerations lead to a specialization in mineral industries. In activities with a high risk, such as wildcat oil exploration, there are stronger incentives for partnerships than in activities that are less risky, such as iron mining.

15. For examples illustrating the "per country limitation" and the "overall limitation" see Jane Graville, *Special Provisions of the Federal Income Tax Affecting the Oil and Gas Industry: A Study of Provisions, Pros and Cons, and Selected References* (Washington, D.C., Congressional Research Service, Library of Congress, August 25, 1972). These mechanics of the tax do not concern us here.

16. Graville, *Special Provisions*, p. 4.

17. For the case of oil, Adelman cites the harmony of interests between the oil company and the oil producing countries, the oil companies acting as tax collectors for the oil producing countries. See Morris Adelman, *Foreign Policy* no. 9 (Winter 1972–1973) pp. 69–107.

18. *The Statutes at Large of the United States*, March 1913–March 1915 (38 Stat. 167), p. 165.

19. See p. 62 of *Regulations* [sic] *45 Relating to the Income Tax and War Profits and Excess Profits Tax under the Revenue Act of 1918, with Addenda Containing all Treasury Decisions to Dec. 2, 1919* (Washington, D.C., U.S. Government Printing Office, 1920).

20. Cited from Joseph Ruskay and Richard Osserman, *Halfway to Tax Reform* (Bloomington, Ind., Indiana University Press, 1970) p. 225.

21. U.S. Department of the Interior, Bureau of Mines, *Federal Mineral Taxation* (Washington, D.C., 1952) Joseph Lerner, principal contributor, p. 80.

22. U.S. Department of the Interior, *Federal Mineral Taxation*, p. 83.

23. U.S. Department of the Interior, *Federal Mineral Taxation*, p. 91.

24. Hearings before the Joint Committee on Internal Revenue Taxation, 71 Cong. 3 sess. (Dec. 9, 10, 11, 12, 1930) pp. 6–7.

25. Anderson, "The Extent of Preferential Taxation."

26. John Gaventa, "Property Taxation of Coal in Central Appalachia," A report for the Senate Subcommittee on Intergovernmental Relations from Save Our Cumberland Mountains, Inc., pp. 8–10.

27. Gaventa, "Property Taxation," p. 12.

28. The biggest coal landowner in Tennessee is the American Association, which is a subsidiary of the London Foreign and Colonial Securities, Inc.

29. Susan Agria, "Special Tax Treatment of Mineral Industries," in Arnold Harberger and Martin Bailey, eds. *The Taxation of Income from Capital* (Washington, D.C., The Brookings Institution, 1969) pp. 101–104.

30. See *General Explanation of the Tax Reform Act of 1969*, pp. 104–107.

31. See Arlon Tussing and Gregg Erickson, *Mining and Public Policy in Alaska: Mineral Policy, the Public Lands and Economic Development*, Report No. 21, prepared for Office of Regional Development Planning, U.S. Department of Commerce (Anchorage, Alaska, University of Alaska College, 1969) for a discussion of discovery appropriation, concession and leasing systems, and their preference for leasing.

32. Wayne Aspinall, "Man, Minerals, and the Environment," speech at the annual convention of the American Mining Congress, San Francisco, California, September 19, 1972. Mikesell notes in passing that "[The] [d]epletion [allowance] has been severely criticized in some developing countries on grounds that it constitutes a charge [compensation to the company] for the value of minerals in the ground, which are regarded as the property of the state and not of the private enterprise exploiting them." Raymond Mikesell, *Foreign Investment in Copper Mining: Case Studies of Mines in Peru and Papua New Guinea* (Baltimore, Md., Johns Hopkins University Press for Resources for the Future, 1975) p. 12.

PART THREE

INTERTEMPORAL EQUITY

7

The Present Value Criterion

Utility is a metaphysical concept of impregnable circularity.

—Joan Robinson

Efficiency and the Distribution of Wealth

THE QUESTION of which criteria to use in "adjusting the rudder" toward a materials policy that will be equitable over the long term is the subject of the next three chapters. In spite of its applicability to problems of taxation, freight rates, and disposal, the efficiency criterion is, in fact, very limited. The (perfected) market will come up with a different efficient allocation of goods and services for each initial distribution of income. As an economist might put it, each efficient allocation of goods and services is conditioned upon a distribution of income or wealth, which functions as a distribution of dollar votes in the marketplace. The efficiency criterion cannot decide between efficient allocations because the choice of the initial distribution of income is logically prior to the workings of efficiency. The best distribution of income is a social question and not one for an economist alone to decide.

Understandably, economists have shied away from such controversial ground and instead of trying to develop criteria that would define the "best" distribution, they have developed economic theory in ways that avoid distributional issues. In the process they have relaxed one limitation of the efficiency criterion. We have described the criterion so far as saying "make no change unless the change hurts no one and helps at least someone." As practically no change hurts no one, this interpretation is very binding. Consequently, the criterion is often interpreted to instruct us to make changes that help some, even at the expense of others, as long as the gainers can fully compensate the losers and still

145

come out ahead. This more relaxed criterion is the Kaldor version of the efficiency criterion. The idea is that efficiency does not require that compensation be made, but only that it could be made.[1] The actual redistribution again is a question beyond the reach of the efficiency criterion. Essentially, the Kaldor criterion allows us to count up costs and benefits no matter where they fall. By this criterion a dollar's benefit counts the same whether it lands on a poor person or a rich one. This is the customary approach used in benefit–cost analysis of projects and policy interventions, and one taken implicitly in chapters 4, 5, and 6.

While the idea of potential compensation frees the efficiency criterion from requiring unanimous consent for a proposed project, the Kaldor version has caused misgivings because it implies that income redistribution is not relevant to project selection and policy making. Clearly some projects and policies may be deemed undesirable because of undesirable income distributional effects, even though they pass the Kaldor test, as long as the potential compensation is not made. To avoid this weakness, economists often recommend that benefit–cost analysis be limited to the evaluation of "small" projects. Small projects are ones with negligible redistributional effects.[2]

Distribution Over Time

So far we have been talking about intratemporal or short-run costs and benefits. But we are mainly concerned about costs and benefits associated with resource depletion and long-lived pollutants whose effects are distributed into the distant future. Economists generally recommend "discounting" long-lived costs and benefits, and here they may part company with the conservationists, who often feel uneasy about the procedure. The economist defends discounting by pointing out that discounting reflects the way people behave and value things. We can follow the economist's argument by looking first at the producer side and then at the consumer side of the finance market.

Producer side

Consider the case of a farmer who borrows $100 at a market interest rate of *i*. With the loan he buys seed that turns into $400 worth of crops at the end of the summer. As long as the $400 is enough to cover expenses (which include fertilizer and his own labor value), the loan, and the interest, the farmer has come out ahead. For him, the repayment next year [$\$(1 + i)$ 100] is worth the smaller $\$100$ he receives now. In general, as long as there is productivity in the economy, it is worthwhile for firms to rent money in order to participate in the economy's productivity.[3]

The farmer will be encouraged by the market to expand his operation to the point where the last $\$100$ he borrows brings just enough crop to cover the loan, interest, and expenses. The interest rate i is a measure of the farm's net marginal productivity. A dollar today is worth $\$(1 + i)$ next year because the intervening time allows him to tie into this productivity for a year. Similarly, for a long-term loan to finance a long-term project of n years, a dollar today is worth $\$(1 + i)^n$ in n years because there is that much longer to tie into the productivity.

Consider two farmers who work identical, adjacent farms (see figure 18). Over a planning period of N years, farmer Grandtotal arranges his growing schedule to maximize the total of his yearly profits:

$$\max \sum_{t=1}^{N} \pi_t \qquad \pi_t = \text{profit in year } t$$

Figure 18. Profits, summed and discounted

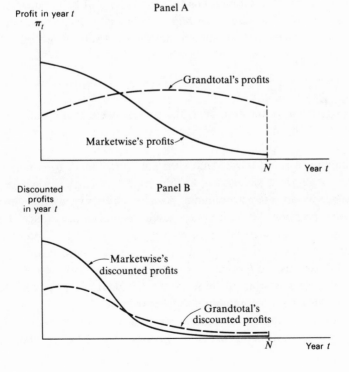

Farmer Marketwise knows that he can duplicate Grandtotal's production schedule. Nevertheless, he shifts the latter's production plan to take some of his profits earlier, even at some sacrifice in their eventual aggregate size. He arranges his plan to maximize the discounted value (present value) of his stream of yearly profits:

$$\max \sum_{t=1}^{N} \pi_t/(1 + i)^t$$

i = market rate of interest or discount rate.

The total sum of Marketwise's profits is less than the sum of Grandtotal's, as can be seen by comparing the areas under the two profit curves in panel A of figure 18; but the discounted value of Marketwise's profits is larger than the discounted value of Grandtotal's, as can be seen by comparing areas of the curves representing annual discounted profits in panel B of figure 18. Who comes out ahead? Marketwise. He knows that his earlier profits are more valuable to him than his later ones because he can earn more interest on his earlier cash receipts by loaning them to other producers in the economy and tying into their productivity. In fact, with fierce competition, the Marketwises will do so much better than the Grandtotals that the latter will be eliminated from the market. Market discipline requires that producers maximize the present value of their profit stream, not the total sum of profits.

Consumer side

Consumers also act as though the present were more valuable than the future. Consumers often borrow at an interest rate, knowing that the increased consumption today will be more than offset by decreased consumption in the future. And when consumers lend, for example, by putting money in a savings bank, they expect to be rewarded for their abstinence by an interest premium. As economists say, by their borrowing and saving behavior, consumers reveal their time preferences toward future and present well-being. A man who is indifferent about whether to spend $1 now or put it in a savings bank at a 5 percent interest rate for a year reveals (to himself) his time preference. With no inflation the $1.05 next year is worth to him just $1 today. He discounts the future value, by his own time preference, by 5 percent.[4]

Suppose we described a consumer's well-being by a function of his consumption: [well-being or utility in time t] = $U(C_t)$, where C_t is consumption in time t. The consumer acts, economists infer, as though he were maximizing a present value of the utility stream,

$$\sum_{t=0}^{N} U(C_t)/(1 + i)^t, \tag{7.1}$$

$$\text{not its sum } \sum_{t=0}^{N} U(C_t), \tag{7.2}$$

where this time i is the consumer's rate of time preference. A consumer who chooses his consumption path by using the equation (7.1) is following a *present value criterion*. The feasible path that maximized (7.1) is said to be optimal under this criterion. For each discount rate, the present value criterion will yield a different optimal path. Note that conceptually we defined i in terms of a commodity (here money) and then applied i to a utility stream in equation (7.1).

The two sides of the money market are, in a sense, symmetrically matched. Producers are willing to borrow at a rental fee and consumers are willing to loan at a rental fee. Market forces tend to bring these two rates together into a single interest or discount rate. ("Interest rate" is usually used when some commodity—money or some other commodity—is being discounted; the "discount rate" is a more general term which is often used for the discounting of utilities as well as commodities.) Of course, in the actual money market one sees many interest rates. The variety of interest rates is due in part to differences in risk. Economists usually take *the* rate of interest to be the riskless rate of interest. In actual markets, differing risk premiums would be added to this rate.

Should We Discount?

So far, what has been described as the economists' defense of discounting is not meant by economists to be a justification of discounting, but the position of a neutral observer who describes without moral judgment the way people behave. When we move from the observation that people in fact discount to the question of whether or not discounting should be a social policy, we find that economists are by no means unified in their opinion. Two highly respected economists, Pigou and Ramsey, thought that the "telescopic faculty," which led people to discount future well-being, was a form of moral weakness. Nonetheless, most economists seem to agree that discounting is the proper approach to problems of intertemporal distribution. Many would like to avoid the moral problem altogether by arguing that it is not their business to judge consumer preferences, but only to recommend the most effective ways of satisfying as many of these preferences as possible. Such acquiescence of course carries with it an implied moral judgment.

In later sections we shall take on the question of in what way, if at all, discounting should be used in determining the long-run distribution of costs and benefits. For now we will note just two things: first, that there is no universal agreement within the economics profession on this question and second, that discounting future utility, contrary to how it may first appear, is not necessarily unfair to the future. To fix ideas and focus on the bare essentials, we will use a few simple, paradigmatic examples.

Consider Robinson Crusoe, cast upon his island with only a stock of corn. He may eat the corn, or plant it knowing it will double each season. Of course he does both, but he must decide how much to save for planting each year. To focus on the investment–consumption decision, we assume he knows he will live exactly N more years. Suppose he follows Pigou and Ramsey in rejecting the "failure of imagination," by which Ramsey disparaged utility discounting. Crusoe instead decides to arrange his consumption and planting schedule, for his whole life, to maximize the undiscounted sum of utilities, subject of course to the production realities. He is following Ramsey's zero discount criterion:

$$\max \sum_{t=1}^{N} U(C_t), \tag{7.3}$$

subject to $C_t + I_t = 2I_{t-1}$; $I_0 = \bar{I}_0$ beginning stock of corn; $0 \leq I_t = $ corn saved for planting in year t; $0 \leq C_t = $ corn consumption in year t.

In this example, the production realities, incorporated in the constraint, are assumed to be particularly simple. There are no planting costs and no harvest costs. This and the models to follow are basically inheritance models. They focus on the distribution over time of the use of the resource base (here the single good, corn), which is a productive but depletable asset.[5] We also assume that Crusoe's utility in any year increases with his consumption that year, but he tends to become sated for larger levels of consumption. At the other end of the scale, for very small levels of consumption, a small increase in consumption adds a great deal to his utility. For any year, Crusoe's utility as a function of his consumption looks like figure 19. As can be seen, the derivative

Figure 19. Utility and marginal utility

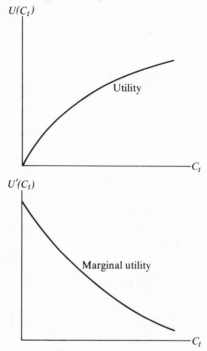

a/ Utility as a function of consumption for any given
year C_t, and marginal utility as a function of consumption for any given C_t.

$dU/dC = U'$ declines with an increasing C; an incremental unit of consumption adds more at low levels of consumption than at high ones. This condition is called "decreasing marginal utility of consumption."

Even with this utility function, Crusoe finds that the Ramsey criterion instructs him to skimp in the earlier years and eat gluttonously in the later ones. The solution to the maximization problem, equation (7.3) is shown in figure 20, and the mathematical details of its derivation are given in appendix E. The reason is quite simple: a kernel sacrificed from consumption in year t, planted and replanted for s years becomes 2^s kernels. Under the Ramsey criterion, productivity favors the future over the present. What finally offsets productivity's instruction to sacrifice in the present for a better future is that eventually 2^s kernels, to an already overfed Crusoe in year $t + s$, is not worth the sacrifice of even one kernel to the starving Crusoe in year t.

Figure 20. Consumption under the Ramsey criterion

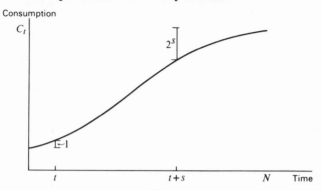

However, suppose Crusoe decides to arrange his planting and consumption schedule on the basis of maximizing the present value of his utility stream. He maximizes

$$\sum_{t=1}^{N} U(C_t)/(1 + i)^t, \tag{7.4}$$

subject to $C_t + I_t = 2I_{t-1}$; $I_t \geq 0$; $C_t \geq 0$; and $I_0 = \bar{I}_0$, where $i =$ Crusoe's discount rate.

In following the present value criterion, Crusoe finds his optimal consumption path is more egalitarian through time. In fact, if Crusoe had chosen the productivity rate as his discount rate, the path would be totally egalitarian. (See appendix E for proof.) Discounting by the resource's natural productivity leads to a concept of fairness in terms of total utility, while zero discounting leads to a concept of fairness in marginal utility. If fairness is to be defined in terms of some form of egalitarianism, which may be too naïve in any case, it would seem more sensible to define it with respect to total utility rather than marginal utility.

Next, suppose that (as illustrated in figure 21) Crusoe had been so unfortunate as to land on the island with a large box of hardtack instead of renewable corn. Crusoe is somewhat consoled, though, having found that the initial stock $\bar{I}_0$ is large enough to provide subsistence for his natural life ($\bar{I}_0/N >$ annual subsistence). At least Crusoe does not have to face the question of when he is going to starve, a question he would have to face if the initial stock had been smaller. If Crusoe decides to discount by the rate of productivity, he quickly notices that $i = 0$ and that equations (7.3) and (7.4) come to the same thing. In this case,

Figure 21. Consumption paths and discounting

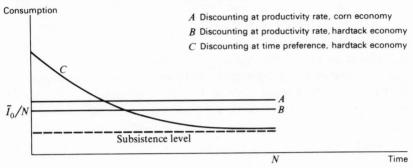

the Ramsey criterion is egalitarian in terms of total utility as well as marginal utility.

But if Crusoe decides to discount by his time preference, and if this is greater than zero, he finds that the present value criterion instructs him to follow the nonegalitarian path C. In a hardtack economy there is no market force to bring the rate of productivity (zero) into harmony with time preference. Even if there were many people trading many nonrenewable goods, there would be no way that market forces could bring the rates of time preference and productivity together (see appendix F).

In trying to find the best allocation path over time for resources and consumption, it is convenient to think in terms of discrete generations and utility functions. In the above examples, each "generation" is collapsed into a single person, and in fact the next generation is the same Crusoe a year later. Of course with real generations there are many people in each, and there is the second distribution problem: how resources and consumption should be distributed among those in a single generation. But in order to focus the analysis on the intertemporal resource allocation and distribution of well-being, we assume in the above example and the ones to follow that each "generation" acts like a single unit.[6] With these assumptions, the problem becomes one of choosing among the infinite number of possible paths of resource allocation and consumption intertemporally, each path being associated with a stream of utility.

As a formal solution, it is tempting to aggregate the utility streams, each stream into a single number, for then the numbers can be directly ranked. The simplest aggregation scheme is to take a weighted average of the utilities, where the weights are a geometric sequence of the discount rate. We now have three possible candidates for an individual's definition of "the discount rate": the rate at which he would loan money or some other commodity, the productivity of the economy, or his "pure time preference" (his comparison of the worth of future utility in terms of present utility). If our desire is to be egalitarian over time in terms of a total measure of well-being, the above examples tell us that the proper discount rate is the rate of marginal productivity of the economy. In other words, if we are going to add utilities over time and if we want to be egalitarian, then we should not maximize the sum of utilities, but a present value of them.

Government Discounting for a Project

So far we have seen that the market encourages both producers and consumers to discount future values. Often governmental agencies undertake projects that generate costs and benefits into the future. In undertaking a project, a dam for example, an agency is acting very much like a firm. It buys materials and labor that would otherwise remain in the private sector.[7] It produces an output, such as flood control or recreation. The output is often in the form of externalities; in fact the non-marketability of output is the usual reason that the private sector will not undertake a worthy project.

When the outputs do not pass through markets, their values are not measured by market prices. Economists are called in to estimate the values of the outputs by benefit–cost analysis. The decision rule in benefit–cost analysis for intertemporal projects is that as long as the discounted value of the benefit stream is greater than the discounted value of the cost stream, the project is worth undertaking. It is the same decision rule as the one used by private firms, except that the outputs are evaluated by economists, not markets.

Discounting has the same role in public projects as it has in private ones. If the government did not discount, but simply added costs and benefits, it would be acting like farmer Grandtotal and would be using resources less productively than farmer Marketwise.

For projects with long lives and with benefits and costs realized at different times, the choice of the government rate of discount often makes the difference in whether or not they pass muster under benefit–cost analysis. In dam construction projects, the costs are concentrated in the present and the benefits—in flat water recreation, flood control, and irrigation—string out into the future. Conservationists who wish to preserve free-flowing rivers and who think that the costs of losing white water recreation are undervalued in the calculations of the Army Corps of Engineers find it to their advantage to argue against the Army Corps' low discount rate. Raising the Army Corps' discount rate from the 2⅝ percent it used in 1962 to 8 percent would have killed off 80 percent of the dam projects approved in that year.[8] The Army Corps, of course, likes a low discount rate because that means more dams to build. Conversely, conservationists may find that the decision to save a redwood forest turns upon whether the Forest Service can be persuaded to use a low discount rate. Because project approval depends very sensitively upon the choice of the government discount rate, various agencies try to choose a rate suitable for their own bureaucratic purposes, while outside groups try to influence the choice toward their desired outcomes. Because of its political consequences, the government rate of discount becomes a strategic number.

Economists would be much more comfortable if there were some neat, clean way to define an ideal government rate of discount. The ideal rate, reflecting consumers' time preference—in either commodity or utility terms—and the economy's productivity, is called the *social rate of discount*. With a logical and unarguable definition of the social rate of discount, economists performing benefit–cost analyses would have a much safer role as neutral technicians. Unfortunately, the social rate of discount is much easier to posit than to define explicitly. After spending a lot of time trying to discover an unassailable definition, economists are beginning to decide that a totally satisfactory definition does not exist.[9]

For these reasons: First, there are imperfections in private markets, the most important one being the corporate income tax. Should the social rate of discount be taken to be the net marginal productivity of a corporation before tax or after tax? If defined to be the rate before tax, the social rate of discount would measure the productivity of resources in the largest part of the private sector. If after tax, the social rate of discount would measure consumers' time preference between present and future commodities. Since the corporate income tax shares nearly half a corporation's net marginal productivity, the difference is considerable. A social rate of discount based on before-tax productivity might be 16 percent; one based on after-tax productivity might be 8 percent. It may be that the corporate income tax is a good tax in that it may be better than other ways of raising money, but it prevents a consistent definition of the social rate of discount.

Second, there are some ways that the government is just not like a small firm. For a small project, the risk is spread over many taxpayers and the risk of any given project going sour is pooled over a large number of projects.[10] For the private market, interest rates can be divided into two parts: a riskless rate and a risk premium. Because pooled government projects are essentially riskless, should the social rate of discount correspond to a riskless bond rate in the private market? That would be one measure of consumers' time preference. Or should the social rate of discount correspond to the riskless rate plus a risk premium? That would be a measure of the marginal productivity in the private sector. Either way, the situation is unsatisfactory. Moreover, for some materials decisions, the potential consequences are too large to be pooled, even by governments. For example, a large-scale project of deforestation may impose risks for future generations, risks that are large even when spread over an entire population. And whose evaluation of risk are we to use, ours or theirs?

Third, governments influence market rates of interest in order to affect short-term goals such as decreasing unemployment or inflation.[11]

Besides these difficulties in defining a social rate of discount, there are additional problems having to do with the fact that those living in a given generation do not function as a single unit. While such intra-generational considerations are being minimized in this book, the impression should not be left that the only difficulties in defining the social rate of discount have to do with mismatching of the above types of time preferences and productivity in the capital markets.[12]

Discounting Social Welfare

So far we have discussed individuals discounting their own future welfare, individual firms discounting their own profits, and government agencies discounting benefits and costs of individual projects. In each case there is the economic argument that discounting promotes economic efficiency by channeling resources into the most productive paths. Economists go further, however. They also often recommend discounting aggregate social welfare. To follow this prescription is to act under the present value criterion, in its most general definition.

In reading the literature on economic growth and natural and exhaustible resources, one often encounters the criterion "maximize

$$\sum_{t=0}^{\infty} f(U^{1t}, U^{2t}, \ldots, U^{Nt})/(1 + i)^t \text{"}$$ (7.5)

This criterion function, or some variant of it, jumps from the page like Athena from Zeus' brow, fully grown. The analysis starts with it. In the usual case it is left to the reader to puzzle out the assumptions underlying it, its interpretations and properties.[13]

While there does not appear to be a consensus on the interpretation underlying (7.5), something of this criterion function, or objective function, can be understood in a straightforward definitional way, at least in formal terms.

The term U^{jt} is the index of well-being (utility) of individual j, who happens to live in generation t. This well-being, or utility, is a function of his consumption and other variables, which are neglected in the exposition. The function f aggregates all the indexes of well-being of individuals in a given generation into a single number. The aggregate social welfare in generation t is

$$W^t = f(U^{1t}, U^{2t}, \ldots, U^{Nt})$$

and f is the *social welfare function*. Conceptually f is a function which starts with a whole sequence of numbers $(U^{1t}, U^{2t}, \ldots, U^{Nt})$ and terminates with a single number, the social welfare of generation t.

In the special case where there is no intertemporal problem because there is only one period, equation (7.5) collapses into a single aggregation, the social welfare function:

$$W = f(U^1, U^2, \ldots, U^N), \tag{7.6}$$

where W = social welfare and f is the social welfare function. This (intratemporal) function has received enormous attention in economic literature where there has been shown a methodological need for an aggregation of individual utilities in order to complete the economic theory of social welfare. One of the prime considerations is how to formulate the theory with as little reliance as possible upon interpersonal comparisons. A second effort is to translate the formulation from nonmeasurable utility terms to quantifiable variables of prices and commodities.[14] Nevertheless, simple and fundamental questions remain as to what assumptions should be built into the aggregation of individual utilities.

Some believe that the social welfare at time t should be the sum of the utilities at a given time:

$$W^t = f(U^{1t}, U^{2t}, \ldots, U^{Nt}) = U^{1t} + U^{2t} + \ldots + U^{Nt}$$

Another way of making the aggregation to which others subscribe is to take the average of the utilities:

$$W^t = (U^{1t} + U^{2t} + \ldots + U^{Nt})/N$$

The two formulations imply enormous differences in optimal well-being and optimal population a few hundred years from now. Summing over all utilities tends toward a "Calcutta solution" that tries to satisfy the present value criterion by adding ever more people, each of whom adds something to the maximand. (The Calcutta solution is intra-temporal in that for a given year the criterion packs in more people to achieve a higher sum of utilities. Even though the well-being of each person goes down, more are added until the sum total of all individuals reaches its peak—in the actual case there is no mechanism to arrest population growth at this optimum. We will see an intertemporal Calcutta solution later.) Maximizing the present value of average utilities means a smaller optimal population and more resources per head. In this case, optimal population is roughly defined by increasing the population only to the point where a further increase brings economies of scale of the market that are more than offset by diminishing returns to environmental services.

While there are fundamental difficulties with the concept of aggregating utilities intratemporally, they are not the essential concern here, and we have avoided them in the preceding sections by assuming that a generation acted like a single unit, a single individual. In this case, $W^t = f(U^t)$ and as U^t is in turn a function of consumption in generation t, we have

$$W^t = f(U^t) = f(U(C_t));$$

that is, social welfare in each generation is some function of consumption in that generation.

Embodied in the criterion (7.5) there is a second aggregation, namely

$$\sum_{t=0}^{\infty} W^t/(1 + i)^t$$

This second aggregation turns another whole sequence of numbers $(W^0, W^1, \ldots, W^t, \ldots)$ into another single number. Both the aggregation of utilities over people at a given time and the aggregation by discounting social welfare W^t over time—procedures typically recommended by economists—incorporate interpersonal comparisons.

Unlike the intratemporal aggregation, the interpretation and analysis of the second aggregation, the intertemporal one, has received remarkably little attention in the economic literature.[15] Below are two different rationales for why we might want to perform the second aggregation. As will be seen, they imply different interpretations of the social welfare function. The whole apparatus together, the discounting of a social welfare function as a guide to social choice, is a more general definition of the present value criterion.

Selfish altruism

To illustrate the rationale, in the initial period (generation) there is just one decision maker, Mr. Nought. The well-being that Mr. Nought enjoys (U) is a function of his consumption level (C_0). But Mr. Nought is an altruist, and he gains satisfaction from contemplating consumption enjoyed by those in the future as well. Thus, Mr. Nought's utility function is

$$U = U^0(C_0, C_1, \ldots, C_t, \ldots),$$

where C_t is Mr. t's consumption in generation t. There is just one person in each generation, and the social welfare from Mr. Nought's point of view is just what Mr. Nought thinks it is. Mr. Nought's utility function is the social welfare function.

It just happens, by the usual convenient assumption, that the effect of each Mr. j's consumption in the future on Mr. Nought's utility is independent of the distribution of all the other utilities, including Mr. Nought were scheduled for the same level of consumption, an extra unit utility function is separable:

$$W = U = U^0(C_0, C_1, \ldots, C_t, \ldots) =$$
$$g^0(C_0) + g^1(C_1) + \ldots + g^t(C_t) + \ldots,$$

where g^i is a different function from g^j. It is important to note that the units associated with $g^t(\cdot)$ are "units of utility enjoyed by Mr. Nought in contemplating the consumption going to Mr. t." While Mr. Nought is altruistic, he is not completely selfless. If a Mr. t in the future and Mr. Nought were scheduled for the same level of consumption, an extra unit going to Mr. t would add less to Mr. Nought's utility than the extra unit going to Mr. Nought himself. We can incorporate this idea of limited altruism and still keep the formulation simple by assuming that $g^t(C_t) = \delta^t f(C_t)$, for some new function f so that:

$$W = f(C_0) + \delta f(C_1) + \ldots + \delta^t f(C_t) + \ldots = \sum_{t=0}^{\infty} \delta^t f(C_t). \quad (7.7)$$

The following interpretation can be given the units of measurement associated with the terms of equation (7.7). Function f is time invariant; it measures the utility of generation t as a function of the consumption of that generation. If generation i and generation j had the same level of consumption, each would enjoy the same level of utility. Thus the units associated with $f(C_t)$ are "units utility in generation t."

The constant δ translates the units of measurement one generation backward. So the units associated with δ are

$$\frac{\text{units utility in generation } t - 1}{\text{units utility in generation } t}$$

The units associated with the term $\delta f(C_1)$ are

$$\frac{\text{units utility in generation } 0}{\text{units utility in generation } 1} \times \text{units utility in generation 1,}$$

or units utility in generation 0. The units associated with $\delta^2 f(C_2)$ are

$$\frac{\text{units in gen. } 0}{\text{units in gen. } 1} \times \frac{\text{units in gen. } 1}{\text{units in gen. } 2} \times \text{units in gen. } 2 = \text{units in gen. } 0$$

And in general the units associated with $\delta^t f(C_t)$ are units utility in generation 0. In the interpretation of selfish altruism, δ represents pure time preference, in terms of present and future utilities.

In the normal case of limited altruism ($\delta < 1$), future well-being is discounted by δ. In the exceptional case where Mr. Nought is completely altruistic, or selfless ($\delta = 1$), future well-being means as much to Mr. Nought as his own; this is the Ramsey case. And finally, we identify δ as a measure of Mr. Nought's time preference. Crudely, it tells us how much more valuable Mr. Nought thinks utility in one period is than in the succceeding one. By writing δ as $1/(1 + i)$, expression (7.7) is the same as (7.5). In this interpretation the present value criterion says that Mr. Nought *should* plan to maximize his own instantaneous utility. Fortunately for the future, Mr. Nought feels satisfaction at the thought of future generations consuming. But this altruism is fundamentally selfish. The reason the present value criterion provides for the future, in this interpretation, is that that provision gives satisfaction to Mr. Nought. If Mr. Nought decides that provision for the future gives him less satisfaction (δ becomes smaller), then the future is worse off; if Mr. Nought decides that provision for the future gives him no satisfaction ($\delta = 0$), then the future is entirely cut off. By definition, maximizing the present value criterion maximizes the welfare of the present generation, Mr. Nought. In this interpretation all valuations are referred back to the vantage point of Mr. Nought and all valuations are made by him. Mr. Nought is the measure of all things; present man is the measure of all generations.

In the market version of this interpretation, there are many people living in a single generation. Still, in this version, all valuations are referred back to the vantage point of the present generation. Only the dollar votes of those living in the present generation count. The market version of this interpretation of the present value criterion says that there should be a consumer sovereignty of the present generation, where future costs and benefits are discounted by the present's rate of time preference. And in this interpretation the present value criterion and the maximization of the present generation's welfare come to the same thing.

Disinterested Fairness

The first interpretation suggests that all decisions are, and should be, based upon a consumer sovereignty of the present generation. The optimal allocation of resources is based upon calculations of the effects of present and future consumption on the present generation's welfare. In the second interpretation, which also leads to the same present value criterion, equation (7.5), maximizing a weighted average of all generations' welfares is the goal, rather than maximizing the welfare of the present generation alone. The weights can be chosen on the basis of fairness between generations. Again, for the exposition we assume that each generation is but a single person.

This time we assume that Mr. Nought's utility function in generation zero is $f^0(C_0)$. Unlike the previous interpretation Mr. Nought does not take into account feelings of satisfaction derived from the contemplation of the consumption of future generations. Each generation t has a similar utility function $f^t(C_t)$, which is a function only of that generation's utility. The units associated with the functions $f^t(\cdot)$ are different from the units of $g^t(\cdot)$ in the first interpretation (selfish altruism). This time the units are "utility enjoyed by Mr. t in consuming his own C_t."

If our concept of fairness is to be egalitarian, we can use the rate of marginal productivity of the economy (a different definition for δ), to derive the system of intertemporal weights $(1, \delta, \ldots, \delta^t, \ldots)$. Maximizing the weighted average of intertemporal welfares

$$W = \Sigma \, \delta^t f^t(C_t), \tag{7.8}$$

we arrive at a criterion of identical form as equation (7.7). This time, however, δ is dimensionless; instead of having units of measurement, it is a pure number. And instead of W being in units utility of Mr. Nought,

W is a weighted average of utilities over all generations. It appears that the second interpretation implies stagnation, but this need not be the case with further assumptions about the treatment of new knowledge, and so forth.

Thus we have two interpretations for the present value criterion, with the important difference that for one the discount factor measures the time preference of the first generation and for the other the discount factor measures the economy's productivity. In the actual world these two interpretations do not boil down to the same thing, for a wedge may be driven between the rates of time preference and productivity. Moreover, there will be differences between the interpretations as the rates of time preference and productivity change over time. Although there is little discussion of the rationales for the present value criterion, it seems that most economists tend toward the first interpretation, using pure time preference in terms of utilities.

We can put the two interpretations of the present value criterion in the context of social choice theory. The problem is to choose a decision rule that will allocate possible consumption streams $(C_0, C_1, \ldots, C_t, \ldots)$ among the affected generations. How do we aggregate individual preferences, one for each generation, into a single (intertemporal) social choice? The first interpretation says that the first generation should be a dictator, its social welfare should be maximized and all the others be discarded, except as they affect the first generation's welfare. In this interpretation the present's decision is made once, for all time, and the present should try to precommit the future to its choice. (Of course, it is often impossible for the present to precommit the future and the future may overturn the present's plan for it.) In the second interpretation the present is not a dictator because the social choice is determined by a weighted average of welfares. This interpretation satisfies the Arrow's nondictatorship postulates for democratic choice. Since the decision rule is to be chosen over a possibly infinite set, it is possible to find social choice rules consistent with all five postulates.[16]

The Present Value Criterion and the Efficiency Criterion

The present value criterion and the efficiency criterion are closely related. Generally the efficiency criterion is used to evaluate specific projects and to analyze failures in particular markets over a fairly short time horizon. The question of intergenerational fairness usually does not come up because everything is considered to happen within one generation or because the redistributional effects are considered small. Sometimes for the purposes of analysis the present generation is assumed to have an infinite time span. We can think of the market version of the efficiency criterion as saying (1) accept the initial distribution of wealth and income intratemporally and intertemporally (all resource control in the present), (2) perfect the markets or simulate them with benefit–cost analysis, and (3) let the market allocate resource usage intratemporally and intertemporally.

The present value criterion says write down a social welfare function and maximize it according to resource and productivity constraints. Generally the concept is used to evaluate the whole economy at once— on the macro level. The connection between the two concepts is that for each distribution of market power in the present and implied inter- temporal allocation of resource usage, there exists a social welfare func- tion and discount rate such that maximization of the present value of this social welfare function under this discount rate leads to the same allocation of resource usage as given under the efficiency criterion.[17] This is the sense of the statement that the present value criterion tends, more or less, to mimic what the market automatically does. In this sense the present value criterion is an intertemporal version of the efficiency criterion.

One can go further to think of the Kaldor version of the efficiency criterion (and generally benefit–cost analysis) falling out of the present value criterion in the following way. Write down the sum of discounted social welfare functions and take its total differential. For a small change resulting from the introduction of a small project, the sum is linearized and changes in the sum are proportional to changes in monetary costs and benefits associated with the project, assuming constant marginal social welfare across time. A particular project is worthwhile whenever it increases the present value of the social welfare function more than the alternatives, one of which is dropping the project. The Kaldor version of the efficiency criterion says the same thing, namely, a project is worthwhile if the discounted value of the net benefits is greater than zero.

Now we can apply some of the ideas underlying the present value criterion to the management of the resource base.

Discounting Depletable "Hardtack" Resources

We begin with the classic analysis made by Hotelling in 1931.[18] Consider a mining company which knows that any given deposit will eventually become exhausted and that it must move on to find and develop other deposits. The exhaustion of a particular deposit is a crisis for neither the mining company nor society because Hotelling assumes that substitutes can be found. The mining company must decide, however, what is the most advantageous rate of depletion of the given deposit. Hotelling first considers the optimal rate of exhaustion from the point of view of the mining company and then from the point of view of society.

If a mineral deposit were a simple inventory, and prices were constant, and the only question was when to place it on the market, the answer would be to market it today. But mineral deposits are unlike inventories in two respects. First, the average cost of extraction from a given deposit increases with the rate of extraction. Doubling the rate of extraction might require new mine shafts and capital equipment. Indeed, it is hard to imagine how high the cost per ton of ore would be driven by an effort to deplete "totally" a large mine in a single year. Second, an owner of an exhaustible resource may expect increases in prices due to future scarcity. Because he expects a higher price next year, a mine owner may be better off slowing his production and saving his stock of ore for the future higher prices.

The two factors, unit costs of production and future prices, jointly determine an expected stream of profits for each time path of extraction. Thus the self-interested competitive mine owner, who maximizes the present value of his profit stream, takes the future effects of depletion into account. Future scarcity, reflected in the expectation of higher future prices, leads each mine owner separately to act like a conservationist in order to maximize the present value of his profit stream. Gray, in an even earlier article,[19] concentrated on the first factor, the variation of cost in relation to scheduling the path of mineral extraction. Hotelling concentrated on the second factor, the effect of depletion on prices.[20]

At each moment in time the company has the choice of leaving a little more ore in the ground or turning it into cash by extracting it. By extracting a little more and putting the cash into investment activities, perhaps new exploration and development, the cash would grow at the market interest rate. On the other hand, ore reserved in the ground to be extracted at tomorrow's future higher prices may grow in value too. Taking into account future prices and costs, each unit of ore could be tagged with a unit profit that depends upon the date of extraction. As long as this unit profit grew at less than the interest rate, it would benefit the company to convert more ore into cash, assuming that mining is profitable in the first place. In this way, Hotelling found that the company was best off when it adjusted its rate of extraction to the point where the profit on a unit of reserved ore grew at just the interest rate. With its rate of extraction so adjusted, the company would be maximizing the present value of its profit stream, over the possible paths of extraction.

It was but a short step for Hotelling to move from a private point of view to a social one. Hotelling reasoned that society is also better off when capital is channeled into its most productive uses. Instead of society being interested in the welfare of a particular company, society is interested in the benefits the company's output provides to people at large. One measure of these benefits is consumer surplus, which is basically the difference between what people would be willing to pay for product output and what in fact they do pay. So, in place of maximizing the present value of the profit stream, Hotelling set about maximizing the present value of the stream of consumer surpluses associated with the flow of output. In other words, Hotelling used a version of the present value criterion to decide what is optimal from a social point of view. The market, as we have just seen, encourages firms to maximize the present value of their profit stream, even with exhaustible resources. Because profits and consumer surpluses are not the same thing, it follows that market forces by themselves may not lead to a social optimum defined by Hotelling's present value criterion. Nonetheless, under competitive conditions Hotelling found that there is a tendency for the market to lead toward optimality, defined from both points of view.

The rate of extraction of depletable resources that is optimal under the present value criterion is efficient in the Kaldor sense. The market rate of extraction, roughly in line with the rate implied by the present value criterion, except for market imperfections, does not guarantee that extraction today will benefit the future, because material may be channeled into short-lived goods, dissipated, and become less available to the future than if the ore had been left in place. The future might well be better off with a slower rate of extraction. But the fact remains that the future could *potentially* be made better off with the perfected market rate of extraction than with a slower rate, with redistributions of wealth and product. So the theory goes.

The Iron Law of the Discount Rate

It is generally recognized among economists that a number of biological resources, like ocean fish, are being overexploited. The reason given is that fish and many other natural resources are treated by the market system as common property resources. However, the market system, even corrected for its failure with respect to common property resources, still tends to bring many biological and geomorphic resources to extinction. In this section we first discuss very briefly the common property misallocation and then consider how discounting spells doom for many biological and geomorphic resources.

In terms of figure 2 in chapter 2, common property resources sit in the environmental sector not owned by anyone. Anyone can gain ownership by direct appropriation, which moves the resource across the boundary into the economic sector. To illustrate, in fishing, the process is by simple capture. One of the costs of a capture is that it lowers the stock for all the other fishermen. Each fisherman counts only his private (internal) costs, from his gear and time, and so forth. He does not count the external cost he imposes on others in terms of the diminished resource base. If there were N fishermen all bearing an equal share of the cost of the diminished resource base, a single fisherman would bear only $1/N$ of the total depletion cost generated by his own catch. He diminishes the resource base for himself as well as all the others, and only to the extent of his own burden is he forced to count the cost of depletion. To the extent he does not count the external cost on others there is overexploitation of the resource base.

By overexploitation economists mean that by allowing fishing under the rule of capture, the world's total harvest is carried past the maximum present value. By restricting the catch, the present value of the entire world catch could be increased. As a remedy, economists recommend international fishing conferences which set quotas for each country, or some other scheme to diminish the common property nature of fishery resources. The 200-mile limit is one such scheme: it is not a complete solution because fish move across boundaries, but it is a step away from the common property problem.

Suppose that somehow conferences are established and they eliminate the common property problem. Quotas are set up which restrict the total world catch just enough to maximize the present value of the biological resource (the potential fish catch). With the common property problem disposed of by assumption, now consider the many biological and natural resources whose productivities are less than the discount rate. Just as in Hotelling's example of the mine, market forces following the present value criterion tend to increase the rate of exploitation of these resources. As they become depleted, there is speculation on future price increases. The rate of exploitation is increased until the unit value of the resource grows, from anticipated future scarcity added to the rate of natural productivity, at the same rate as the discount rate. For slow-growing biological assets, a rate of absolute decline is optimal under the present value criterion. In other words, the motivation of resource reservation slows down the decline but guarantees that each year the "optimal" size is less than the optimal size the year before. If there is no resource stock size for which the productivity reaches up to the discount rate, and there are still unit profits from harvesting, the process continues until the resource is wiped out. This is as it should be under the present value criterion.

Hotelling applied his analysis narrowly to a nonrenewable resource that is not vital—such as ore from a single mine when there are substitutes. But the present value criterion applies as well to renewable resources and in principle even to resources that are vital to survival. Those natural resources whose productivity is greater than the discount rate will be expanded if possible, and those whose productivity is less than the discount rate will be decreased if possible. The present value criterion may transform renewable resources into essentially nonrenewable resources, time-dated for exhaustion, as is true in some cases for timber.

Just as in the case of mining, which Gray analyzed, there is a tendency for the unit costs of extraction for productive resources to increase as the stock of the resource is depleted. The last few whales are harder to find because they are dispersed more and more thinly over the oceans. If the costs of extraction of a biological resource rise enough to eliminate the profit from extraction while the population size is large enough to reproduce, then the resource has a chance to survive even if its biological productivity is less than the discount rate.[21]

The path toward extinction of whales is shown in figure 22. The situation for many ocean fish is probably considerably better than for whales. Most fish have a biological growth rate, for some population size, sufficient to meet the discount rate. An international agreement that monopolized the control of the world catch and maximized its present value would probably protect most commercial fish from extinction. Some whales may have a natural growth rate less than the market discount rate and may be marked for extinction by the present value criterion. A perfectly efficient whaling conference may find that a gradual elimination of entire species is optimal under this criterion.[22]

The iron law of the discount rate is the harsh side of the present value criterion; there is also a "conservationist" side. When all the management and exploitation costs are counted in, the present value criterion

Figure 22. Annual Blue Whale catch, 1930–1960

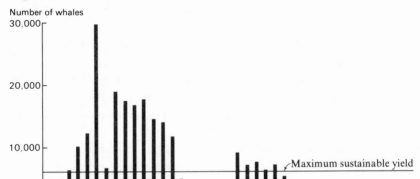

may call for a lower annual harvest than would be obtained by maximizing the sustainable yield as it is often defined in practice. In practice, sustainable yield criteria often neglect management costs and consequently push the activity further. But when the asset yield is defined in terms of its net value (yield minus carrying costs), then sustainable yield concepts may be more "conservative" than the present value criterion.

Ethics in a Hardtack World

To sharpen the moral conflict between the present and the future, we return to the case of Robinson Crusoe cast upon his island with a stock of nonrenewable hardtack. Previously, we had assumed that the stock was large enough so that Crusoe could live out his natural lifespan (N years). In that case, if he discounts by the hardtack productivity, which is zero, he arrives at an egalitarian solution; if he discounts by his time preference, he eats well in the beginning and austerely at the end. Either way, it is his life and his choice as to what to do with it. It is clear, though, that if he chooses in the beginning to discount by time preference, he is more likely to regret this choice in his later years.

The ethical problem becomes much tougher if the initial stock is not sufficient for a lifetime's subsistence. If the last few years are very important to him, he can stretch out his life as long as possible by only eating enough to subsist each day (plan A in figure 23). But this solution means that he will be miserably hungry every day of his life. This, in effect, is an intertemporal Calcutta solution. (See appendix G for mathematical details.)

Alternatively, he can live somewhat better in the beginning at the cost of an earlier death. This way he will have at least a few pleasant years.[23] If he chooses to use a present value criterion and discounts by what he judges in the beginning to be his set of time preferences, his plan of consumption is likely to look like C in figure 23, and if by the rate of productivity (zero), like B. With either form of the present value welfare criterion, he essentially decides to commit suicide in order to live better in the present. This is certainly not the kind of moral choice one would like to have forced upon him.

The moral problem can be still worse, however. Suppose that instead of deciding only for his own life, Crusoe must decide for others as well. Suppose Fletcher Christian and his band, Tahitian wives and all, were thrown up upon a barren island with a huge stock of hardtack, enough for several generations, and with no means of escape. Then the first generations are forced into the position of deciding which generation will be the last one. Suppose, further, that the first generation voted and decided to follow a present value criterion, using the first generation's time preference for the discount rate. Suppose each following generation adheres to the implied consumption plan, which is C in figure 23 (appropriately reinterpreted from Crusoe to Christian and his band), and you happen to be born ten years before N_c. As you grow up, it is explained to you that the world is going to end very shortly because earlier generations wanted to live well. This is obviously the basis for a conflict between the points of view of the present and the future. You might well call out to the ghosts of the first generation, demanding by what right

Figure 23. Alternative consumption plans

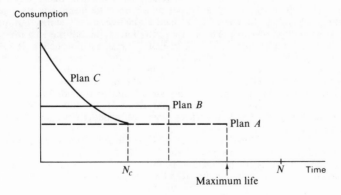

it made its decision. It would be hardly satisfying to hear the answer, "We took a vote of all those present and decided to follow our own time preferences."

In the selfish altruism version of the present value criterion so far discussed, there is no way of resolving a conflict between generations over how resources should be allocated. Everything is done from the point of view of the present; it is their time preference, and everything is discounted back to them. While many economists realize the inability of the present value criterion to resolve conflicts across generations, they may not recognize it as a serious failure. They tend to think that the world economy is not a hardtack one, but an investment one in which the future will be better off than the present. For this reason, they argue that such a failure of consistency is not important. Conservationists, on the other hand, tend to think that the world has certain hardtack tendencies and may, unless steps are taken, drift irrevocably into a hardtack economy. For them the failure is more serious.

Notes

1. Nicholas Kaldor, "Welfare Propositions of Economics and Interpersonal Comparisons of Utility," *The Economic Journal* vol. 49 (1939) pp. 549–552, reprinted in Kenneth Arrow and Tibor Scitovsky, eds. *Readings in Welfare Economics* (Nobleton, Ontario, Richard Irwin, 1969) p. 388.

2. Harberger treats the distributional impact of most projects as a minor problem, saying that the distributional impact of one project is likely to be small compared with distributional changes from the general drift of the economy. See Arnold Harberger, "Three Postulates of Applied Welfare Economics: An Interpretive Essay," *Journal of Economic Literature* vol. 9, no. 3 (Sept. 1971) pp. 785–797, and particularly p. 787.

3. The economy need not be growing for productivity to exist. One hundred dollars' worth of seeds can turn into $400 worth of crop whether or not GNP is sitting still. On the other hand, without productivity the economy would soon starve.

Productivity is a slippery concept that can be defined in many ways. For the purposes of this book, we take "productive asset" to mean one that generates something of value. In contrast, a "nonproductive asset" stores but does not generate something of value. This is all a little imprecise, but the idea may become clear in the examples that follow. A bag of flour is not productive. It has value, but the only way to obtain it is to use it up. It only stores value. Similarly, ore in a mine is not productive. The "something of value" in this case is the metal stored underground. This something may become more or less valuable as market conditions change, but the metal is only stored, not generated. The defining characteristic of a nonproductive asset is that there is no way to obtain its value without depleting it. There are three types of productivity important for our discussion:

1. Machine. A machine is productive when it saves more time and trouble than is embodied in the machine itself. By cleverly designing more roundabout and elaborate processes of production, people are able to generate a greater saving of effort than was originally embodied in the construction of the machine.

2. *Corn.* Biological productivity is the easiest to understand. A farmer can start out with a few seeds in the fall and end up with hundreds the following year. The time and trouble in bringing biological productivities to harvest can be fully compensated for by the basic productivity of the natural asset itself. Otherwise there would be no farmers, ranchers, and fishermen.

3. *Grand Canyon.* People often do not think of geomorphic assets as productive. But clearly the "something of value" in the Grand Canyon is not a finite something that is stored and used up as people enjoy the area. The Grand Canyon or wilderness areas (and Rembrandts too for that matter) are capable of indefinitely generating value without depletion. They are like perpetual yield bonds which forever spin out interest without wearing out the principal. (In times of inflation, which erode the value of long-term bonds, they may be considerably better.)

Unlike perpetual yield bonds, the three types of productive assets generate, in an economic sense, "real" somethings of value instead of financial transfers. The first type is man-made productivity, while the latter two are by and large natural productivities.

4. With inflation greater than 5 percent, saving will be at a negative rate of interest. As we have recently seen, saving still takes place at negative rates of interest, presumably for precautionary motives.

5. In the sense defined in footnote 3 in this chapter, geomorphic assets such as the Grand Canyon are also productive but depletable. See footnote 12, chapter 1, noting the emphasis on inheritance models.

6. A commonly used device to focus attention on the intertemporal distribution problem is to assume that consumption is split equally among those of any given generation. See, for example, Robert Solow, "Intergenerational Equity and Exhaustible Resources," *Review of Economic Studies,* Symposium on the Economics of Exhaustible Resources, vol. 41 (supplement 1974) pp. 29–45. For a discussion of the conditions under which the well-being of the members of a generation can be aggregated and treated as a single unit, see Karl-Göran Mäler, *Environmental Economics: A Theoretical Inquiry* (Baltimore, Md., Johns Hopkins University Press for Resources for the Future, 1974) chapter 4, section 11.

7. If there is unemployment of labor or capital, then a government project need not preempt all its resources from private use. If the government is able to use resources that would otherwise be idle, the cost of the project from the point of view of society as a whole is somewhat reduced. See Robert Haveman and John Krutilla, *Unemployment, Idle Capacity, and the Evaluation of Public Expenditures: National and Regional Analysis* (Baltimore, Md., Johns Hopkins University Press for Resources for the Future, 1968).

8. John Ferejohn, "Congressional Influences on Water Politics" (Ph.D. dissertation, Stanford University, July 1972) pp. 45–46.

9. W. J. Baumol, "On the Social Rate of Discount," *American Economic Review* vol. 58, no. 4 (1968) pp. 788–802.

10. This type of risk is quite different from the type of risk that often concerns conservationists. The economist is talking about the risk involved with the failure of a project, small compared with the whole economy. Conservationists are concerned more with risks of large disasters.

11. And fourth, as we have seen in appendix F, even in the absence of the above market distortions, market forces may not bring productivity into harmony with time preference.

12. Stephen Marglin describes one type of externality in which those in the present do not act like a single unit, thus making the social rate of discount more elusive. See Stephen Marglin, "The Social Rate of Discount and the Optimal Rate of Investment," *Quarterly Journal of Economics* vol. 77, no. 1 (February 1963) pp. 95–111.

13. Examples can be found in Robert Strotz, "Myopia and Inconsistency in Dynamic Utility Maximization," *Review of Economic Studies* vol. 23 (1955–1956)

p. 167; Kenneth Arrow and Mordecai Kurz, *Public Investment, the Rate of Return and Optimal Policy* (Baltimore, Md., Johns Hopkins University Press for Resources for the Future, 1970) p. 11; Tjalling Koopmans, "Some Observations on 'Optimal' Economic Growth and Exhaustible Resources," Cowles Foundation Discussion Paper no. 356, March 28, 1973, p. 3; (Koopmans uses the same "hardtack" and "sheep" paradigms as are used in chapters 7, 8, and 9 of this book); Richard Gordon, "A Reinterpretation of the Pure Theory of Exhaustion," *Journal of Political Economy* vol. 75, no. 3 (June 1967) p. 277; Vernon Smith, "An Optimistic Theory of Exhaustible Resources," California Institute of Technology Social Science Working Paper no. 39 (April 1974) p. 3; Oscar Burt and Ronald Cummings, "Production and Investment in Natural Resource Industries," *American Economic Review* vol. LX (1970) p. 579; C. G. Plourde, "Exploitation of Common-Property Replenishable Natural Resources," *Western Economic Journal* vol. IX, no. 3 (Sept. 1971) p. 256; and Neil Vousden, "Basic Theoretical Issues of Resource Depletion," *Journal of Economic Theory* vol. 6 (April 1973) pp. 126–143.

14. Mäler discusses some of the conditions under which one translates from nonmeasurable utility terms to quantifiable variables of prices and commodities. Karl-Göran Mäler, *Environmental Economics*, chapter 4 and especially sections 6, 7, and 11.

15. In view of the great efforts economists have made in the past thirty years for the intratemporal case to avoid interpersonal comparisons in the theory of economic welfare, their willingness to make such comparisons in the intertemporal theory of welfare is somewhat surprising. Perhaps the willingness is prompted by the realization that it clears the way for models of great mathematical elegance or by the perception that it is a normative statement of what the market tends, more or less, to do by itself.

16. The "almost anywhere dominates" criterion satisfies all five of Arrow's desirability conditions. Consumption path $(C_0, C_1, \ldots, C_t, \ldots)$ almost everywhere dominates path $(C_0', C_1', \ldots, C_t', \ldots)$ if $C_t > C_t'$ for all but a finite number of t; if $C_t > C_t'$ for an infinite number of t and $C_t' < C_t$ for an infinite number of t the two paths are "socially indifferent" under the criterion. The criterion is a generalization of majority voting; there are obvious shortcomings with a criterion which neglects a possibly very large minority, but the main interest is in demonstrating that Arrow's five postulates are not inconsistent over an infinite number of generations. I am indebted to John Ferejohn for pointing this out to me. See Kenneth Arrow, *Social Choice and Individual Values* (2nd ed., New York, Wiley, 1966) pp. 24–31; and Henry Wan, *Economic Growth* (New York, Harcourt Brace Jovanovich, 1971) p. 302.

A stricter version of the "almost anywhere dominates" criterion is the "everywhere dominates" criterion. For a proposed project to become a chosen project, this criterion would require that every generation be made better off. This criterion is a generalization of unanimity voting; in other terms, it is a criterion for Pareto improvement with the requirement for actual compensation. This criterion can be contrasted with the present value criterion that permits potential Pareto improvements with potential compensation. The difference between potential Pareto improvements and actual ones is the difference in intertemporal fairness. I am indebted to Myrick Freeman for suggesting the criterion of actual Pareto improvement.

17. See Milton Weinstein and Richard Zeckhauser, "Use Patterns for Depletable and Recyclable Resources," *Review of Economic Studies*, Symposium on the Economics of Exhaustible Resources, vol. 41 (supplement 1974) p. 71 and especially footnote 2 on that page.

18. Harold Hotelling, "The Economics of Exhaustible Resources," *Journal of Political Economy* vol. 39, no. 2 (1931) pp. 137–175.

19. L. C. Gray, "Rent Under the Assumption of Exhaustibility," *Quarterly Journal of Economics* vol. 28 (1914) pp. 466–489, reprinted in Mason Gaffney,

ed., *Extractive Resources and Taxation* (Madison, Wisc., University of Wisconsin Press, 1967) pp. 423–446.

20. I am indebted to Chandler Morse for his comparative discussion of Gray and Hotelling. See Chandler Morse, "Depletion, Exhaustibility, and Conservation" in William A. Vogely, ed., *Economics of the Mineral Industries* (3d ed., New York, American Institute of Mining, Metallurgical, and Petroleum Engineers, 1976).

21. See Vernon L. Smith, "Economics of Production from Natural Resources," *American Economic Review* vol. 58, no. 3 (June 1968) pp. 409–431 for an elegant discussion of the interaction of the common property phenomenon, rising costs for depletion, congestion in extractive activities, and the possibility of biological growth of the resource stock. He shows that by its nature private profit can in many cases eliminate the resource stock altogether.

22. Besides the common property resource phenomenon, there is a second class of externalities that is associated with whales. People like to see whales and they like to know that the species exists (existence value); in addition to these evaluations, whales may benefit the ocean environment in unknown ways. The benefits of these externalities do not accrue to any whaling conference and would not accrue to one even if the conference acted like a perfect monopoly. The best the conference can do for itself is to maximize the present value of the tangible whale products. It has no way of setting quotas, and so forth, to capture these external benefits (the psychic and intangible ones). The rational (that is, internal profit-maximizing) whaling conference will ignore them and consequently overharvest, according to the efficiency criterion.

Many natural assets have nonmarket external benefits associated with them. These are often not taken into account, even by government agencies charged with protecting the "public trust"; but the point is that even if these externalities were taken into account, the "iron law of the discount rate" tends to eliminate any asset if its productivity, including the external benefits, is lower than the discount rate.

23. Unfortunately, this ethical dilemma is not just a textbook one. Victims of some cancers are faced with the choice of chemotherapy which may add a few weeks of life at the cost of making each week more uncomfortable than without the therapy.

8

The Conservation Criterion

The earth belongs in usufruct to the living.
—Thomas Jefferson

The Conservationist Ethic

IN CONTRAST to the economists, the conservationists do not spell out criteria in precise mathematical detail. It is not even clear what the definition of "conservation" is. While the view of the economist is a little like a theology, the view of the conservationist is more like that of a religion. That is to say, the former is likely to give rise to a closed system of ideas, the latter to a less analytically precise system of values. One explanation of this vagueness is in the conservation movement's political origins.[1] As a political movement it used slogans, made compromises, and was tempered by the personalities of its leaders. Hays dates the first conservation movement from 1890 to 1920,[2] and at its peak, when Theodore Roosevelt and Gifford Pinchot were in power, it was remarkably successful. Roosevelt tripled the amount of forest under control of the Forest Service, ostensibly out of the greedy hands of private industry. The conservation movement spilled over from natural resources to anti-industrialization, anti-immigration, trust-busting, and pure food laws, among other things.

As with all political movements, conservationists were tempted to make their movement appear to be all things to all people. Gaffney attributes to Pinchot the slogan that conservation stood for "the greatest good for the greatest number over the longest time." Who could be unhappy with this echo of Bentham, except perhaps the mathematician who wonders how to maximize the same thing in three different ways, all simultaneously. A 1910 *Outlook* article summed up the conservation

174

movement: "A great many people are in favor of conservation, no matter what it means."[3]

It does seem clear, however, that the conservation movement received much of its original impetus from the view that many of the world's resources were like so much hardtack, to be used up as slowly and wisely as possible. Pinchot wrote:

The five indispensably essential materials in our civilization are wood, water, coal, iron, and agricultural products. . . . We have timber for less than thirty years at the present rate of cutting. The figures indicate that our demands upon the forest have increased twice as fast as our population. We have anthracite coal for but fifty years, and bituminous coal for less than two hundred. Our supplies of iron ore, mineral oil, and natural gas are being rapidly depleted, and many of the great fields are already exhausted. Mineral resources such as these when once gone are gone forever.

If [coal] can be preserved, if the life of the mines can be extended, if by preventing waste there can be more coal left in this country after we of this generation have made every needed use of this source of power, then we shall have deserved well of our descendants.[4]

Faced with the spectre of running out of vital resources, conservationists thought it immoral for the present to waste depleting stocks. Barnett and Morse have distilled from the conservationist literature three rules to avoid waste:

1. The regenerative capacity or potential of renewable resources (such as forests, grazing land, cropland, water) should not be physically damaged or destroyed.
2. Renewable resources should be used in place of minerals, insofar as physically possible.
3. Plentiful minerals resources should be used before less plentiful ones, insofar as physically possible.[5]

To this list we can add the modern stressed dictum:

4. Nonrenewable resources should be recycled as much as possible.

Barnett and Morse point out that these are not the rules of an economy guided by individual consumer sovereignty.[6] In this country concern over resource scarcity, and in particular over the threat of timber famine, goes back at least a century. Carl Schurz, secretary of the interior, forecast in his annual report of 1877 that there was only a twenty-year supply of timber.[7] Clepper cites other and earlier warnings.[8]

Two factors have caused reserve estimates to be frequently revised upward. First, the estimates were, and are, increased by new discoveries. This factor is of temporary comfort, because the world is, after all, of finite dimension. The second factor, however, may have no ultimate limit: new technology has substituted new materials for depleted ones and has cheapened the cost of mining inferior ores. Barnett and Morse spend a good part of their book trying to find out whether or not technology has kept pace with depletion over the past hundred years. Using price data constructed by Potter and Christy[9] for many basic materials, they tentatively concluded that most prices of raw materials, corrected for inflation, have fallen in the past century. The big exception is timber, the costs of which have steadily risen, and are still rising. In their analysis, it was not possible to unscramble the effects of new discoveries and those of technological change. Of course the past century can hardly be taken as a guide to the next century. The enormous tracts of land that were opened up in the past century were quite literally a last frontier. Neither the path of technology nor the search for new resource bases, such as the sea, is bound by previous history.

While it is fortunate from our point of view, the fact that resource scarcities did not follow on Pinchot's and the other conservationists' schedules undermined the conservation movement. Like the boy who cried wolf, conservationists found that their warnings aroused less response the more they were revised.

After several decades of decline, the conservation movement has re-emerged. A convenient date for its reappearance is 1962, the time of publication of Rachel Carson's *Silent Spring*. The conservation movement is still growing, so that one can only speculate as to what will prove to be its dominating ideas and achievements. Many of the ideas sketched below go back to the earlier movement and many further back to the classical economists, Malthus, Ricardo, and Mill. But in this modern version of the conservation movement, the emphasis has changed and this is what I will try to describe.

In *Silent Spring* the burden imposed upon the future is not the preemption of a finite stock of nonrenewable resources, but the accumulation of poisons in the environment. The limits are perceived in the carrying capacities of the environment. The emphasis shifts to the long-run effects of pollution and threats to environmental systems. When economists see market failures caused by pollution, they generally recommend some sort of administrative action; most likely effluent taxes or standards. Often these remedies are analyzed as though their administration were both costless and perfectly efficient. To the contrary, many active conservationists, who have dealt with regulatory agencies, perceive sharp limitations to administrative carrying capacities. An agency's ability to deliver an economist's theoretically optimal effluent tax is limited by an inevitable degree of incompetence, the bureaucracy's own interests, and outside industry pressures.

With this mistrust of government's ability to deliver, how then, can the activists demand environmental cleanup, which implies greater governmental intervention?[10] Their answer is to encourage conditions under which carrying capacities, both social and natural, are less strained. With a more benign technology, emissions are more easily assimilated by the environment and are thus less costly pollutants. Moreover, in this case the economists' optimal effluent tax is closer to zero, so that administrative incompetence is less costly. And with sufficiently benign pollutants, the efficiency gains from effluent taxes are more than offset by administrative costs and errors so that the optimal tax, taking all the administrative costs into account, is zero. Similarly, with a world population that slowly diminishes to one or two billion, there is a smaller press on environmental assimilative capacities, resulting in both a smaller need for administrative remedy and a greater margin for error.

Technology is mistrusted because it is perceived as a principal cause of environmental costs and long-run dangers. There are many chronicles of technology's negative role, from *Silent Spring* to the *SST and Sonic Boom Handbook*. Most of the technological dangers discussed are the outcomes of post–World War II discoveries, and share a McLuhanesque feature. The dominant symbol of the nineteenth century "mechanical society" is the assembly line. One can see the parts and figure out the system by watching how one thing moves into another. In the "electrical society" of the twentieth, the relationships between parts are hidden, like the electrical flows in a television set. So, too, with technology. In the nineteenth century one could see the technology. Forests were stripped ever more efficiently with more modern machines but the effects were visible. In contrast, pesticides in the environment are unseen, as are leakages of "normal radiation releases" from a fission power plant. Modern technological hazards are more invisible; one has to infer the dangers. One has to be trained to think that one part in a million can be important. A century ago air pollution was mostly visible black soot, now it is much more complicated, with its pollutants more deadly and less visible. The greater uncertainty of the long-run effects of new technology and its greater invisibility make technological progress an untrustworthy ally.

In addition, there is another variant of Gresham's law that favors technical change with higher long-run uncertainty and greater invisibility.

The natural selection of the market favors those technological improvements least likely to run into governmental prohibition; that is, ones whose effects are least visible and definite.

Improvements in technological capabilities allow the processing of enormous quantities of low grade ores; toxic trace substances are released in such quantity as they scatter that they become regional problems. In the old-fashioned Gresham's law, bad money drives out the good, because each person wants to spend paper money and hoard gold. Each one wants to keep for himself the solid buying power of gold and socialize the uncertainties of the weaker currency. With the new variant of Gresham's law, internal costs are traded for dispersed, uncertain, and publicly borne costs (external costs). New technology makes these trades more possible.

Nonetheless, many conservationists now view technical progress, no matter how untrustworthy, as a necessary ally. Unlike their predecessors, they do not think of material resources as being necessarily like hardtack, with fixed amounts of supply. To varying degrees, they have accepted the Barnett–Morse thesis that technology can create substitutes and lower costs of increasingly inferior resources, thus changing nonrenewable resources into renewable ones. However reluctantly, they agree that without technical progress we are doomed to a hardtack economy. Because their goal is to preserve the long-run livability of the planet, they have no alternative but to accept technology.[11]

The possibilities of technical progress mean that we can escape the ethical problem of a limited number of generations living in a hardtack world. However, the ethical problem reemerges in the actual world in a deeper form. Even though we do not *necessarily* live in a hardtack world, there are many ways in which we can make the planet less livable or even uninhabitable in the short span of a century or so.

The locus of the ethical problem for the conservationist may be clearer if we think in terms of three simple economies. Two of them we have discussed as hardtack and corn economies. The third is a manna economy, which is an idealization of countless traditional societies. There is no economic growth, no population growth, and no depletion of resources. Such societies live off only renewable resources by hunting and gathering. Their efforts are small compared with the resource base, which can renew itself no matter what the efforts of the hunters and gatherers are. Each generation makes no mark on the world, leaving to the next generation a world in the same condition as it was a generation previous. It is in a practical sense a complete recycle economy. All the flows are recycled, except solar energy flows. This economy enjoys a kind of social immortality. Until the far-off day when something happens to the sun, there is no reason that human existence cannot go on generation after generation. It is not a "free lunch" economy because each generation has to work hard for its sustenance, but it is a "manna" economy in the sense that the same stream of potential consumption flows to all generations. There is no ethical dilemma because the actions of one generation have no effect on the resource base for succeeding generations. The manna economy is a primitive spaceship earth.

There is a more modern, and to most people, a more attractive version of this idea of spaceship earth. In this version, technical progress is used to raise the standard of living over time. To achieve a more comfortable social immortality, we need not limit ourselves to exploitation of only recyclable flows. We need not decrease our consumption of coal to the rate it naturally forms. Technology is channeled and stimulated sufficiently to offset the tendency toward rising costs as the better grade ores are depleted. Instead of a long-run steady state in flows, the sophisticated version recognizes that to achieve social immortality it is sufficient to maintain costs for service flows forever constant. Technology renews the depletable resources.

The ethical question in this context is not the inherently depressing one of how to live best in a hardtack economy, but the prior one of how to choose between the different economic regimes (manna, hardtack, and corn).[12] Though it is a deeper question, the answer, at least in broad outline, is much easier for the conservationist. To the conservationist, the moral imperative is to establish institutions and incentives that keep the economy in its corn and manna regimes and to prevent it from drifting into a hardtack one, in its important features.

A Criterion

For protection against gradual extinction by market forces, conservationists recommend that many natural assets be managed on a sustainable yield basis. To do this one must of course first identify the assets to be so managed. Presumably not every organism and every natural environment is to be preserved in perpetuity, only the most "important" ones.

Beyond this, it is often recommended that assets be managed not merely on a sustainable yield basis but on a maximum sustainable yield basis. There are many examples of this concept in practice: in forestry, fishing, agriculture, and the management of wildlife populations. The concept spills over into petroleum recovery in the slightly different variant of maximum economic recovery (MER), and it underlies some of the enthusiasm nuclear engineers have for the liquid metal fast breeder reactor (LMFBR), which squeezes a much higher energy recovery from uranium than other methods. For many of these areas, including petroleum recovery and the LMFBR, economists have argued that maximizing the sustainable yield or just maximizing the yield over a short period is economically inefficient and inconsistent with present-value maximization of economic benefits.

When there are many interacting assets, it is not always clear what is meant by maximizing the sustainable yield for each one. It is often possible to increase the sustainable yield of one species by sacrificing a little of the sustainable yield of a competing one. More troublesome is the fact that one can keep increasing the sustainable yield of many natural assets by pouring more resources into their management. Where is the process to stop? Samuelson offers an unambiguous definition of maximum sustainable yield: that perpetually repeatable (or steady state) yield with the maximum yield net of management costs averaged over the production cycle. Because there is no appearance of a discount rate in this definition, this sustained yield criterion differs from the present value criterion.[13]

Sustainable yield concepts are usually recommended on the grounds that they protect the resource base from gradual extinction. The conservationist recommendation of sustainable yield management is often met by an industry countersuggestion of exploitation up to the maximum limit of sustainable yield. Under a market test, or under the efficiency criterion, exploitation would not be carried further than the point where an incremental increase in the management and exploitation costs is larger than the resulting gain in the value of the yield. Management on a maximum sustainable yield basis may go further, especially if some of the management costs are externalized upon the government (as with the Forest Service) or the public at large (as with pollution costs), or if the management costs are neglected entirely in the calculation of maximum sustainable yield. Thus, while the present value criterion does not guarantee the survival of a resource base, it may be more conserving than the application of a sustainable yield concept, especially a maximum yield one.

The implications of various sustainable yield and present value criteria can be seen in terms of a simple corn-manna economy. In this economy there is a single resource which satisfies all subsistence needs. It grows in forests and, like trees, increases in bulk and hence value, slowly at first, then quickly, and finally slowly as it becomes old. The first generation stumbles upon a forest of trees, uniformly (randomly) distributed in age. The first generation's problem is to decide in what time pattern to harvest the trees. When a tree is cut or dies naturally, another sapling springs up in its spot. There is a limited amount of space in the forest and a constant number of trees at any given time. Of course, if the first generation cuts down all the trees, it will leave nothing but saplings for the future, and if it cuts nothing down, it will "waste" those aging trees that would have been lost to the future anyway.

The yield of a single tree can be plotted (figure 24) as a function of its age, yield $= f$(age). If the first generation chose the criterion of maximum yield per tree, it would cut trees of age A, at their time of death and just as they are beginning to rot.[14] In this case, society does not have the highest annual (and perpetual) consumption, however, because the product $f(A)$ is spread across the whole period of the tree's natural life A. Annual perpetual consumption would be higher if society adopted the criterion to maximize the average sustainable yield per tree. With this criterion, society would cut trees of age B. The yield per tree would be lower, but the time between harvests on a given plot of land would be lessened enough to raise the sustainable yield per year. In this

Figure 24. Yield of a single tree as a function of time between harvests

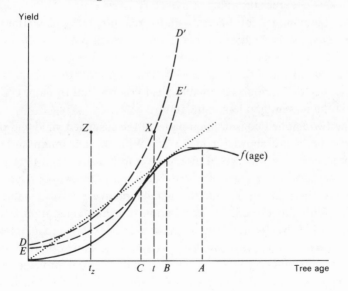

simple economy there is no labor required for planting or harvesting, and, with no management costs, maximum sustainable yield and maximum sustainable net yield come to the same thing.

Society could, however, decide to use a present value criterion and discount by time preference i (there being no other discount rate in this economy besides the natural rate of tree growth, which circularly varies according to which criterion is chosen). In this case the optimal age of harvest can be shown by using "equal-value intertemporal contours." In spite of their formidable name, these contours have a simple meaning and definition. Choose any point on the vertical axis (for example, D) and let it grow at the discount rate i. Thus, point X, t years from now has a vertical height $X = D(1 + i)^t$. We can easily compute the "present value of X units in future time t" by the present value criterion. The present value is

$$X/(1 + i)^t = \frac{D(1 + i)^t}{(1 + i)^t} = D$$

By definition, all the points on an equal-value intertemporal contour have the same value from the point of view of the present, if it uses the present value criterion with discount rate i. To draw another contour, one starts with another point on the vertical axis (for example E) and lets it grow at the discount rate. Any point, for example Z in figure 24, lies on some contour which relates its value at time t_z to its present value (where the contour cuts the vertical axis). The contour will be familiar to bankers who plot the value of monetary assets over time.[15]

The optimal age of harvest, under the present value criterion, is determined by the highest feasible contour, which is EE'. With a harvest age of C years, society maximizes the present value of any given tree.[16] Applied to all trees, the present value criterion leads to a younger forest than under the various sustainable yield criteria, and to more consumption in the present and less in the future.

The two implied consumption paths of the sustained yield and present value criteria are shown in figure 25. With the maximum sustainable yield criterion, the first generation does a little better than later generations, because it can feast off the overage trees (trees over B years old, in figure 24), in setting up the maximum average sustainable cycle (SS'). With the present value criterion, the first generation does still better (PP') by feasting on a larger number of overage trees (age greater than C years in figure 24). The present value criterion also admits the possibility that GG' may be optimal. The present value criterion may keep lowering the optimal age of trees for harvest, generation by

Figure 25. Consumption paths under differing criteria—initial abundance

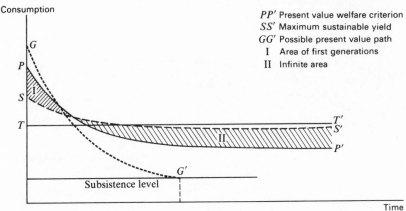

generation, until the aggregate forest yield is brought below the subsistence level. Perhaps if the criterion is chosen by only those in the present, the present value criterion might be chosen. If the criterion were chosen by all generations, it is hard to imagine that the little extra welfare for the first generations (associated with area I in figure 25) would be allowed to dominate the potential improvement for all later generations (associated with the infinite area II). In this case, the sustainable yield criterion is closer to another criterion, the "intertemporal maximin criterion," which requires society to maximize the welfare of the worst-off group. This criterion often leads to egalitarian sharing over time, as shown by TT'.

On the other hand, if the first generation had not stumbled into a fully developed, naturally grown forest, but had been placed on a scrubby island, it might take many generations of sacrificed consumption in order to bring the forest to its maximum sustainable yield. In this case (figure 26) the first generation is likely to be the worst-off generation, even with the present value criterion, and the maximin principle would rank the present value criterion over the maximum sustainable yield criterion. But if society, in opting for a sustainable yield criterion, decides it is not necessary to reach the state of maximum sustainable yield as soon as possible, much of the burden on the present can be shifted from its shoulders. It may seem worth it from the point of view of all generations that the first few generations should sacrifice a little more than they would under the present value criterion (with the discount rate chosen by the first generation), if it results in an eventual permanent increase in welfare, in spite of the fact that this situation violates the maximin

Figure 26. Consumption paths under differing criteria—initial scarcity

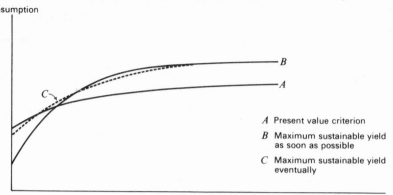

Consumption

A Present value criterion

B Maximum sustainable yield
as soon as possible

C Maximum sustainable yield
eventually

Time

criterion. A gradualist sustainable yield criterion, rather than a maximum sustainable yield as soon as possible, may be more attractive to the first (present) generation, which after all has a certain veto power. One might say sustainable yields are all right if they don't cost too much to my generation, but the calculation need not be reduced entirely to the basis of selfish altruism. Part of the calculation may rest on valuations of entire consumption streams from the perspectives of different generations.

We can apply some of these ideas to the actual economy, and in particular, to nonrenewable virgin materials as follows. First we deal with the problem arising from the fact that there are many depletable virgin materials: Should each one be managed on a maximum sustainable net yield basis? That would be too rigid an approach, not allowing for some materials to become superseded by others and dropped from the economy's inventory of resources. We, therefore, identify the important, or vital, virgin materials to be included in such an index. The selection of such materials is not too hard and many lists have been made, for defense and other purposes. Suppose there are N materials. For a base year, perhaps this year, we write down the prices and quantities of these virgin materials as they enter the economy. Then for each succeeding year we compute a price index of the extractive sector:

$$I_t = \sum_{i=1}^{N} \frac{p_{it}q_{io}}{p_{io}q_{io}},$$

where p_{io} is the price of the ith virgin material in the base year; p_{it} is the price of the ith virgin material in the tth year; q_{io} is the quantity of the ith virgin material introduced to the economy in the base year; q_{it} is the quantity of the ith virgin material introduced into the economy in the tth year.

For this composite, we could define a maximum sustainable net yield, in the sense Samuelson defines it. However, while conservationists wish to enhance certain geomorphic and biological resources (such as wilderness areas and forests), they appear to have a more modest condition in mind for workaday materials such as minerals—preservation of the resource base. In this spirit we can compare the price index of the extractive sector I_t with the general price level by dividing I_t by the GNP price deflator D_t. If we can keep the "real" price of the composite of virgin materials (I_t/D_t) constant or declining we are maintaining a "sustainable" yield of virgin material resources. Barnett and Morse have surmised that the real prices of most extractive materials have not increased in the past century; we can define a *conservation criterion* as stating that this hypothesized condition *should* be maintained. This is clearly different from the present value criterion, which would maximize the present value of each material resource separately. In the present value criterion there is no provision for a perpetual steady state with respect to the resource base. It could be, of course, that this provision is unnecessary and we could learn to live without a virgin material resource base.[17] But this would reverse a long-term trend—year by year we are becoming more dependent on the virgin material resource base.

In order that the costs of virgin materials be kept nonincreasing, one should forecast the price pressures on these materials. One begins by trying to understand past price behavior in terms of its major component effects: How much of the long-term decline in the past century was the result of new discoveries; how much was a result of better extraction technology; how much was a result of changes in intensities of factor inputs and their price changes; how much was illusory because pollution costs were not counted; and how much was the decline offset by rising costs from depletion? To forecast the future pressure on virgin material prices, one would have to guess the strength of these components in the future. If the real prices of virgin materials are moving up or are threatening to do so in the next decade or so, then some remedial action is appropriate, under the conservation criterion.

Probably the simplest policy instrument is the severance tax, which is a price instrument. By raising the nominal price of virgin materials, a severance tax hurries along the substitute technologies to find new substitutes including more scrap usage and a more efficient usage, physically, of virgin materials. Fortunately, implementing the conservation criterion does not require delicate forecasting and fine tuning. While there is a great deal of volatility in the short-term price movements of many commodities, the important trends in materials prices are long term, with leisurely oscillation, if any. Thus, if there is evidence of increasing costs in the extractive industries, as there has been for the past several years, it would be possible to remove the depletion allowances and substitute severance taxes of perhaps 10 percent and then wait twenty years to see if that was the right amount of policy intervention to stabilize the prices of the extractive sector (the real prices of the extractive sector are counted net of severance taxes and other taxes and tax subsidies).

It should be noted that this definition of the conservation criterion carries with it the typical index number problems. The "market basket" of virgin materials is their composition in the base year. The more the composition of virgin materials changes over time, the less well I_t/D_t defines the real price of virgin materials in composite. And more fundamentally, the price index, like other price indexes, fails to incorporate quality changes. For this reason it might prove to be unnecessarily strong in the long run. Suppose, for example, we gradually learn how to squeeze three times more GNP out of the same old mix and amounts of virgin materials, but over the same period the cost of each material doubles. Our index number calculation tells us that virgin materials have become more expensive and suggests that measures should be initiated to return to the old level of costs. But actually we are doing better than before because we have learned to stretch our materials further; their "quality" has improved. With large-volume basic materials these changes happen and diffuse through the economy slowly, over decades. Over the years, we may find that if the real expenditure on the extractive sector $[(D_t/I_t)(\sum_i p_{it} q_{it})]$ is declining, the conservation criterion may be considered unnecessarily conservative and we might want to relax it a bit. While there are the typical index number problems associated with the definition of the conservation criterion, there are some advantages in treating the whole virgin material sector as if it were a single asset. Such treatment does not require that each material be renewed and allows substitutions among materials.

Because we live in a world of uncertainty it is really too simple to require that I_t/D_t be kept nonincreasing, and it is not in the spirit of the conservation criterion to require merely that the expected value of the index be kept nonincreasing. Suppose in some target year we plot our

best estimate of I_{20}/D_{20} as a random variable with probability distribution in panel A of figure 27. Here the mean or expected value of the
index is m_1, but there is a rather large probability, equal to area A, that
the real cost of virgin materials will rise after all. Because the idea behind the conservation criterion is to provide insurance that these costs
do not rise, it is necessary to look at more than expected values. Suppose further that with 10 percent severance taxes the probability distribution of I_{20}/D_{20} is shifted leftward, as in panel B. With the severance
tax, the chance of rising virgin material costs is greatly diminished, to
area B. The point is, that even with severance taxes there is no insurance, with probability one, that depletion costs will not be imposed
upon the future in the form of higher virgin material costs. Just as in
the case of long-lived pollutants, some of which may prove to be
extraordinarily lethal, there is no way of completely protecting the
future. In both cases, as in the formulation of macroeconomic policy,
tradeoffs must be made. A zero rate of inflation may be too expensive
to try for, while a 4 percent rate may be "acceptable." In the same way
a zero-sized chance of rising virgin material costs may be too expensive
to achieve, and the problem is to find the most appropriate "area B."

Just as there is no neat way of determining what is the most appropriate rate of inflation, there is no easy way of determining the most
appropriate area B. The purpose of defining the conservation criterion

Figure 27. Future price index as a function of the severance tax

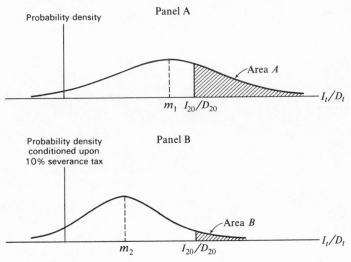

as done above and of making the preceding remarks is to establish a context in which the important policy issues can be formalized explicitly.

Motes and Beam-motes

The conservation criterion, or at least, its more ordinary manifestation as a sustainable yield criterion, is often criticized on the grounds that it does not maximize the present value of the yield's benefits. This reasoning is surely wrong. It is no more appropriate to conclude that the sustainable yield criterion is invalid because it does not satisfy the present value criterion than it is appropriate to conclude that the present value criterion is invalid because it does not satisfy the sustainable yield criterion. One cannot use one criterion to bludgeon another. They are on the same logical level. The most one can say at this point is that the two criteria conflict; they imply different states of the world.

One can judge a criterion, however, by its implications and by the conditions under which it leads to desirable consequences. We have seen that it is possible to view the natural resource sector much as a single productive asset, even including "nonrenewable" virgin materials. No criterion emerges as clearly superior to all others. But it is clear that there is a world of difference between the statements, "The earth belongs to the living" and "The earth belongs in usufruct to the living."

Notes

1. Harold J. Barnett and Chandler Morse, *Scarcity and Growth: The Economics of Natural Resource Availability* (Baltimore, Md., Johns Hopkins University Press for Resources for the Future, 1963) p. 72.
2. Barnett and Morse, *Scarcity and Growth*, p. 50.
3. Barnett and Morse, *Scarcity and Growth*, p. 96.
4. Gifford Pinchot, *The Fight for Conservation* (New York, Doubleday, 1910) cited in Barnett and Morse, *Scarcity and Growth*, p. 76.
5. Barnett and Morse, *Scarcity and Growth*, pp. 80–81.
6. Barnett and Morse, *Scarcity and Growth*, p. 81.
7. Barnett and Morse, *Scarcity and Growth*, p. 86, fn. 11.
8. Henry Clepper, *Professional Forestry in the United States* (Baltimore, Md., Johns Hopkins University Press for Resources for the Future, 1971) pp. 135–136.
9. Neal Potter and Francis T. Christy, Jr., *Trends in Natural Resource Commodities: Statistics of Prices, Output, Consumption, Foreign Trade, and Employment in the United States, 1870–1957* (Baltimore, Md., Johns Hopkins University Press for Resources for the Future, 1962).
10. Mancur Olson, "Introduction" to "The No-Growth Society," symposium issue of *Daedalus, Journal of the American Academy of Arts and Sciences* (Fall 1973) pp. 8–9.
11. It is interesting to note a parallel shift in perspective in work done at Resources for the Future and its predecessor, the Paley Commission. During World

War II, enormous quantities of resources were used up and shortly after the war there were some misgivings about the adequacy of the U.S. resource base to meet the greatly increased and steadily increasing demand for raw materials. The commission made projections of demand up until 1975 (many but not all of which turned out to be remarkably accurate) and inventoried some of the supply options. The Paley Commission found that the period of unlimited resource availability, for the United States, was over, but the perspective was optimistic: U.S. materials, which were growing relatively more scarce and expensive, could be supplemented with foreign trade; the resource stock could be greatly expanded by new technology, which was benign; and there was little or practically no mention of pollution and other environmental problems associated with material extraction and processing; markets worked for the benefit of consumers and market failure was negligible. Over the years the emphasis has greatly changed. Now pollution and congestion problems, residuals management, and other market failures have become a prime focus. Nor is new technology considered unquestionably benign: see, for example, Allen V. Kneese, "The Faustian Bargain," *Resources* (a periodical published by Resources for the Future) Sept. 1973.

12. The economist, by contrast, often thinks in terms of the characteristics of a particular regime. Within a model incorporating an economic regime, he searches for the implications of a present value criterion. Having twice reduced the scope of his search, he does not consider his inquiry an ethical one.

13. Paul A. Samuelson, "Economics of Forestry in Evolving Society," November 1974, p. 26. This informal paper sets out several of the issues of present value and sustained yield management of the timber resource base and sketches the historical development of ideas.

14. In the initial transition period, the first generation would also harvest over-age trees of age greater than A.

15. Under the present value criterion, these contours are social indifference curves. The present generation is indifferent between time-dated values on any given contour.

16. This solution is not quite correct, because the site value of the land is being neglected, along with the management costs. But for the purposes of illustration this omission is not important. The present value criterion requires

$$\max_{t_1, t_2, \ldots t_n, \ldots} \sum_{j=1}^{\infty} (f(t_j) - L) / (1 + i)^{t_j}$$

rather than

$$\max_{t_1} f(t_1) / (1 + i)^{t_1},$$

which is what we have done.

17. Solow mentions this possibility in Robert M. Solow, "The Economics of Resources or the Resources of Economics," *The American Economic Review* vol. LXIV, no. 2 (May 1974 Papers and Proceedings) p. 11.

9

The Criteria Reconciled

> *To each according to his threat advantage is not a principle of justice.*
> —John Rawls

IN THE PRECEDING two chapters I have described two conflicting intertemporal criteria and a little of the spirit of each. But as we have seen in chapter 8, one criterion is not "incorrect" because it conflicts with another. Different criteria embody different desiderata and work with varying suitability in different situations. In deciding how to select and use criteria, the proper way to proceed is to write down the properties and implications of each criterion and the conditions under which each is most suitable. Once this is done it may be possible to select a criterion or combination of criteria that best matches the existing conditions and social goals.

There is an analogy here with statistical estimators. In some situations a maximum likelihood estimator gives results different from those obtained by a best linear unbiased estimator. This does not mean that one estimator is right and the other wrong. The statistician knows that each estimator has certain desirable properties that emerge with varying strengths depending on the characteristics of the problem at hand. The statistician makes his choice of estimator on the basis of what "optimality" properties are most important to him and on the basis of the characteristics of the statistical problem. Under one set of circumstances, one estimator may be chosen; under another set, another estimator.

In this chapter we follow the same general approach. We proceed by drawing up a short list of categories and then scoring the properties of first the present value and then the conservation criterion against this list. Some of the properties have already been developed and need only

190

to be brought together. The intention is to be illustrative in method rather than exhaustive in detail. In this context, the discussion shows that "optimum" is a relative word, meaning little by itself and drawing its meaning from a particular criterion. As the criterion changes so does its meaning. Besides this observation, enough detail emerges to show that the analogy with statistical estimators is not completely parallel. With statistical estimators the choice is usually one or the other of the candidate estimators, and all the candidates are on the same level. But an enumeration of the properties of the present value and conservation criteria suggests that they may be best viewed not as conflicting substitutes but as nonconflicting complements on different levels of analysis.

"Optimality" Properties of the Present Value Criterion

1. *Administration.* The present value criterion is nearly self-administering, since it recommends, by and large, what markets automatically do. Because there are millions of product designs and other decisions having to do with material allocations, this is no small virtue.

2. *Completeness.* The present value criterion is complete. By itself in principle it is enough to yield a complete allocation of materials, goods, and services in the economy.

3. *Intertemporal Fairness.* The present value criterion, or at least the selfish altruism version of it, favors the present generation over future generations. In the selfish altruism interpretation of the criterion, maximization of the criterion coincides with maximization of the welfare of the present generation. Although not a criterion based upon intertemporal fairness, the present value criterion, being nearly laissez-faire, may be more practical than other criteria based upon intertemporal fairness. Appeals to fairness should not imply such self-denial that the present generation would not live with a fairer criterion. Each present generation, after all, has to administer the criterion.

4. *Efficiency.* The present value criterion is efficient in principle, and efficiency is one of the chief virtues of the criterion. However, intertemporal efficiency is not always easy to analyze. Difficulties arise, for consideration of intertemporal efficiency, when utility functions are made inseparable by the existence of intertemporal externalities. In principle the criterion is still applicable, but in this case it becomes something of an unwieldy and empty formalism. We look at this case in 6 below.

5. *Permanent Livability.* The present value criterion makes no guarantee about livability of the future. In chapter 7 we saw that the "iron

law of the discount rate" eliminates slow growing assets. This property is true even when the assets are vital to survival in the future. This formal property has been mentioned before, but it is so often misunderstood that it is illustrated further in appendix H.

6. *Intertemporal Consistency.* The present value criterion is inconsistent intertemporally. A criterion when followed by the present generation gives a plan of resource use not only for the present but also for the future. The same criterion followed by the next generation gives another plan from that time onward. It is a desirable condition for the two plans to be in harmony for the time of their overlap, from the next period or generation onward. In general the present value criterion does not have this attribute.

This does not mean that we want a criterion that is so rigid that it could not be revised with new information and unanticipated changes in preferences and other conditions. However, the inconsistency of the present value criterion is deeper than this type of flexibility. The criterion is inconsistent even in a world of perfect knowledge and perfect certainty. Because this attribute, or lack of it, has not been previously mentioned, it will be discussed in some detail here.[1]

Imagine Crusoe again on his island with his pile of hardtack, but this time with the certain knowledge that he will be rescued on the hundredth day. As in chapter 7 he scratches in the sand his present value calculation of utility over the hundred-day period:

$$\underset{C_1, \ldots, C_{100}}{\text{maximize}} \sum_{t=1}^{100} U(C_t)\delta_t \tag{9.1}$$

$$\text{subject to} \sum_{t=1}^{100} C_t = \bar{C}$$

Here, $\bar{C}$ is his initial stock of hardtack and U his utility function, but this time his discount factor δ_t is not geometric. The special-case geometric discount factors and a possible sequence of Crusoe's general discount factors are plotted in figure 28. Crusoe solves the maximization problem in equation (9.1), his optimal plan of hardtack consumption, day by day. The resulting plan (plan A) is shown in figure 29. The nonproductivity of hardtack coupled with Crusoe's positive time preference leads to higher consumption in the earlier days. All this calculation takes place on day one. But, still in the first day Crusoe has plenty of time and he wonders what the calculation would look like on day two. Crusoe subtracts day one's consumption, dropping "yesterday's" consumption

Figure 28. Geometric and nongeometric discount factors

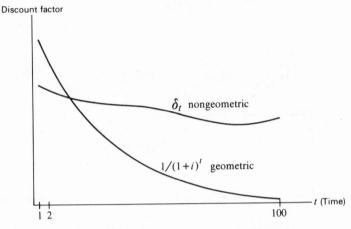

from the calculation, moves the discount factors forward one day, and resolves the problem in equation (9.2). (The first discount factor says how much tomorrow's utility is worth in terms of today's utility, so as the perspective changes by a day, he moves the entire sequence of discount factors forward to keep them current.)

$$\text{maximize} \atop C_2, \ldots, C_{100} \quad \sum_{t=2}^{100} U(C_t)\delta_{t-1}$$

$$\text{subject to} \sum_{t=2}^{100} C_t = \bar{C} - C_1 \tag{9.2}$$

From the perspective of day two his optimal plan of consumption is B in figure 29. Here we have what Strotz called an intertemporal tussle. We are assuming that Crusoe is living in a world of perfect certainty: he knows his preferences, he knows his resources, and there are no surprises. He also knows that his optimal plan drawn up on day one will not be followed from day two onward. He will break the plan by eating x less than what plan A calls for. He knows this with certainty when he makes the calculations on day one. What sense is there in drawing up an optimal plan from the perspective of day one if it will not be followed on day two; and if in fact it is not optimal from the perspective of day two onward? Perhaps Crusoe could somehow chain himself to the original plan, optimal from the vantage point of day one. Presumably this would make him happier on day one, but less happy for the rest of the days.[2]

Figure 29. Consumption plans implied by various criteria

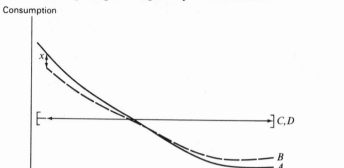

Note that Crusoe can make an irreversible decision which could not be modified on later days: he could eat all the hardtack on the first day. In less dramatic ways, the present often resolves the intertemporal tussle by locking the future into irreversible decisions.[3] This way of resolving the intertemporal inconsistency of the present value criterion is to make the present generation a stronger dictator.

Intertemporal inconsistency is not inevitable. Suppose, for example, that Crusoe follows the egalitarian criterion "share equally the hardtack over the days that are left." On day one Crusoe divides the hardtack into a hundred equal piles and plots the plan (plan *C*, the line segment in figure 30). Again with time on his hands he decides on day one to redo the allocation from the perspective of the next day. He removes the first day's ration and divides the rest into ninety-nine equal piles. The optimal plan implied by the egalitarian criterion from the vantage point of day two, plan *D*, the double arrow on the overlap coincides with the optimal plan from the vantage point of day one. For the present value criterion, the same criterion applied to different vantage points in time leads to different plans; for the egalitarian criterion, the same criterion leads to the same plan for the overlapped periods.

There is a further subtlety relating to the intertemporal inconsistency of the present value criterion. The inconsistency of the present value criterion just described arises from the general form of the discount factors when they are not in a geometric sequence. In the formulation, we have counted the well-being of day one's consumption from the vantage point of day two as a sunk benefit, over and done with and

Figure 30. Discount factors from the perspective of day *k*

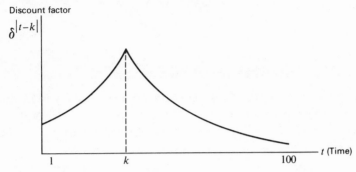

counted at zero. [Note that $U(C_1)$ does not appear in equation (9.2).] This is traditional practice in benefit–cost analysis—not to count the past because it is irrevocable. But our problem is a little different. Crusoe is evaluating an entire consumption plan from the vantage point of day two before the plan is enacted, even before consumption on day one. As Crusoe scratches on the sand on day one, he is in a position to contemplate how entire plans will be evaluated from different vantage points.

In the selfish altruism interpretation of the present value criterion, Crusoe feels utility in contemplating consumption on days distant from his present vantage point. The utility from contemplated distant consumption declines as the distance increases. In the interpretation of selfish altruism, why should not Crusoe feel utility in contemplating consumption distant in the other direction, in the past? We have the same reason to think that he feels utility in remembering consumption in the past as to think that he feels utility in contemplating consumption in the future. The easiest assumption is that Crusoe enjoys "good memories" but the "altruism" Crusoe feels for the past drops off symmetrically with distance as it is assumed to drop off for the future. The easiest model is that both drop off geometrically. In this case Crusoe's criterion from the vantage point of day one is

$$\text{maximize} \sum_{t=1}^{100} U(C_t)\delta^t$$
$$C_1, C_2, \ldots, C_{100}$$

$$\text{subject to} \sum_{t=1}^{100} C_t = \overline{C}$$

which is the same as equation (9.1) except that the discount factors are now in a geometric sequence; and the criterion from the vantage point of day two is

$$\underset{C_1, C_2, \ldots, C_{100}}{\text{maximize}} \quad \sum_{t=1}^{100} U(C_t)\delta^{|t-1|} \qquad (9.3)$$

subject to the same resource constraint as above.

With this "before time" version of the present value criterion, the discount factors from vantage point k decline from both sides of day k, as in figure 30. Normally when the past is really past it makes no difference to consider it in a decision process; there is no changing it and its consideration adds nothing. But in our example the calculations are made on day one, "before time began." On day one he calculates how various plans will look from different vantage points. He knows as much about how day one's consumption will look from day two as how day two's consumption will look from day one. Under the assumption of perfect certainty this calculation is much the same as the one commonly used in the application of the present value criterion where Crusoe is assumed to know on day one what his utility will be from consumption on day two in order to translate this utility backward to day one by his discount factor.

Evaluating entire consumption plans out of time, or before time, leads to intertemporal inconsistency with the present value criterion, with or without geometric discount factors as long as these factors decline forward and backward from each vantage point. In the actual world, of course, the past is really irrevocably past, but in thinking about fairness and what kind of decision principles the future would like us to use, it is appropriate to evaluate decisions from future perspectives, forward and backward, before they are made.

7. *Conditional Evaluations.* The present value criterion is not suited to the evaluation of intertemporal externalities. Many assets, particularly natural ones, are valued at one time, in part upon beliefs about their use at other times. For example, the present generation is likely to be less willing to preserve some endangered species if it believes the next generation will carelessly wipe it out. Alternatively, if the present could bargain with the next generation, it might offer increased efforts of preservation in return for the next generation's greater efforts as well, the next generation bargaining with the following one, and so forth. If they were possible, such bargains, perhaps among all generations at once, might be mutually advantageous to all generations. The enjoyment of many natural assets is enhanced by the contemplation of their permanence. This observation applies to virgin materials as well. Our valuation

of our efforts to preserve the resource base for all generations by providing substitutes and new technology diminishes the more we believe that the next generation will negate these efforts. Similarly, our interest in protecting the environment from radioactive wastes or other long-lived pollutants increases the greater we believe the next generation's effort will be. There is little point in carefully storing our radioactive waste if the future negates these efforts by its own carelessness.

Assets whose valuation depends upon beliefs about their future use may be called *conditionally valued assets*. The conditionally valued assets of interest to us can be split into two parts: the physical part of the asset, or its service flow (the virgin material flowing from the ground), and the permanence value (value from contemplating the permanence of the resource base).[4]

Obviously there are no market mechanisms taking into account conditionally valued assets and simulating mutually advantageous trades across time. In other words, there is no way that markets can internalize the potential benefits from more efficient management of conditionally valued assets. Likewise, the formal version of the market criterion, the present value criterion, is not suited to deal with conditionally valued assets. The typical assumption about separability sweeps away the phenomenon of conditionally valued assets from analysis. To drop the assumption of separability would eliminate much of the mathematical elegance of the present value criterion.

Without the possibility of intertemporal trades, one might conclude that the externalities associated with conditionally valued assets are irrelevant. On the contrary, when markets fail to include externalities, it is the role of benefit–cost analysis to estimate the values of the externalities, which often fall upon the future, and to include them in the calculation of total costs and benefits. The problem of estimating future evaluations exists for normal consumption goods. In both equations (7.7) and (7.8), social welfare is a function of utility from future consumption. For normal goods to be consumed in the future, the problem of clairvoyance is often handled by assuming that future generations have the same basic utility functions as we do. This approach could be used as well to estimate each generation's valuation of "permanence" in conditionally valued assets.

The phenomenon of conditionally valued assets is, in fact, a very general one, and there are many attempts to deal with it. There are "bargains" with the future to establish state and federal parks (to "lock them up" for permanent protection), "perpetual care" grave sites, and professorial chairs. (Intermixed with attempts to increase intertemporal efficiency benefiting all generations may be simpler efforts to dictate to the future for the present's own benefit.) These bargains are one-sided since the future does not participate in the decisions. Though the future cannot bargain directly with the present, there is little doubt that the present's valuations are in fact conditioned upon its beliefs about the future's actions. Were this not so, there would scarcely be any basis for contracts, and no point in developing common law.

One of the important ways that people deal with conditionally valued assets is to assert and act as though they were jointly owned over time. Thus, in the case of virgin materials, people often assert that the earth's endowment of natural resources belongs not only to the present but to all generations. And in the case of waste generation, it is often asserted that the environment, which receives the wastes, also belongs to all generations. This point of view conflicts with the "selfish altruism" interpretation of the present value criterion. By placing conditionally valued assets in the context of intertemporal externalities, we formalize the conservationist's intuition that the market mix of assets is inappropriate: there are too few conditionally valued assets with positive value, such as wilderness areas, and too many conditionally valued assets with negative value, such as radioactive wastes.

In summary, the present value criterion is something of a fair-weather criterion. It works well when markets work well. When the consequences are long run, when there are issues of intertemporal fairness, or when there are externalities, the criterion is less helpful.

"Optimality" Properties of the Conservation Criterion

For the same list of properties we can briefly contrast some of the characteristics of the conservation criterion.

1. *Administration*. The conservation criterion is not self-administrating. It involves making estimates of future costs of resources, imposing severance taxes on virgin materials, and adjusting the tax as conditions and information change. Because of the long-run nature of the problem, the adjustments would be slow, decade by decade.

2. *Completeness*. The conservation criterion is a partial criterion. By itself it does not imply a complete allocation of virgin materials, let alone all the rest of the goods and services in the economy. It is embedded in a larger market process.

3. *Intertemporal Fairness.* The conservation criterion attempts to provide a fair use of the resource base intertemporally. It does so by keeping the resource base essentially intact, and thus preserving a world of equals among generations. Again the conservation criterion is a partial criterion; it does not attempt to provide fairness in all its dimensions, but only in the use of the physical resource base.

4. *Efficiency.* In principle the conservation criterion is unlikely to be efficient intertemporally. But if, for example, a severance tax is the only practical way of shifting resource ownership and control toward the future, then the criterion may be efficient under a different distribution of resource ownership than would occur under the present value criterion.

5. *Permanent Livability.* The primary purpose of the conservation criterion is to keep the resource base intact. This may be seen as a necessary condition for permanent livability, but not the only condition required.

6. *Intertemporal Consistency.* If each generation preserves the resource base for the next generation, then the resource base is preserved for all generations. Thus the application of the criterion by one generation does not result in a plan for all time, as in the case of the present value criterion, but just from one generation to the next. And so we do not compare many overlapped plans from different vantage points in time. Instead we can look at the complete plan formed by each generation's link to the next in its resource use and preservation. The complete plan is harmonious with each generation's application of the criterion, as it was derived from each application, and in that sense, the conservation criterion is intertemporally consistent.

7. *Conditional Evaluations.* The conservation criterion does not take into account explicitly the implicit trades which could benefit both present and future in the use of the resource base. Nonetheless, one can think of the existence value of the resource base as a public good through time and the severance tax as an instrument promoting that public good. The conservation criterion favors the view that the resource base should be managed as though it were jointly owned over time. Joint ownership is one way of handling the externalities associated with conditionally valued assets.

In summary, the conservation criterion is something of a foul-weather criterion. It appears unnecessary when things are looking up, but it provides insurance against threats to the resource base decades hence. It is particularly suited for the analysis and illustration of certain aspects of intertemporal fairness.

A New Social Contract Theory

How are we to decide between the two types of criteria? If the selection is to be made on the basis of of a vote, we can imagine the party platforms and slogans: "The present value criterion stands for efficiency and productivity" and "Guarantee the future's right to life with the conservation criterion." The fact that it is hard to imagine society actually making this sort of constitutional choice reminds us that society is not accustomed to making explicit choices of intertemporal criteria. If we stretch our imaginations to allow representatives from the future to participate in an up-or-down vote between criteria, it is hard to think that the present value criterion would prevail without some modification. To an assembly of representatives drawn from all generations, this criterion would not look much more attractive than the scheme of vesting total ownership and management of the oceans' fisheries to one country this year, to another the next year, to another the following year would look to an assembly of present-day countries.

One may object that it is unrealistic to attempt to analyze how social choices might be made by representatives from all generations, a procedure already mentioned. In fact, social choices have to be made by the present generation and that one only—that is the reality of time. This observation is certainly true but it misses the point. Because of the one-way nature of time, economic productivity, and the flow of environmental costs, certain questions important to materials policy and environmental economics in general become remarkably difficult to conceptualize. Among these are: "What are our obligations to the future?" "What is intertemporal fairness or justice?" and "When can we say that the future 'regrets' a decision made by the present?" The point is that by thinking in terms of an intertemporal social contract it becomes easier to conceptualize these questions by an "operational" definition of intertemporal fairness.

Recently John Rawls has revived and developed a theory of social compacts as a basis for ethics.[5] Interestingly, Rawls devotes most of his effort to the intratemporal case, with only passing reference to the intertemporal one. Yet because of the asymmetries of time, his approach may be even more helpful in the intertemporal case than in the intratemporal one.

In the intertemporal case we consider that constitutional rules might be adopted if it were possible to convene an assembly of representatives from all generations. The representation is of a very particular sort.

No one knows his place in society, his class position or social status; nor does he know his fortune in the distribution of natural assets and abilities, his intelligence and strength, and the like. Nor, again, does anyone know his conception of the good, the particulars of his rational plan of life, or even the special features of his psychology such as his aversion to risk or liability to optimism or pessimism. More than this, I assume that the parties do not know the particular circumstances of their own society. That is, they do not know its economic or political situation, or the level of civilization and culture it has been able to achieve. *The persons in the original position have no information as to which generation they belong.* [Emphasis added.][6]

The reason for this "veil of ignorance" is that it rules out certain considerations in the assembly's decision making. "No one knows his situation in society nor his natural assets, and therefore no one is in a position to tailor principles to his advantage."[7]

On the other hand, "It is taken for granted, however, that they know the general facts about human society. They understand political affairs and the principles of economic theory; they know the basis of social organization and the laws of human psychology."[8]

With these assumptions the members of the assembly constitute a world of equals. There is no basis for bargaining and coalition formation; what is reasonable to one will be reasonable to all; they will decide unanimously. There is no need to have representatives from every generation, a few chosen randomly will do. In fact, just one chosen randomly is enough. "[I]t may be helpful to observe that one or more persons can at any time enter this [original] position, or perhaps, better, simulate the deliberations of this hypothetical situation, simply by reasoning in accordance with the appropriate restrictions."[9]

The "original position" and the "veil of ignorance" are not entirely fantasies to guide philosophical intuition. There were elements of both in the U.S. Constitutional Convention. At the time, the structure of American society was remarkably formless. Some of the delegates came from well-to-do backgrounds, some from impoverished families. There was great uncertainty as to where one's immediate descendants would come out in the social scale. With such a comparative veil of ignorance it was wise to define checks and balances and rules of law that would be fair to thieves and magistrates.

With this discussion in mind we come to Rawls' definition of fairness. Rawls defines just or fair rules as those that would be chosen in an original position under the appropriate veil of ignorance and general knowledge.

In the algebraic examples given earlier we have several times alluded to the problem of representing future generations in decisions which affect them. Occasionally we have inquired what might happen if the future generations could express their preferences or if there could be a vote among all generations. To move from this rudimentary consideration of intertemporal fairness to the Rawlsian framework involves just one small step. In the algebraic examples we assumed that each generation knew its place in time and the effect of that place upon its welfare. To move to a Rawlsian framework we draw the veil of ignorance a little further. We assume that the representatives are ignorant as to which generation they will be born into, although they still have a detailed knowledge of the implications and properties of the intertemporal welfare criteria.

Here we depart a little from what appears to be Rawls' interpretation of the original position for intertemporal constitution making. Rawls appears to be thinking primarily about the intertemporal problem as one of choosing the fair rate of saving. The present bestows a lump of homogeneous capital—valuable and benign—to the future. In this scheme of things the first generation is likely to be the worst off. In our interpretation, the composition of the heritage to be passed on is crucial. The future may be saddled with risks of catastrophic costs, or it may be slowly impoverished with depleted resource bases and long-lived wastes. With this "general knowledge" the delegates in the original position are likely to frame the intertemporal problem quite differently, and this difference is likely to affect the selection of intertemporal criteria.[10] Rawls also appears to favor the idea that all the representatives are chosen from the same generation but they are ignorant as to which generation they belong. We are assuming that the original position is made up of delegates drawn from all generations, again with ignorance as to which generation each belongs. In the original position, specified by the general knowledge available and the form of representation, the delegates are to meet and write a "constitution"—they are to choose the rules of the game, including the intertemporal welfare criterion.

We now can clarify a couple of heretofore foggy concepts. In a trivial sense it is often said that the present always regrets the actions of the past. No matter how much the past saves and provides for the present, the present always prefers that the past had done more. But suppose that some intertemporal welfare criterion is unanimously chosen in the original position. This criterion implies some effort of saving and some mix of assets to be passed on to each generation. This mix and level of savings effort is intertemporally fair by definition. In actual time, a present generation could still trivially regret that the past had not been more altruistic, but it could have no regrets in the sense of fairness. Alternatively, if the past had saved less or provided a mix of assets inconsistent with what could emerge from a criterion chosen in an original position, then that would be the basis for genuine (Rawlsian) regret.

Similarly we now can dispose of the question, What are our obligations to the future? In the selfish altruism interpretation of the present value criterion there are no obligations whatsoever. But in the Rawlsian context our obligation to the future can be defined as the duty to follow criteria which would emerge from an original position. The obligation is time invariant; as actual time shifts from generation to generation the obligation remains the same.

One of the important ideas of the original position is that it links all generations together with a common perspective. In the original position there is no shift in time perspective from one generation to another; all are treated on the same basis. Just as in the Constitutional Convention, there was no discounting of the future, and in both cases the focus was on all time. The constitutional delegates wanted to establish a framework of government in which the political market could function forever.

One can imagine the delegates in the original position quickly agreeing upon the requirement of permanent livability, which incidentally rules out a sole reliance upon the present value criterion. But then, after this quick agreement, they might cast around for some time trying to find an operating principle to guarantee permanent livability.[11] After some discussion, one could imagine that the delegates might agree that the simplest thing to do would be to settle for the rule of thumb that each generation should be intertemporally self-sufficient. In this way one generation could follow another indefinitely, but each generation would be required to look only one or a few generations ahead. And finally, after more discussion the conservation criterion might be chosen as a workable method of promoting intertemporal self-sufficiency.[12]

With their general knowledge of the properties of various criteria, it would be clear to the delegates that the conservation criterion by itself is incomplete. They would like the day-to-day details of economic decisions to be handled in some desirable way, from the point of view of all generations. Once permanent livability is guaranteed, as far as it is possible, by the conservation criterion, the delegates might find the market version of the present value criterion, the efficiency criterion, very attractive. It is largely self-administrating; it imposes few obligations upon each present generation because it coincides with selfish maximization; it minimizes waste by tending toward economic efficiency.

The delegates would quickly realize that there is no reason that there must be an either/or choice between the criteria. They do not clash head-on. One looks to the long run, the other to the short run. And most important, one criterion sets the conditions in which the other works at its best. The impact of the conservation criterion, implemented by severance taxes, is on the boundary in figure 2. Severance taxes are like import tariffs collected at a relatively small number of entry ports to the economy. Inside the economic sector, given these entry fees, markets are encouraged to allocate efficiently (and the efficiency criterion requires the markets to be perfected as much as possible). By modifying the flows across the boundary between the environment and the economy, myopic markets can be encouraged to be consistent with long-range social goals. In estimating possible future dangers in order to modify the boundary flows, there is no discounting and no simple adding of utilities or social welfare functions across generations; within the boundary, inside the economy proper, there is discounting as is usual with markets.[13]

It may be useful to retrace our steps over the last three chapters. In chapter 7 we described some of the properties of the present value criterion, in chapter 8 some of the properties of the conservation criterion. From there we developed the idea that criteria are to be judged on the basis of their properties and the conditions under which they are to be used. This idea was illustrated by the analogy with statistical estimators. By a further look at the properties of the two criteria, it emerges that they belong on different conceptual levels. Using the Rawlsian construct of the original position, we were able to define intertemporal fairness and to suggest an interlocking relationship between the two criteria.

This relationship will be familiar to economists. The analysis of markets is called price theory or microeconomic theory. In developing this theory, economists often posit a particular context within which markets are assumed to operate: reasonably full employment, reasonably low inflation, sufficient information, and so forth.[14] These latter conditions describe a macroeconomic context without which markets may not function satisfactorily, and consequently these conditions are often treated as macroeconomic goals. The conservation criterion can be considered just one more macroeconomic goal. Viewed as an instrument to achieve the conservation criterion, a severance tax is analogous to the progressive income tax. Intratemporally, the progressive income tax is used to promote a more socially acceptable or fairer distribution of income, market power, and hence, well-being. Intertemporally, the severance tax could be used to promote a fairer distribution of resource use and control across generations. Both the severance tax and the progressive income tax can be considered as instruments to establish a more suitable context for the interplay of the microeconomic forces of the market.

Within this context is the domain of the goal of market efficiency. A statement of this goal, the efficiency criterion, in intertemporal terms is the present value criterion. For one macroeconomic context, partly specified by the intratemporal and intertemporal distributions of income and resource control, the present value criterion will lead us to one solution; for another context with a different distribution of wealth and resource control, the present value criterion will lead us to another solution. The conservation criterion functions at the macroeconomic level establishing a context for markets; the present value criterion functions at the microeconomic level of market efficiency. For policy analysis and prescription both levels are needed.

This dichotomy between the macroeconomic context and the microeconomic market has not always existed. Nineteenth century classical economists thought that what we now call macroeconomic goals—full employment, stable prices, and so forth—would be achieved automatically by the micro forces of the unfettered market. The classical economists used the metaphor "invisible hand" to express their faith that the micro forces of the market would harmonize with desired macro conditions. This was the economic variant of the idea of harmony which spread through all enlightenment thinking and shows up most strikingly in Leibnitz' philosophy.

Years of business cycles, chronic unemployment, inflation, and concentration of wealth have changed the thinking of economists. Keynes designed his theory specifically to incorporate the idea that chronic unemployment could be the result of micro market forces. Harmony in economics has become modified by a limitation in scope. Unlike classical economists, post-Keynesians do not count upon the invisible hand for macro problems (they still do for micro ones).

There is a similar situation with respect to the conservationist goals. Many people still think that while the goal of future livability is an admirable one, there is no need to design special policy instruments to achieve it. Let the micro forces work themselves out—they will automatically achieve future livability.[15]

Many people still think that while the goal of holding constant the costs of material production is basically a good one, there need be no special policy tool such as a severance tax to achieve it. Market forces will automatically keep the costs of material production constant. However, this thinking is giving way to the idea that micro forces will not automatically provide food, energy, and other materials at constant or declining costs. For 100 years the cost of wood production has not been kept constant by market forces, and the government is betting hundreds of millions of dollars a year that the private market will not by itself develop technology to provide substitute energy materials in a timely fashion. As our ability to degrade the environment grows, we can no longer assume that somehow nature (or markets) will harmonize our actions with the conditions for permanent livability. Worse than the boy who cried wolf prematurely are the villagers who too carelessly thought that the wolf would never come.

Notes

1. Part of the intertemporal inconsistency of the present value criterion has been elegantly modeled by Strotz. See Robert Strotz, "Myopia and Inconsistency in Dynamic Utility Maximization," *Review of Economic Studies* vol. XXIII (1955–1956) pp. 165–180.

2. Strotz affirmed that the intertemporal tussle is a frequent occurrence in daily living. People join Christmas clubs in January, locking themselves into monthly payments and knowing that they will regret the club membership in July, but they hope that the entire yearly plan will appear optimal from the vantage point of December. Strotz, "Myopia," p. 173.

3. For a discussion of irreversibilities, see John Krutilla and Anthony Fisher, *The Economics of Natural Environments: Studies in the Valuation of Commodity and Amenity Resources* (Baltimore, Md., Johns Hopkins University Press for Resources for the Future, 1975) chapter 3.

4. The latter is a public good over time. One generation's contemplation of the resource base's permanent existence does not detract from another generation's contemplation of permanence. The inefficiency of markets in dealing with conditionally valued assets is analogous to the inefficiency discussed by Stephen Marglin in "The Social Rate of Discount and the Optimal Rate of Investment," *Quarterly Journal of Economics* vol. 77 (February 1963) pp. 95–111; and by Amartya K. Sen in "On Optimising the Rate of Saving," *The Economic Journal* vol. LXXI (September 1961) pp. 479–496. What Sen called the "isolation paradox" is a certain public good aspect of altruism toward the future. To paraphrase Marglin: Just as I am willing to save something toward increasing welfare in the next generation, I am even more pleased to have you save toward the future. Without a social agreement, a certain small amount will be saved. But I would be better off if I could strike a bargain to save more on the condition that others saved more. And others would be better off, too. Hence a private solution to the savings problem is not efficient.

Efficiency may be improved by a political solution whereby my contribution is the price I pay to get others to contribute. For Sen and Marglin the public good aspect was the feeling of altruism shared by people in the present generation, and the political logrolling occurs among those in the present.

The case of the intertemporally, conditionally valued asset is an intertemporal version of the isolation paradox, and the logrolling for efficiency is among succeeding generations.

5. John Rawls, *A Theory of Justice* (Cambridge, Mass., Harvard University Press, 1971) sections 24 and 44, especially.

6. Rawls, *A Theory of Justice*, p. 137.

7. Rawls, *A Theory of Justice*, p. 139.

8. Rawls, *A Theory of Justice*, p. 137.

9. Rawls, *A Theory of Justice*, p. 138.

10. Rawls, *A Theory of Justice*, pp. 286–289.

11. It must be admitted, however, that this and the following is not Rawls' inference about intertemporal welfare criteria chosen in the original position. While Rawls favors the maximin criterion intratemporally, he rejects it intertemporally on the grounds that it prevents too much the development of civilization. Robert Solow concurs with this criticism of the maximin criterion in the intertemporal case ("Intergenerational Equity," *Review of Economic Studies,* Special Issue, Symposium on the Economics of Exhaustible Resources [November 1974] pp. 29–46). Instead Rawls posits a golden rule of savings. Each generation should make an effort at saving equal to the effort it would like its immediate predecessor to undertake.

12. This is not to say that severance taxes are necessarily the best instrument for achieving the conservation criterion, or that the conservation criterion defined in·chapter 8 as the maintenance of price indices for natural resources is necessarily the best criterion for promoting permanent livability. These concepts, nonetheless, illustrate one approach to the problem of intertemporal fairness. For another example that also follows the Rawlsian approach, though to a lesser extent, see Orris Herfindahl and Allen Kneese, *Economic Theory of Natural Resources* (Columbus, Ohio, Charles E. Merrill, 1974) pp. 387–391.

13. Note the difference between "no discounting" and "discounting at a zero rate," which is equivalent to adding the social welfare functions over time—the Ramsey criterion (7.3).

14. For an example of a microeconomic analysis within a posited context of "a given state of economic affairs," see Richard Leftwich, *The Price System and Resource Allocation* (New York, Holt, Rinehart and Winston, 1964) the entire book but especially pp. 8–9.

15. Richard Nixon expressed this idea of harmony in regard to the optimal population size: "I have a basic faith that the American people themselves will make sound judgments regarding family size and frequency of birth, judgments that are conducive both to the public interest and to personal family goals." *The Washington Post,* May 6, 1972, p. A1.

10

Conclusion

A NATIONAL "policy" often emerges as the result of an accretion of numerous individual decisions, subject to different pressures, and made over a long time, rather than from plans and goals formulated by a governing body. The consequence of such a process is that the policy, formed after the fact, takes on some of the contradictions accumulated over separate and disparate decisions. Our present materials policy falls into this category; it is a piecemeal affair.

It is not the intention of this book to prescribe a specific package of remedies for our existing *de facto* materials policy, but to offer a coherent way to look at material flows, a way that can be used in the formulation of materials policy. We can think of the formulation of this policy on three levels. At the most elementary level (discussed in chapters 2 and 3) there is a "large" quantity of waste generated, a "low" amount of recycling, and direct concern for resource availability in the future. At this level the approach to materials use and the remedies prescribed are in the piecemeal tradition of our existing "policy"—subsidies on recycling, product specification, and so forth. As in the existing policy, this approach is a collection of particular responses to particular pressures. The difference is that some of the pressures and perceptions are new, and some of the prescribed remedies tend to be in the conservative direction.

As seen in chapter 2, at this level the focus is too narrow. In terms of the analogy with the sailing ship mentioned in chapter 1, the focus is like setting a particular sail without taking into account the balances among the sails. There is no relationship of one sail to another, no way of telling whether copper should be recycled at one rate and iron at another. By concentrating on an increase in recycling, one may inadvertently shorten durability. Or, as in the case of voluntary recycling efforts, direct intervention may be self-defeating. Moreover, at this level of analysis there is no way of telling whether such factors as product durability and recycling rates are at their optimum.

At the second level we take a step back to look at how markets work and examine specific failures in the system. It can be seen from chapters 4, 5, and 6 that correction of a single market failure leads to the improvement of several specific conditions concurrently. For example, elimination of the tax preferences for virgin materials would simultaneously increase the rate of recycling, increase product durability, decrease waste generation, and increase conservation of materials.

A market standard operates at this level. By this standard, the efficiency criterion, we can determine in principle the best balance in material flows, when there are no economic inefficiencies. At this second level we focus on the balance among the sails. For any particular course upon which the ship sails we can define the proper or efficient balance among the sails. We can tell how the rate of recycling of copper should be balanced against the rate for iron, or the durability of a product against the waste generated in its production. According to this criterion, the standard perceptions seen at the elementary level are all correct: the quantity of waste is too large, the rate of recycling is too low, there is too much depletion. It is at this level that particular policy directives can be readily formulated.

Consider the pricing structure for freight, electricity, and other forms of energy. The current structure favors users most sensitive to price, the largest users. In the past, the justification has been that volume discounts to the larger users built up capacity, whether in railroad tracks or in power generators, in order to take advantage of possible economies of scale. In the case of freight transportation, it happened that bulk materials such as scrap and virgin materials were the intended beneficiaries of this pricing structure, but that virgin materials benefited more. In the case of energy pricing also, the result has been to move extra materials around in the economy: fuel materials, materials for plant and generating equipment, and materials associated with the consumption of energy. However, the efficiency criterion tells us that there is a cost associated with such demand pricing. A wedge is driven between the price of a material and its marginal cost, a wedge that distorts the price signal to downstream users of materials. In both freight rate making and energy pricing this distortion has been neglected. As discussed in chapter 4, the issue is a complicated one involving tradeoffs of competing goals. Nevertheless, the policy direction inherent in the efficiency criterion is clear:

move away from demand pricing and toward marginal cost pricing. This move would tend to conserve materials.

At this same, second level of analysis, the efficiency criterion guides us on the taxation of materials industries. Having noted low recycling rates, high rates of waste generation, and the relatively light tax burden on virgin material industries, one may find it easy to recommend equal tax treatment for secondary material industries. And in fact there have been many legislative proposals to extend the tax preferences on virgin materials to scrap materials as well. The efficiency criterion tells us that such a move would compound the materials problem. The result would be more material flowing through the economy, with increased costs of energy and capital to move the material around. There would likely be some saving in virgin material extraction and waste discharged to the environment, but this saving would come at unnecessarily high cost. The appropriate move, according to the efficiency criterion, would be to eliminate the tax preferences for virgin material. This has been done, in part, for major oil companies, but not for other materials industries.

The efficiency criterion also guides us on disposal costs at this level. The criterion tells us that the disposal costs associated with a product— collection, processing, and final disposition—should be borne by the product itself, as far as is practicable. If there were no implementation costs, the efficiency criterion would tell us that there should be disposal fees, just as there should be effluent fees for air and water pollutant emissions. When the costs of implementation are taken into account, the efficiency criterion sometimes guides us toward deposit systems, because they are very nearly self-administrating and the costs of implementation are internal to the product cycle and those using it. In most cases, where deposit systems are not feasible, the costs of implementing a disposal fee system must be balanced against the loss of economic efficiency from not having disposal costs internalized in the product.

From the perspective of this second level of analysis, recycling, durability, and materials conservation are not considered goods in themselves. The focus is on making the market work better. As the market becomes a better allocator of material uses, recycling, durability, and conservation will take care of themselves.

Efficiency analysis suggests a way to evaluate long-run costs that may be associated with depletion or the generation of certain wastes. These costs can be discounted at the market rate of interest or a corrected form of this rate. While the efficiency criterion has long been a staple of the economic literature on depletable resources, it is probably safe to say that this criterion has not been an important concept in the legislative process in the past.

For the third level, treated in chapters 7, 8, and 9, we take another step back to see where the economy as a whole is heading. At this level we focus on the rudder. There are varying views as to what attention needs to be focused on the rudder. One view is that no attention need be paid at all. The ship is on automatic pilot—the same wind that falls upon a balanced set of sails is harnessed to the rudder's adjustment. In this view, the economy sails safely into the future much as Joshua Slocum sailed a thousand miles across the Pacific without adjusting his steering mechanism. According to this view, market forces provide a satisfactory balance between new technology and depletion, and the generation of long-lived wastes is not cause for concern. But as we have seen, this view is an expression of faith, not a conclusion to be drawn from the analysis of markets, even perfect markets.

In another view, the view developed in this book, the course of the economy should not be determined solely by the automatic pilot of market forces. Like Slocum's craft, the economy can rely on its automatic pilot of market forces only under special, smooth-sailing circumstances. To adjust the rudder of the entire economy in its use of materials, it is necessary to look ahead fifty or seventy-five years. Different principles apply to the adjustment of the rudder than to the setting of the sails. The resource base is shared intergenerationally, and the questions are: Will it be shared fairly? In its use of materials how can the economy be kept from drifting into unlivable futures? Even perfect markets could not answer these questions. To set and balance the sails requires considerations of economic efficiency; to adjust the rudder requires considerations of fairness. There are interconnections. Once the sails are set in balance, they can be maintained in balance while the rudder is adjusted. Moreover, knowledge of the sails' balance tells us something about feasible courses toward which the rudder can be adjusted.

In earlier chapters we saw models showing how economies could drift into unlivable futures and how this could be prevented by policy action. Some renewable resources can be managed on a sustained yield basis, some "nonrenewable" resources can be renewed by new substitutes and new technology, and some resources can be depleted without cost to the future. The proper mix and intensity of policy actions are obviously difficult questions. While it is clear that, in a fundamental sense these are questions of fairness, it is not clear what is a fair resolution of these questions.

We saw, however, that some headway can be made in defining a fair resolution by imagining an agreement among representatives of different generations deciding on the management of the commonly owned resource base. In this framework it was suggested, though by no means proved, that a minimal requirement would be to keep the resource base essentially intact over time. By way of illustration we also saw that an ad valorem severance tax on virgin materials could be used as a policy instrument to preserve the resource base intact. As an alternative, the Forest Service follows a practice of the allowable cut, which is tied to targets for "adequate" forest size 150 years from now. As another alternative, certain areas are set aside for future use. This is not to say that all methods of resource preservation are sensible; the point is that consideration of a fair use of the resource base is a legitimate and important concern in the formulation of materials policy.

A materials policy based in part on the conservation criterion is simple but probably counter-intuitive. It suggests that when virgin materials threaten to become increasingly costly they should be made more expensive nominally, perhaps by severance taxes, now. Often people think just the opposite: when virgin materials threaten to become more costly they should be subsidized in order to keep prices constant to the consumer. The problem with the latter approach is that it encourages the expenditure of more resources than may be returned from the effort, in the short term; in the long term, it leads to a mismatching between the rate of depletion and technological renewal.

Of the three levels of consideration for the formulation of materials policy, the first, direct level is perhaps the most relied upon at present. And of the three levels it is the least suitable, because its focus is too close. In the formulation of materials policy there should be a mixture of the second and third levels, at the same time bearing clearly in mind that there are quite different principles applying to each level. For a materials policy we need to know how to set the sails and how to adjust the rudder. In the past both skills have been neglected.

In earlier times it was harder to change the resource base from generation to generation. Traditional societies lived primarily off renewable resources. And while it certainly is not true in all cases, in many cases the resource base was passed on from one generation to another in essentially replicated form. Since the industrial revolution, however, our dependence on nonrenewable resources has grown enormously and during the same time, the reach of technology has grown commensurately. Although it is something of an oversimplification, it may still be said that past generations did not have the power to destroy the resource base even if they wanted to, but we do. With the size and power of modern economies comes the greater need to look ahead and see where our economies are going.

Appendixes

APPENDIX A

Flexibility of Material Intensities

ALTHOUGH IT IS CLEAR that materials, including energy materials, are basic to the economy, there still remains the question of how much flexibility there is to sustain a given standard of living with differing amounts of materials and energy. At one extreme there is the view that there is no flexibility at all. In testimony supporting special tax provisions favoring the mining industry, Rolla Campbell, general counsel to the Island Creek Coal Company, asserted that, "It is a generally known fact that the standard of living of every country is in direct ratio to its per capita consumption of mechanical energy."[1] In this statement there is the implication that increased subsidization of the energy sector would increase the standard of living.

In support of this view, reference is often made to a graph that plots energy consumption per capita against GNP per capita for many countries (figure A-1). As can be seen, countries which have more GNP per person also consume more energy per person. But much of the linearity can be explained by the simple observation that richer countries (ones with higher GNP per capita) tend to consume more of everything, including energy and other raw materials.[2] The question we are interested in is a different one. How little or how much energy (or material) does it take to produce a dollar's worth of GNP? This is the question of flexibility, and to help answer it we plot energy per dollar GNP against GNP per capita in figure A-2.

As can be seen in figure A-2, in terms of energy intensiveness, the United States is by no means the most gluttonous user of energy. From the graph it appears that there is a great deal of flexibility in how much energy it takes to produce a dollar's worth of GNP. One generalization is that it appears that countries with large extractive sectors (South Africa, Venezuela, Norway, and Canada) are more energy intensive.

Corresponding plots show an increasing and somewhat linear relationship between metals per capita and GNP per capita, nonmetal minerals per capita and GNP per capita, and timber per capita and GNP per capita. (The linearity is considerably less strong than that suggested in

Figure A-1. International comparisons of energy per capita

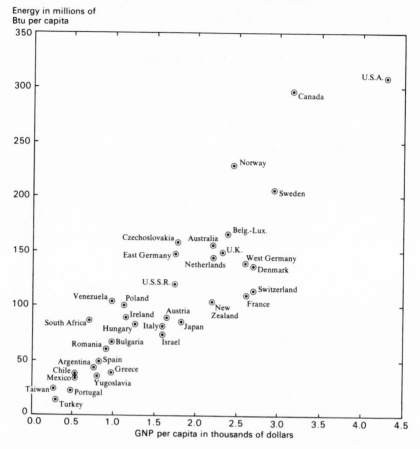

Energy in millions of
Btu per capita

GNP per capita in thousands of dollars

figure A-1). And as in the case of energy, when we shift to the more appropriate intensity measures (in terms of materials per dollar GNP), the linearity vanishes altogether, as can be seen in a comparison of the correlation coefficients in table A-1.

Another way to gather evidence about the long-term flexibility of the economy is to record its intensity of material and energy usage for the United States over time. According to the National Commission on Materials Policy, over the past seventy years in this country the materials

Figure A-2. International comparisons of energy intensity

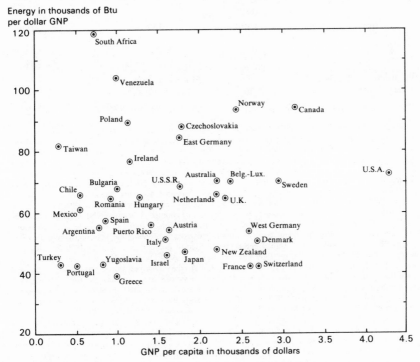

Energy in thousands of Btu
per dollar GNP

GNP per capita in thousands of dollars

intensiveness has gradually declined by about half.[3] And of course while the amount of material embodied in each dollar of GNP halved, the standard of living has greatly increased. In the case of energy, Landsberg notes a decline in its intensity, energy consumption per dollar GNP, over the past three decades.[4]

Economic theory tells us that if we subsidize material and energy extraction we can achieve material and energy intensities that are too high to be efficient. With too high material or energy intensity we could *increase* economic well-being by *lowering* the intensity, quite to the contrary of the implication sometimes drawn from a casual reading of figure A-1.

Table A-1. Correlation Coefficients of Intensity and GNP per Capita

Materials	GNP per capita	Materials	GNP per capita
Energy per capita	.89	Energy per dollar GNP	.02
Metals per capita	.47	Metals per dollar GNP	−.05
Nonmetal minerals, per capita	.36	Nonmetal minerals, per dollar GNP	.11
Timber per capita	.60	Timber per dollar GNP	−.22

Sources: GNP per capita for 1968 for socialist and nonsocialist countries was determined from table 11 in the appendix to *Energy, Economic Growth, and the Environment,* Sam H. Schurr, ed., and was calculated by Joel Darmstadter (see notes to table). The figure for Iceland was separately obtained from AID Doc. RC-W·138, "GNP Growth Rates and Trend Data by Region and Country" (April 30, 1970). GNP per capita for 1969 was obtained from AID Doc. RC-W-138, as above, except for the socialist countries where a percentage change in per capita income was derived by comparing index numbers for 1968 and 1969 as listed in the *U.N. Statistical Yearbook (1971),* table 177, National Accounts, and this percentage change was applied to the GNP per capita figure for 1968 as discussed above. Total GNP for 1968 was obtained from AID Doc. RC-W-138, named above, except for socialist countries where the GNP per capita for 1968 as determined by Darmstadter was multiplied by total population as found in *U.N. Statistical Yearbook (1971),* table 18, Population. (Population for 1968 was derived by dividing the 1970 mid-year estimate of population by the total average annual percentage change in population from 1963–1970 for each year going back to 1968.) Total GNP for 1969 was obtained from AID Doc. RC-W-138, named above, except for socialist countries where GNP per capita for 1969, derived as described above, was multiplied by total population for 1969, which was derived using the same basic procedure as discussed for obtaining 1968 total population figures. (All per capita and total GNP figures are ultimately based on 1968 constant U.S. dollars. Total GNP is in billions of these dollars. Socialist countries use "gross material product" as a measure of total economic product, and Yugoslavia uses "net material product".)

Energy per dollar GNP was obtained from table 11 in Schurr's book, cited above (see notes to Schurr's table). This figure is in thousands of Btu's per dollar of GNP for 1968. Apparent consumption of non-metal minerals per dollar GNP was calculated for 1969 by netting out import and export trade figures from the production of nonmetal minerals in each country and then dividing by the total GNP for 1969 (see above) for each particular country. The figures are from *Minerals Yearbook, International Reports, 1970,* prepared by the Bureau of Mines, U.S. Department of the Interior. Where figures were given in volume terms, they were converted to weights by use of density and conversion tables from the *Chemical Engineers' Handbook.* Any figure that amounted to less than 500 metric tons per year was excluded. U.S. figures were from *Minerals Yearbook, United States, 1970.* Apparent consumption of metal minerals per dollar GNP was calculated for 1969 by netting out import and export trade figures from the production of metal minerals in each country and dividing by the total GNP for 1969 (see above) for each particular country. Production of crude ore was usually the representative figure used for determining domestic production of metal minerals. Trade figures include crude ore and other basic and semimanufactured forms of metal minerals. (Imports and exports of finished products using materials derived from metal were not included in these tables.) The figures are from *Mineral Yearbook, International Reports, 1970,* as cited above. Any figure that amounted to less than 500 metric tons per year was excluded. U.S. figures were from *Minerals Yearbook, United States, 1970.* Apparent consumption of timber per dollar GNP was calculated for 1968 by netting out import and export trade figures from production of timber in each country and dividing by the total GNP for 1968 (see above) for each particular country. Production of timber in its crude form (coniferous and nonconiferous round wood) was the representative figure used for determining domestic production of timber. Trade figures include round wood and other basic and semimanufactured forms of timber products. (Imports and exports of finished products using materials derived from timber were not included in these tables.) The figures are from *FAO Yearbook of Forest Products, 1969,* tables P1 and T1–T8. Where figures were given in volume terms, they were converted to metric tons by use of a general round wood weight-to-volume conversion factor which was derived from the average densities of coniferous sawlogs and broad-leaved tropical sawlogs and which assumed approximately equal densities for sawlogs and round wood. These density and conversion tables (tables B3 and C) are in the appendix to the FAO yearbook under "Standard Conversion Factors." Any figure which amounted to less than 500 metric tons per year was excluded.

Notes

1. U.S. Congress, Ways and Means Committee, *Tax Revision Compendium* (Washington, D.C., U.S. Government Printing Office, November 16, 1959) vol. 2, p. 1049.

2. Figure A-1 (or a similar plot of energy per capita against GNP per capita) can be found in Sam Schurr, "Energy," *Scientific American* vol. 209, no. 3 (September 1963) p. 112; (Edward Mason may have made the first such plot, with 1952 figures); Joel Darmstadter et al., *Energy in the World Economy* (Baltimore, Md., Johns Hopkins University Press for Resources for the Future, 1971) p. 66; V. E. McKelvey, "Mineral Resource Estimates and Public Policy," U.S. Geological Survey, *United States Mineral Resources: Geological Survey Professional Paper 820* (Washington, D.C., U.S. Government Printing Office, 1973) p. 10; Chauncey Starr, "Energy and Power," *Scientific American* vol. 225, no. 3 (September 1971) p. 38; and Earl Cook, "The Flow of Energy in an Industrial Society," *Scientific American* vol. 225, no. 3 (September 1971) p. 142. Some of the authors indicate that much of the correlation can be explained as a move out along Engle curves— richer countries tend to consume more of everything—but some appear to subscribe to Campbell's narrower view.

3. National Commission on Materials Policy, *Materials Needs and the Environment: Today and Tomorrow* (Washington, D.C., U.S. Government Printing Office, 1973) p. 3-3.

4. Resources for the Future, *Annual Report,* 1973, p. 34.

APPENDIX B

Definition and Geometry of Elasticity

THE ELASTICITY OF SUPPLY is a measure of the responsiveness of the amount supplied to a price change. It is defined to be the percentage change in quantity resulting from a 1 percent change in price. Geometrically, the elasticity of supply (or demand) at a point on the curve is the distance along the tangent from the point to the horizontal axis divided by the distance from the point along the tangent to the vertical axis. This can be seen in figure B-1 by noting that triangles BEC and ACD are similar; thus

$$\frac{AC}{BC} = \frac{p}{q(dp/dq)} = \frac{dq/q}{dp/p}$$

Figure B-1. Elasticity of supply

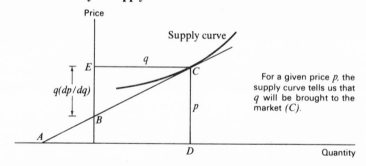

For a given price p, the supply curve tells us that q will be brought to the market (C).

The supply is defined to be *elastic* if a 1 percent change in price implies a greater than 1 percent change in quantity supplied, and *inelastic* if a 1 percent change in price implies less than a 1 percent change in quantity supplied. By the geometry, supply is elastic if the tangent hits the vertical axis before the horizontal, and inelastic otherwise.

ICC Burden Studies

BURDEN STUDIES depend on the ICC's allocation of costs. Basically, all the costs of a given railroad are totaled for a year's operation. Eighty percent of these costs are considered variable and are to be allocated over the individual railroad operations.

An operation might be driving a locomotive a mile or turning a switch. Each operation is a cost factor. The variable cost of a particular shipment is computed by adding the cost factors over the shipment's whole route. The United States is divided into seven cost areas, and a cost factor for the same operation is computed for each area. For two years, 1966 and 1969, a 1 percent sample was taken of all freight traffic. To arrive at the variable cost of the shipment of a particular commodity, the cost factors are added over each shipment of that commodity in the sample and the average taken. For a shipment beginning in one cost area and ending in another, an average of the two sets of factors is taken, with the implicit assumption that the route splits the operations of each type half in one territory and half in the other.

A discussion and critique of the 80 percent variable rule can be found in Meyer or Friedlaender.[1] Our problems concern mainly the cost factors. The basic difficulty is that those factors are computed as averages over different situations. The concept is useful for distinguishing different costs arising from different types of freight cars. For example, the cost factor of moving a boxcar one mile in the New England territory is 31 cents, and a gondola 36 cents. In this case the "cost factor" is well defined and related to the inherent differences between a boxcar and a gondola. But what does the concept tell us about the cost of moving a gondola from A to B with an empty backhaul and the cost of moving the same car from C to D without an empty backhaul. Here the differing situations are averaged out in computing the cost factor for this type of car.[2] Because the differences in backhaul probabilities are averaged out, the cost factor approach tends to overestimate the cost of moving scrap with a low probability of empty backhaul, and underestimate the cost of moving ore in the same type of car but with a high probability of empty backhaul.

Similarly, cost factors average out variations that result from moving trains of different lengths. Multiple car shipments save on switching and terminal costs. But the cost factor for moving a boxcar a mile is the average cost of moving a boxcar a mile. Thus, the cost factor overestimates the cost of moving a unitized trainload of boxcars and underestimates the cost of moving a single boxcar. In this case the cost factor tends to underestimate the cost of moving scrap, which usually moves in single car shipments, and to overestimate the cost of moving ore, which often travels in trainloads.

How can the cost factor approach deal with the following problem related to scrap shipments? While ore shipments generally travel over the same routes time after time, scrap shipments travel over changeable routes, in small lots, and over different railroad lines. Consequently, there is a much greater chance for cars belonging to railroad X to get misplaced on railroad Y, a situation that apparently is very common. When railroad X temporarily loses a car, it also loses the car's revenue. The loss is shared with railroad Y, which pays railroad X per diem fees for the lost car. Jointly, railroads X and Y have to spend more than for cars carrying virgin material. One result is that railroads consider moving scrap a nuisance; another result is a shortage in gondola cars, which primarily move scrap. From 1951 to 1970, the total gondola fleet decreased by 35 percent, even though scrap demand increased.[3]

Presumably these problems could be solved with computerized accounting of the location of freight cars. But how do these complications get taken into account in the cost factors, which tell us, on average, the cost of moving a gondola one mile? The answer, unfortunately, is that they do not. The most important differences in cost between primary and secondary shipments are averaged out of the analysis.

Aware of the difficulties inherent in the ICC's burden studies, the Environmental Protection Agency contracted for its own study of the effect of freight rates on recycling. The contractor, Moshman Associates,[4] decided that in spite of the difficulties the ICC cost factors were "the best available data" on marginal costs of freight shipment because they were the only existing data. The approach, however, was somewhat different from that in the burden studies. Instead of using all the shipments on the waybill of a particular commodity, the Moshman study matched routes of competing scrap and virgin commodities. For example, 35 of the 130 shipments of scrap aluminum on the waybill were selected. For each of these 35 shipments, Moshman traced out the route and computed the mileage in each cost territory. The cost factors were then averaged with weights proportioned to the distances in each cost territory.

To find the cost of a particular shipment, these averaged cost factors were added over the shipment's route. For each car type and each cost territory, there were just four cost factors. For example, in the New England cost area, the cost factors for a gondola are as follows:

line cost factor per ton mile	0.0037
line cost factor per car mile	0.3620
terminal cost factor per carload	42.76
terminal cost factor per ton	0.0028

To compute the cost of a single car shipment inside this cost region Moshman used the formula

$$\text{Cost} = [0.0037 \text{ (tons)} + 0.3620] \cdot \text{(miles)} + 2 [0.0028 \text{ (tons)} + 42.76]$$

In order to compute the cost of a shipment inside a single cost area, all that is needed from the waybill is the number of tons shipped and the distance. An n car shipment would have a computed cost of n times the single car shipment. While there are some differences between Moshman's results and those of the burden study, the results are much the same because both approaches fundamentally rely on the ICC's cost factors.

Notes

1. John Meyer, Merton Peck, John Stenason, and Charles Zwick, *The Economics of Competition in the Transportation Industries* (Cambridge, Mass., Harvard University Press, 1960) appendix A, pp. 274–276; and Ann Friedlaender, *The Dilemma of Freight Transport Regulation* (Washington, D.C., The Brookings Institution, 1969) appendix A, pp. 191–194.

2. Cost formulas allow different empty return ratios on aggregate bases.

3. Herschel Cutler, "Role of Transportation in Disposal of Obsolete Metallic Waste," *Waste Age* vol. 1, no. 4 (July-August 1970).

4. Moshman Associates, *Transportation Rates and Costs for Selected Virgin and Secondary Commodities*, a study for the U.S. Environmental Protection Agency, 1973.

Taxes and Inefficiencies

Inefficiency in the Factor Market

INEFFICIENCY in the factor market was first analyzed by Harberger.[1] To see the argument in its simplest form,[2] imagine an investor choosing between similar investments, one in an extractive industry and the other in a manufacturing industry. Both generate the identical stream of gross income $(Y_0, Y_1, \ldots, Y_T)$, both require the identical stream of costs $(C_0, C_1, \ldots, C_T)$, and neither generates any externalities. Judged by their present value, the two investments are of equal social value. The two investments differ in one respect, however. They receive different tax treatment. Because of this, there will be less incentive to invest in the manufacturing industry than in the extractive one. Since the costs for both investments are the same and the benefits are the same (measured by the net income), for efficiency there should be the same incentive to invest in either industry. We can measure the difference in strengths between the incentives to invest, this difference being an inefficiency incentive, by analyzing how much an investor will be willing to pay for the income stream in each industry. He will pay up to the present value of the net income after taxes. If he invests R in the manufacturing industry, he is allowed to deduct a depreciation charge (R/T) each year from his taxable income. With a 50 percent income tax rate, his tax each year t is $0.5(Y_t - C_t - R/T)$, so that his net income after taxes, in year t is

$$(Y_t - C_t) - 0.5(Y_t - C_t - R/T),$$

and the present value of the after-tax net income stream is

$$0.5\sum_{t=0}^{T}(Y_t - C_t)/(1 + i)^t + 0.5R\sum_{t=0}^{T}1/T(1 + i)^t = 0.5Y + 0.5dR, \quad (D.1)$$

writing $\Sigma 1/T(1 + i)^t$ as the discount factor d and $\Sigma(Y_t - C_t)/(1 + i)^t$, the present value of the net income stream, as Y. The investor has an incentive to buy the manufacturing asset up to the point where R equals the present value of the after-tax profit stream, equation (D.1). In this case $R = 0.5Y + 0.5dR$ or, solving for R,

$$R = Y/(2 - d) \tag{D.2}$$

For the extractive asset, the investor is allowed more generous deductions. He is allowed to deduct the full amount of his exploration and development expense in the first year,[3] and he is allowed a percentage depletion deduction every year. If he invests S in the first year (all assumed to go into exploration and development), his tax is $0.5(Y_0 - C_0 - S - pY_0)$, and in every other year t his tax is

$$0.5(Y_t - C_t - pY_t),$$

so that the present value of his net income after taxes is

$$0.5Y + 0.5S + 0.5p\Sigma Y_t/(1 + i)^t \tag{D.3}$$

Percentage depletion is applied to gross income (Y_t). In this example it is useful to think of the amount of the depletion deduction as a fraction of the net income and to think of the present value of the depletion deductions as a fraction of the present value of the net income stream. We define this latter concept as

$$p' = p[\Sigma Y_t/(1 + i)^t]/Y$$

Introducing p' will simplify the algebra. As before, the investor has an incentive to buy the mineral asset up to the point where his expenditure S equals the present value of the after-tax net income stream, equation (D.3). In this case $S = 0.5Y + 0.5S + 0.5p'Y$, or, solving for S, we have

$$S = Y(1 + p') \tag{D.4}$$

Now we can see how much greater is the incentive to invest in the mineral rather than the manufacturing asset by dividing S by R.

$$S/R = (1 + p')(2 - d)$$

To estimate d, the asset life T and the discount rate i are all that are needed. Harberger assumed i to be 10 percent. To estimate p' Harberger divided the depletion deduction actually taken by net income. His estimated parameters and calculated inefficiency incentives are in table D-1. The value of 1.95 for S/R for petroleum means that because of the favorable tax treatment, an investor is willing to pay 1.95 times more for a petroleum asset than for a manufacturing asset with the

Table D-1. Inefficiency Measures

Materials	T	d	p'	Inefficiency intensity S/R
Petroleum	10	.65	.45	1.95
Sulfur	20	.43	.35	2.12
Iron	25	.36	.30	2.13
Copper	20	.43	.25	1.96
Lead and zinc	20	.43	.45	2.27
Coal	30	.30	.35	2.30

Source: Arnold Harberger, "Taxation of Mineral Industries," Joint Economic Committee on the Economic Report, *Federal Tax Policy for Economic Growth and Stability* (Washington, D.C., U.S. Government Printing Office, 1955) pp. 448–449.
For meaning of column head symbols, see text.

identical costs and net income stream. Resources (capital) in the form of machines, and so forth, flow inefficiently from manufacturing industries into mineral industries. The ratio S/R is a measure of the intensity of the inefficiency. Thus the inefficiency incentive in the use of capital is greater in the sulfur, iron, copper, lead and zinc, and coal industries than in the petroleum industry, which has come in for the greatest attention concerning tax preferences. The 1.95 figure for petroleum does not mean, however, that the investment in that industry is twice what it should be. It means that because investors are willing to pay more for a stream of net income in the petroleum industry, the economy ends up with an investment balance such that a unit of capital used in the mineral industries produces smaller streams of net income than could be obtained by shifting the unit of capital into manufacturing industries.

As capital flows inefficiently into the mineral industries, several things can happen: (1) costs can be driven up; (2) rents, which are determined by the difference between the best and worst deposits being mined, are driven up as development increases and spreads to the worse prospects; (3) the quantities of minerals extracted increase; and (4) virgin mineral material prices soften as more virgin material is dumped on the market.[4] We are most interested in the effects on prices and quantities, but the Harberger analysis does not tell us how his inefficiency incentive toward too much capital in the extractive industries distributes itself among the four possible effects listed above.

Steiner refined the analysis to take into account the facts that not all the investment expenditures in mineral industries are expensed and that depreciation rules are more generous in manufacturing industries than the straight-line method Harberger used (depreciation deductions can be greater than R/T in the earlier years of production and smaller than

R/T in the later years, although they still add up to R over all the years). With these adjustments, Steiner found the inefficiency incentive on capital investment in petroleum to be more like 1.5 than Harberger's 1.95. Agria, using newer data for her estimates of the parameters, made the same adjustments as Steiner and added one of her own. She took into account the effect of severance taxes, which to some degree could be expected to offset the preferential features of mineral taxation. Agria found that severance taxes were small when compared with the tax savings implied from the percentage depletion and expensing, and her results were very similar to Steiner's.

The results of the line of analysis developed by Harberger, Steiner, and Agria show that the present tax system produces inefficiencies in the use of capital in the extractive industries. The results also provide estimates of the relative sizes of the incentives toward inefficiency, but not in terms of prices and quantities. In these analyses capital is a factor and Agria show that the present tax system produces inefficiencies in the factor market, but nothing about how the inefficiency is transmitted into the product market.

Inefficiency in the Product Market

In his criticism of the Harberger analysis outlined above, McDonald defended the depletion allowance and shifted the focus from inefficiency in the factor market to inefficiency in the product market.[5] He did this by a very simple method, which was to assume that all the effects of the tax provisions were concentrated on prices and none on profits, costs, or rents. McDonald defended the special tax treatment of minerals on the grounds that it offsets inefficiencies in the product market implied by a uniform income tax. Once we assume that effects of favorable tax treatment of minerals are shifted forward into prices, then we can also assume that the effects of the income tax itself are shifted forward into prices. Imagining for a moment that there were no special provisions for mineral taxation (that the effective rates of the income tax were uniform), forward shifting of the income tax would distort product prices upward for both manufactured products and mineral products. McDonald argued that uniform taxation would hit mineral industries especially hard and that consequently uniform taxation would distort mineral prices more than those of manufactured products. He then carried the argument further by calculating that the special tax provisions for minerals just offset the extra distortion in mineral prices, leaving the ratio of product prices about the same as it would be in the absence of any tax at all. Because efficiency on the product level requires that the ratios of product prices be the same after tax as they would be before the tax,[6] McDonald concluded that instead of preventing efficiency, the special provisions for minerals promote efficiency. Since we are especially interested in efficiency on the product level, McDonald's argument is important to us.

McDonald argued that mineral industries are relatively more risky and capital intensive than other industries. These two factors are the reasons that a uniform income tax would increase prices more for minerals than for other industries. Where there is more risk, investors will insist on a risk premium which is added onto the rate of return. An income tax shares the return; with a higher rate of return the pre-tax profit will be larger and hence the tax will be larger. With the assumption that the tax is shifted forward, a greater risk means that more tax burden will be shifted onto prices. Second, the income tax is assumed to be a tax on capital. The more capital intensive an industry, the greater the fraction of capital and profits in output. With a higher capital intensity, the income tax will be spread over a larger fraction of output. The percentage increase in prices needed to cover the income tax will be in direct proportion to the fraction of pre-tax profits in output.

McDonald estimated that for petroleum the rate of return after tax on invested capital was about twice the rate for manufacturing (24 to 12 percent) and that the capital intensity (measured by the ratio of stockholders' equity to sales output) was about two and a half times larger in petroleum than in manufacturing. Putting these two factors together, he found that it would require a depletion deduction of 21.5 percent of gross income to offset the extra distortion caused by risk and capital intensity, assuming forward shifting. Since the effective rate of the depletion deduction for petroleum was 22 percent for the time McDonald was making his estimates, he concluded that the percentage depletion deduction happened to be almost exactly the right amount.

The uncanny coincidence of McDonald's result invited review by other economists. Eldridge found McDonald's estimate of the rate of return for petroleum to be much too high.[7] Using other data, Eldridge found that the rate of return for petroleum for the average domestic operation was about the same as in other industries, around 12 percent. And, in fact, it is the position of the petroleum industry itself that the rates of return after taxes are in line with those of other major industries in the United States.[8] If we take the rate of return for petroleum to be 12 percent (equal to the rate for manufacturing) and recompute the percentage depletion needed to cancel the extra burden on petroleum from the income tax, we get 8.6 percent, instead of McDonald's 21.5 percent.

Implicitly McDonald is assuming that the full adjustment of the extra burden of the income tax is to be taken up by the percentage depletion allowance. Musgrave pointed out that the income tax has a built-in adjustment for risk in its allowance for loss offset against taxable income.[9] He uses this idea to explain why there need not be a risk premium in the petroleum industry (there appears to be none in the industry figures). Furthermore, as we saw in the section on capital gains, more risky industries actually have advantages under the present income tax law.

Steiner pointed out that McDonald did not consider the offsetting effect of expensing provisions for the mineral industries. Taking these into account, Steiner suggests that the distorting tendency of the income tax might be offset by these provisions alone, with no percentage depletion.[10] McDonald acknowledged these and other criticisms, saying that "all of them may have at least some validity."[11]

Where are we left? First, it should be remarked that even if McDonald had been right in his calculation and that a 21.5 percent depletion deduction was just the right adjustment to offset the burden of the income tax, we would only be trading one inefficiency for another. That is, by allowing the special tax provisions for mineral industries, we accept Harberger's type of inefficiency in the allocation of capital resources. If we eliminate the special provisions, we remove Harberger's type of inefficiency, and accept McDonald's. To the extent that the income tax is a tax on one factor of production, it is generally impossible to remove both types of inefficiency at once; we are stuck with at least one type of inefficiency. Accepting the criticisms of McDonald's position, we find that with the existing special provisions we have both types of inefficiency, one in the factor market and the other in the product market.

But McDonald gives us more. We can use his assumption of full forward shifting to develop an upper bound for the effect on prices of all the tax provisions for the extractive industries, the uniform ones as well as the special ones.
We start with

Y = gross income (sales)

P_b = income before taxes (gross income minus nontax costs)

t = present effective tax rate, for mineral industry

t' = present effective tax rate, for manufacturing industry

P_a = income after taxes

Let $b = P_b/Y$ be the fraction of gross income represented by income before taxes. Suppose that the present effective rate t for the mineral industry is raised to the rate for manufacturing t' and the full effect is shifted forward into higher prices (higher Y gross income). If at the same time that the effective tax rate moved from t to t', a negative sales tax were placed on mineral output, we ask how large would the tax have to be to leave the mineral industry just as well off (and prices unchanged) as it was with its previous low effective tax rate but with no subsidy on sales? In this way we can take into account the effects of uniform taxation as well as the special provisions that are especially favorable to the mineral industries. By definition $bY = P_b$ and $(1 - t)P_b = P_a$. Now we increase prices, and hence gross income by ΔY, just enough so that when we raise the tax rate in the mineral industry to the same effective rate as other industries the after-tax income remains unchanged: $(1 - t') \cdot (P_b + \Delta Y) = P_a$.

Dividing by Y and rearranging, we have

$$\frac{\Delta Y}{Y} = \frac{P_a}{Y(1 - t')} - \frac{P_b}{Y}$$

or

$$\frac{\Delta Y}{Y} = \frac{(1 - t)bY}{(1 - t')Y} - \frac{bY}{Y}$$

and

$$\frac{\Delta Y}{Y} = b \left(\frac{t' - t}{1 - t'} \right)$$

In other words, if mineral industries were given a $\Delta Y/Y$ negative sales tax and the same effective tax rate as other industries, they would be just as well off.

It is easy to obtain a lower bound to an estimate for b in the case of a firm which is able to take percentage depletion without bumping into the 50 percent of net income ceiling. Such firms were in the majority in 1960, as can be seen from table D-2, and are probably even more numerous today, with the slightly lower rates of percentage depletion. Consider a firm with a 22 percent depletion deduction and with sufficient net income before taxes to be in column 1 of table D-2. To be in column 1, $0.22Y < 0.5P_b$ so that $P_b/Y = b > 0.44$. A source for t can be found in detailed data on eighteen major petroleum firms, released by the American Petroleum Institute. Using aggregates from this data, Wright and Cox estimated the effective tax rate of these firms to be about 8.5 percent.[12]

With $t = 0.1$, $t' = 0.4$, and $b = 0.44$, $\Delta Y/Y = 15$ percent. We can interpret the 15 percent by thinking of a hypothetical mineral firm now

Table D-2. Depletion on Domestic Properties Claimed in 1960, by Type
(percentage)

Mineral categories	Based on gross income rate	Based on net income	Adjusted basis
All mineral products	73	19	8
Mineral products receiving percentage depletion at:			
27½	75	17	8
23	51	33	16
15	80	19	n.a.
Metals	85	14	1
Nonmetals	73	26	n.a.
10	41	56	4

Source: Resources for the Future, "A Program of Studies for Non-Fuel Mineral Policy," a report to the Office of Science and Technology, Feb. 1, 1968, p. ix–7. This table also appears on page 317 of the *President's 1963 Tax Message.*

paying an effective tax rate of 10 percent, thanks to the special tax provisions and its ability to exploit uniform provisions. If the effective tax rate were then raised to match the rate in other industries but at the same time the government paid the mineral firm a negative sales tax of 15 percent, the firm would be as well off as before the changes, assuming that the tax is shifted forward each time. Under the assumption of forward shifting, the favorable tax treatment of minerals is worth a price subsidy of 15 percent. However, this does not mean that if mineral firms began to pay the same effective tax rates as other firms the prices of virgin materials would rise 15 percent. They would rise only to the extent that the tax is in fact shifted forward. Thus the term $b[(t' - t)/(1 - t')]$ sets an upper bound on the price effect of the favorable tax treatment of minerals.

Because we are interested in the competition between primary and secondary materials, it is useful to compare how the present effective tax rates could affect prices, again under the assumption of full forward shifting by all firms. Setting the initial tax rate t equal to zero, we obtain the price effect of the income tax compared with a situation of no income tax when the upper bound is $b[t'/(1 - t')]$. For illustrative purposes we might have the following situation:

	b	t'	Price effect (percent)
Manufacturing	0.1	0.4	7
Petroleum	0.33	0.1	4
Scrap	0.25	0.4	17
Hard minerals	0.33	0.2	8

This assumes that the hypothetical scrap firm's capital intensity is midway between the intensities of a petroleum and a manufacturing firm. A scrap firm that is also capital intensive, which they are rapidly becoming, may have an income tax price burden considerably worse than the competing virgin material firm. This illustration also assumes that the effective federal tax rate for hard mineral firms is about 20 percent and that these firms are about as capital intensive as petroleum firms.[13] With these assumptions and with McDonald's assumption of forward shifting, we arrive at a result quite different from McDonald's: instead of the special tax provisions leading to neutrality in the product market, they lead to a rather strong inefficiency in the product market between primary and secondary industries. This inefficiency is roughly measured by the difference in the illustration between 17 and 4 percent, the price effects for scrap and petroleum, or 17 and 8 percent, the price effects for scrap and hard minerals. These numbers are for illustrative purposes; they are too imprecise for firm conclusions. Nonetheless, they suggest that we may have both types of inefficiencies at once. We have Harberger's inefficiency in the factor market because of the special provisions lightening the taxation of capital for extractive industries. And we may have McDonald's inefficiency in the product market because of the price effects. From an efficiency point of view, one might tolerate these two distortions—if one distortion worked in favor of the extractive industries and one against—as a kind of least bad compromise justified by the need for a corporate income tax. But when both misallocations work in favor of the extractive industries there is no such justification.[14]

Notes

1. Arnold Harberger, "The Taxation of Mineral Industries," *Federal Tax Policy for Economic Growth and Stability*, 84 Cong. 1 sess. (November 1955) pp. 439–449. The analysis was refined by Peter Steiner in "Percentage Depletion and Resource Allocation," *Tax Revision Compendium*, U.S. Congress, House Committee on Ways and Means, Nov. 16, 1959, vol. 2 (Washington, U.S. Government Printing Office, 1959) pp. 949–966. It was extended by Agria, "Special Tax Treatment of Mineral Industries," pp. 77–122.

2. The following recasts Harberger's argument to conform with the previous algebra.

3. In this example Harberger assumed that the mineral investor can expense all his costs. Steiner and Agria take into account that not everything is expensed and that more liberal depreciation than the straight-line form is allowed in manufacturing.

4. Any increase in profits is competed away by assumption in Harberger's analysis.

5. Stephen McDonald, "Percentage Depletion and the Allocation of Resources: The Case of Oil and Gas," *National Tax Journal* vol. XIV, no. 4 (1961) pp. 323–336.

6. This condition is not quite appropriate, for there are second-order effects of income taxes, but McDonald does not consider these effects.

7. Douglas Eldridge, "Rate of Return, Resource Allocation and Percentage Depletion," *National Tax Journal* vol. XV, no. 2 (1962) p. 217.

8. See, for example, Myron Wright, *Tax Reform, 1969*, Hearings before the Committee on Ways and Means, House of Representatives, 91 Cong. 1 sess. (1969) p. 3169.

9. Richard Musgrave, "Another Look at Depletion," *National Tax Journal* vol. XV, no. 2 (1962) p. 206 and in particular, footnote 3.

10. Peter Steiner, "The Non-neutrality of Corporate Income Taxation—With and Without Depletion," *National Tax Journal* vol. XVI, no. 3 (1963) pp. 250–251.

11. Stephen McDonald, "Percentage Depletion, Expensing of Intangibles, and Petroleum Conservation," Mason Gaffney, ed., *Extractive Resources and Taxation* (Madison, Wisc., University of Wisconsin Press, 1967) p. 284. McDonald admitted that his assumption of forward shifting onto prices "assumes an unrealistically elastic long-run supply of capital; that the observed high rate of return in the extractive phase of the petroleum industry is not attributable to risk; that the high capital intensity of petroleum extraction is in large part due to wasteful over-drilling induced by state regulations; that percentage depletion itself contributes to high capital intensity by motivating integrated buyers to overprice petroleum (so as to increase the allowance), which attracts entry and creates overcapacity under market-demand regulation of production; and that the tax benefits of the special provisions are absorbed largely in increased rents."

12. The effective rate is the tax paid divided by the entire tax base, which includes both domestic and foreign income. This is the appropriate definition under the national efficiency point of view. For an enlightening discussion of various definitions and their uses, see Arthur Wright and James Cox, "The Economics of the Oil Industries Tax Burden," *The Petroleum Industry's Tax Burden*, Washington, D.C., Taxation with Representation, 1973. More complete information on effective tax rates for material industries has recently become available on 10-K forms.

13. Anderson, "The Extent of Preferential Taxation."

14. The three estimates of the effect of taxation on virgin materials differ in their assumptions. The first (11 percent) depended on Treasury estimates of "excess" and industry calculations of what would be the tax with and without the special provisions. The second series of estimates only included the effect of the percentage depletion deduction, when it was "pure" subsidy and when it did not bump into the 50 percent of net income ceiling. This last estimate, in this section, took into account uniform as well as special provisions, the fact that virgin material industries are more capital intensive than most, and the tax effect on competing industries as well.

APPENDIX E

Lagrangian Details

1. Ramsey model, equation (7.3).

Form the Lagrangian

$$L = \sum_{t=1}^{N} \left[U(C_t) + \lambda_t(2I_{t-1} - C_t - I_t) \right]$$

The first-order conditions are

$$\frac{\partial L}{\partial C_t} = U'(C_t) - \lambda_t = 0 \tag{E.1}$$

and

$$\frac{\partial L}{\partial I_t} = 2\lambda_{t+1} - \lambda_t = 0 \tag{E.2}$$

By (E.2),

$$\lambda_t = \lambda_0(2)^{-t} \tag{E.3}$$

Using equation (E.1) and substituting equation (E.3), we have

$$\frac{U'(C_t)}{U'(C_0)} = \frac{\lambda_0(2)^{-t}}{\lambda_0}, \tag{E.4}$$

so

$$U'(C_t) = 2^{-t}U'(C_0)$$

As can be seen by figure 19, for a smaller $U'(C_t)$, $U(C_t)$ is larger, and so too is C_t. This is implied by the assumption of diminishing marginal utility of consumption. So as t increases, $U(C_t)$ and C_t increase, as is shown in figure 20.

2. Present value maximization, equation (7.4).

Form the Lagrangian

$$L = \sum_{t=1}^{N} \left[U(C_t)/(1 + i)^t + \lambda_t(2I_{t-1} - C_t - I_t) \right]$$

Following the same steps as before, we have

$$U'(C_t) = (1 + i)^t(2)^{-t}U'(C_0)$$

236

In this and the Ramsey model (case 1) the natural rate of productivity is 100 percent. If Crusoe discounts at the rate of productivity, he sets $i = 1$, and we have $U'(C_t) = (2)^t(2)^{-t}U'(C_0) = U'(C_0)$, so that his "optimal" consumption path is egalitarian; C_t is constant each period, as shown in path A, figure 21.

3. Present value criterion when productivity is zero.

In this case the Lagrangian is

$$L = \sum_{t=1}^{N} \left[U(C_t)/(1 + i)^t + \lambda_t(I_{t-1} - C_t - I_t) \right],$$

and the first-order conditions are $U'(C_t)/(1 + i)^t - \lambda_t = 0$ and $\lambda_{t-1} - \lambda_t = 0$. This means that $\lambda_t = \lambda_0$ for all t, so $U'(C_t) = \lambda_0(1 + i)^t$. And as long as $i > 0$, $U'(C_t)$ increases with t, implying that $U(C_t)$ and C_t decrease with t. With i equal to time preference and greater than zero, we have path C in figure 21. With i equal to the rate of productivity, which in this case is zero, we have path B in figure 21.

APPENDIX F

Inconsistency Between Time Preference and Productivity

THIS TYPE of market failure can be explained in the context of loan-able funds. As illustrated in figure F-1, in a "normal" financial market, the schedule of willingness to borrow for productive purposes (A) is a negative function of the interest rate i. The willingness to lend (B), for any purpose, rises with the interest rate (both are per unit of time). Assuming that there is no demand for consumption loans, we find the equilibrium interest rate of i_0, in panel I, where funds loaned equal funds borrowed per unit time. The rate i_0 measures both the lender's marginal time preference and the borrower's marginal productivity.

To the producer's willingness to borrow, we can add the consumer's desire to borrow. In panel II the schedule for consumption loans is plotted as C, also a negative function of the interest rate. The horizontal sum of C plus A is D, the total willingness to borrow as a function of the interest rate. This time the equilibrium is at i_1, which is higher than i_0 but still measures both consumers' time preference and producers' marginal productivity.

Now we move to a hardtack economy where the marginal productivity is zero for all levels of borrowing. Keeping the same willingness to lend

Figure F-1. Inconsistency of time preference and productivity

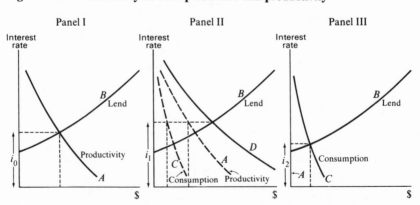

238

(*B*) and desire for consumption loans (*C*), we now have *A* coincident with the vertical axis—there is no willingness to borrow for production purposes at any interest rate. This time the equilibrium interest rate is i_2 which measures only time preference but not productivity, which is clearly zero. This is the situation in Crusoe's hardtack economy. It also occurs in Robert Strotz' "Myopia and Inconsistency in Dynamic Utility Maximization," *Review of Economic Studies* vol. XXIII (1955, 1956). (Strotz has positive time preference and zero productivity.) An actual example of this type of economy occurred in P.O.W. camps in Germany where there were market rates of interest for borrowing and lending cigarettes. The cigarettes, which were issued in monthly lots like manna, had a zero productivity rate, of course.

APPENDIX G

Intertemporal Calcutta Worlds

IN THIS ILLUSTRATION of intertemporal Calcutta worlds, the productivity is zero, the number of periods (N) is to be chosen, but for each period of existence consumption must be at least at subsistence level $(\tilde{C})$. If there were no subsistence restriction and for a fixed N and with discounting at a zero rate $(i = 0)$, section 3 of appendix E would show that the optimal plan is egalitarian $(C_t = I_0/N)$. Thus for a fixed N small enough so that the egalitarian consumption is feasible $(I_0/N \geq \tilde{C})$, the egalitarian path is optimal under the present value criterion, with $i = 0$. The remaining problem is to choose N.

We begin with $N = 1$, and ask if

$$\sum_{t=1}^{N} U(I_0/N) = NU(I_0/N) \text{ can be improved by increasing } N. \quad \text{(G.1)}$$

The differential of (G.1) is

$$(dN)U(I_0/N) - NU'(I_0/N)I_0/N^2 dN$$

We should keep increasing N as long as this differential is positive; and it is feasible to do so as long as the new, longer, more austere egalitarian programs still provide subsistence. In other words, we should keep increasing N as long as

$$U(I_0/N) - (I_0/N)U'(I_0/N) > 0 \quad \text{(G.2)}$$

and

$$I_0/N \geq \tilde{C}$$

Condition (G.2) is the same as

$$U'(I_0/N)\frac{I_0/N}{U(I_0/N)} < 1 \quad \text{(G.3)}$$

By condition (G.3) we keep lowering each period's egalitarian consumption until the elasticity of U increases to 1 or we meet the subsistence level barrier first.

In appendix B the geometry of elasticities is developed. The elasticity of quantity demanded (horizontal axis) with respect to price (vertical axis) is shown to be the distance from a point of tangency along the tangent to the horizontal axis divided by the distance from the point of tangency along the tangent to the vertical axis. Here the roles of the variables are reversed: we wish to show the elasticity of U (measured on the vertical axis) with respect to consumption (on the horizontal axis). Thus the elasticity is the distance from the point in question to the vertical axis divided by the distance to the horizontal axis. With the type of utility function shown in figure 19 and starting with $N = 1$ (eat everything in the first period and only one period of survival), the elasticity is $AB/AC < 1$ (figure G-1). Condition (G.3) tells us that we can increase

$$\sum_{t=1}^{N} U(C_t)$$

Figure G-1. Choosing N

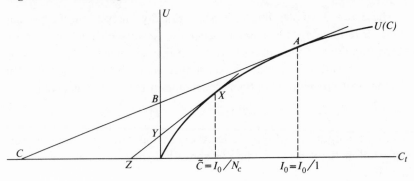

Figure G-2. Importance of cardinality

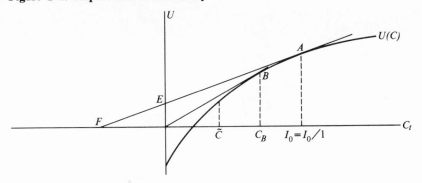

by increasing N, and by decreasing egalitarian consumption. As can be seen in figure G-1 the elasticity increases as C decreases and we increase N, the number of "years" of survival, until we hit the subsistence barrier $\tilde{C}$. Even at $\tilde{C}$ the elasticity is still less than 1 ($XY/XZ < 1$), but we can go no further. Discounting at a zero rate and with a utility function like the one of figure 19, the present value criterion selects egalitarian subsistence consumption, over the longest number of "years," as optimal. This case is also shown as plan A in figure 23.

This result, the intertemporal Calcutta solution, is critically dependent upon the form of the utility function. Suppose, in order to incorporate the idea that the Calcutta solution entails misery for low levels of consumption, we simply translate the utility function downward: for low levels of consumption, utility is negative (figure G-2). As before, we start at I_0 with elasticity $AE/AF < 1$, and move to the left. This time we find that the elasticity is brought up to unity at B before consumption is brought down to the subsistence barrier. This is the same as path B in figure 23.

These two examples illustrate how critically analysis by the present value criterion depends upon cardinality. Results change with linear transformations of the utility function. In the case where $i > 0$, present value "optimal" consumption is no longer egalitarian, for each N. By section 3 of appendix E optimal consumption for each N is given by

$$U'(C_t) = \lambda_0(1 + i)^t$$

To find the optimal N (aptly called the terminal date) we could in principle follow the same procedure as above but the mathematics would be messier.

On the Optimality of Extinction

IMAGINE AN ECONOMY with a single productive good, rice. For simplicity, each year coincides with a generation. The amount of rice consumed in generation t is r_t; the stock existing in that year is R_t; hence the amount left over for planting for the next generation is $R_t - r_t$. The stock of rice harvested by the following generation is proportionate to the amount planted the preceding generation. Thus we have the production condition

$$R_{t+1} = (1 + g)(R_t - r_t) \qquad \text{(H.1)}$$

Here the constant g is the natural growth rate of rice. If g were zero, the economy would eventually starve, but with a sufficiently high g it is possible for succeeding generations to eat better and better.

From generation Nought's point of view, the social welfare function, according to the interpretation of selfish altruism, is a function of consumption of all generations:

$$W = U^0(r_0, r_1, \ldots) \qquad \text{(H.2)}$$

and following the usual assumptions about separability and time preference

$$W = U(r_0) + \delta U(r_1) + \delta^2 U(r_2) + \ldots.$$

We also make the usual assumption that U exhibits decreasing marginal utility of consumption. By a typical specification of U, $U'(r)$ goes to infinity as r goes to zero. This means that the graph of U starts straight up as in figure H-1 and is a little stronger than the assumption embodied in figure 19. The assumed form of U is meant to incorporate the basic facts of life and to keep the maximization from immediate extreme solutions (for example, the present eats everything the first year and the economy ends in that year).

The problem now is to maximize

$$\sum_{t=0}^{\infty} U(r_t)\delta^t$$

Figure H-1. Utility function with infinite marginal utility at zero consumption

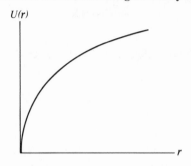

$$
\text{subject to} \quad
\begin{aligned}
R_{t+1} &= (1 + g)(R_t - r_t) \\
R_t &\geq 0 \\
r_t &\geq 0 \\
R_0 &= \bar{R}_0
\end{aligned}
$$

where δ expresses time preference and $\delta = 1/(1 + i)$

We form the Lagrangian:

$$
L = \sum_{t=0}^{\infty} \left\{ U(r_t)\delta^t + \lambda_t[(1 + g)(R_t - r_t)] - R_{t+1} \right\} + \lambda_0(\bar{R}_0 - R_0)
$$

and write down the Kuhn–Tucker conditions:

$$
\frac{\partial L}{\partial r_t} = U'(r_t)\delta^t - \lambda_{t+1}(1 + g) \leq 0 \tag{H.3}
$$

$$
\frac{\partial L}{\partial R_t} = (1 + g)\lambda_t - \lambda_{t-1} \leq 0 \tag{H.4}
$$

But for (H.3) to be satisfied with strict inequality, we must have $r_t = 0$.
As $U'(r) \to \infty$ for $r \to 0$, we are assured that (H.3) must be satisfied by an
equality. Furthermore, for $r_t > 0$ we must have $R_t > 0$, so (H.4) must
also be satisfied with equality.

With equality condition (H.4) we have

$$
\lambda_t = \lambda_0(1 + g)^{-t}
$$

and substituting this into equality condition (H.3) we have the solution in
terms of the marginal utility of the social welfare function (H.5).

$$
U'(r_t) = \lambda_0[(1 + i)/(1 + g)]^t \tag{H.5}
$$

where λ_0 is some positive constant. In the solution everything depends on
whether or not g is bigger than i. If the rate of natural productivity is
bigger than the rate of time preference, U' will shrink from generation to

Figure H-2. Consumption paths depending on generation Nought's time preference

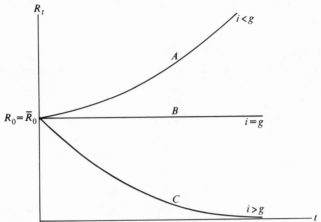

generation so that social welfare is growing; if $g = i$, U' is constant and consequently so is social welfare each generation; and if the rate of time preference is bigger than the rate of natural productivity, U' grows, implying that social welfare declines (asymptotically) to zero. The cases are illustrated in figure H-2.

The result is closely related to the formulation by Irving Fisher,[1] as can be seen by dividing equation (H.5) for generation $t - 1$ by the same equation for generation t:

$$\frac{U'(r_{t-1})}{U'(r_t)} (1 + i) = (1 + g) \tag{H.6}$$

On the left-hand side, the rate of time preference is translated from utility terms to commodity terms by the ratio of marginal utilities (the ratio of first derivatives evaluated in succeeding generations).

The units of $(1 + g)$ are $\dfrac{\text{units rice in generation } t}{\text{units rice in generation } t - 1}$, for any $t \geq 1$;

the units of $U'(r_t)$ are $\dfrac{\text{units utility in generation } t}{\text{units rice in generation } t}$;

and the units of $(1 + i)$ are $\dfrac{\text{units utility in generation } t}{\text{units utility in generation } t - 1}$, for any $t \geq 1$

So the units for equation (H.6) are:

$$\frac{\dfrac{\text{utility in gen. } t - 1}{\text{rice in gen. } t - 1}}{\dfrac{\text{utility in gen. } t}{\text{rice in gen. } t}} \qquad \frac{\text{utility in gen. } t}{\text{utility in gen. } t - 1} = \frac{\text{rice in gen. } t}{\text{rice in gen. } t - 1}$$

In multiplying $(1 + i)$ by the ratio of marginal utilities, we translate the dimensions on the left-hand side from utility terms to commodity terms.

According to Irving Fisher, the commodity version of time preference, which is the whole left-hand side of equation (H.6), tends to be equilibrated in the market to the rate of capital productivity, which is expressed by the right-hand side. This means that the condition for maximization of the present generation's welfare, equation (H.6) according to the present value criterion, is automatically achieved by market forces.

The situation with respect to the welfare of future generations can easily be shown with an Irving Fisher-like diagram if we restrict ourselves to a two-generation case. Nothing is lost by looking at the two-generation case, for in this example, whatever pattern is established between one generation and the next is perpetuated throughout time. We now consider the utility function $U^0(r_0, r_1)$ and a diagram of its indifference curves in figure H-3.[2]

The slope of an indifference curve is found by taking the total differential and setting it equal to zero:

$$\text{slope} = \frac{dr_1}{dr_0} = \frac{-\partial U^0/\partial r_0}{\partial U^0/\partial r_1}$$

and in our example

$$\frac{\partial U^0}{\partial r_0} = U'(r_0) \quad \text{and} \quad \frac{\partial U^0}{\partial r_1} = U'(r_1)\,\delta,$$

so we have the slope of an indifference curve equal to

$$\frac{-U'(r_0)}{U'(r_1)}\frac{1}{\delta} = \frac{-U'(r_0)}{U'(r_1)}(1 + i)$$

The productivity constraint is given by straight-line segments of slope $(1 + g)/1$. The meaning of this is that one unit of rice in generation Nought can be translated into $(1 + g)$ units in the next generation. The solution to the maximization problem occurs where these two slopes are equal. If consumption is declining, the solution will take place to the right of the $45°$ line. We can tell whether the economy, following the present value criterion, will grow or collapse by comparing slopes of the (social) indifference curve and the productivity constraint at the $45°$

Figure H-3. Case where time preference is greater than productivity

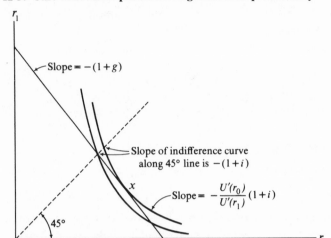

line. On this line r_0 and r_1 are equal, hence the ratio $U'(r_0)/U'(r_1)$ is unity and falls out of slope expression (H.4). For a given productivity fixed by nature, everything depends on the rate of time preference. If i is greater than g, an indifference curve cuts the productivity constraint from above at its intersection with the 45° line as in the diagram, ensuring that the solution will be found to the right of the 45° line and that the economy is on its way to collapse, as long as it follows the present value criterion as dictated by the first generation. It is essential to observe that in the Irving Fisher formulation there is no tendency for market forces to bring i and g into equality; Fisher is asserting that market forces tend to bring the left- and right-hand sides of equation (H.6) into equality. (At point x in figure H-3 the left- and right-hand sides of equation (H.6) are brought into equality.) Thus there is no implication that the present value criterion, or Fisher's market version of it, tends toward an egalitarian solution over time (C in figure H-2).

In this first example, with some initial austerity, evergrowing consumption and stocks of rice are feasible (A in figure H-2) but we may find that the present value criterion selects C as "optimal."

In the second example there are two goods in the economy, one faster growing than the other: g_1 is the growth rate of fast-growing rice and g_2 the growth rate of slow-growing whales. We assume an explicit form of the social welfare function given by

$$U(r_t, w_t) = r_t^\alpha w_t^\alpha,$$

where r_t is rice consumption in generation t; w_t is whale consumption in generation t; and $0 < \alpha < 1/2$ to ensure decreasing returns to the scale of consumption.

The problem, according to the present value criterion, is to maximize

$$\sum_{t=0}^{\infty} r_t^{\alpha} w_t^{\alpha} \delta^t$$

subject to $R_{t+1} = (1 + g_1) (R_t - r_t)$; $W_{t+1} = (1 + g_2) (W_t - w_t)$; $R_0 = \bar{R}_0$; and $W_0 = \bar{W}_0$

Again we form the Lagrangian:

$$L = \sum \{ w_t^{\alpha} r_t^{\alpha} \delta^t + \lambda_{t+1}[(1 + g_1)(W_t - w_t) - W_{t+1}]$$
$$+ \mu_{t+1}[(1 + g_2)(R_t - r_t) - R_{t+1}]\} + \lambda_0(\bar{R}_0 - R_0) + \mu_0(\bar{W}_0 - W_0)$$

and write down the first-order conditions (with the same argument for equality constraints as above with the Kuhn–Tucker conditions):

$$\frac{\partial L}{\partial w_t} = 0 \text{ and } \frac{\partial L}{\partial W_t} = 0,$$

which implies

$$\alpha w_t^{\alpha-1} r_t^{\alpha} \delta^t = \lambda_0 (1 + g_1)^{-t}; \tag{H.7}$$

and

$$\frac{\partial L}{\partial r_t} = 0 \text{ and } \frac{\partial L}{\partial R_t} = 0,$$

which implies

$$\alpha w_t^{\alpha} r_t^{\alpha-1} \delta^t = \mu_0 (1 + g_2)^{-t} \tag{H.8}$$

Because of the special choice of utility function and production functions, a little algebra leads to an explicit solution.

Dividing (H.7) by (H.8), we have

$$\frac{r_t}{w_t} = \frac{\lambda_0}{\mu_0} \left[\frac{1 + g_2}{1 + g_1} \right]^t \text{ or } r_t^{\alpha} = k_1 w_t^{\alpha} (1 + g_2)^{\alpha t} (1 + g_1)^{-\alpha t} \tag{H.9}$$

where k_1 and the k_i to follow are positive but unimportant constants. By (H.7)

$$r_t^{\alpha} = k_2 w_t^{1-\alpha} \delta^{-t} (1 + g_1)^{-t}$$

Substituting for r_t^{α} into (H.9), we have

$$k_2 w_t^{1-\alpha} \delta^{-t} (1 + g_1)^{-t} = k_1 w_t^{\alpha} (1 + g_2)^{\alpha t} (1 + g_1)^{-\alpha t}$$

or

$$w_t^{(1-2\alpha)} = k_3 (1 + g_1)^{t-\alpha t} (1 + g_2)^{\alpha t} \delta^t \tag{H.10}$$

And by symmetry

$$r_t^{(1-2\alpha)} = k_4 (1 + g_1)^{\alpha t} (1 + g_2)^{t-\alpha t} \delta^t \tag{H.11}$$

Putting (H.10) and (H.11) together, we have

$$(w_t r_t)^{(1-2\alpha)} = k_5 (1 + g_1)^t (1 + g_2)^t \delta^{2t}$$

so

$$U(w_t, r_t) = w_t^\alpha r_t^\alpha = k_6 \left[\frac{1 + g_1}{1 + i} \times \frac{1 + g_2}{1 + i} \right]^t \frac{\alpha}{1 - 2\alpha}$$

and $\dfrac{\alpha}{1 - 2\alpha}$ is a positive constant.

In other words, everything depends on whether the rate of time preference is sufficiently high so that $(1 + i)$ is bigger than the geometric mean of the growth factors, that is, whether or not $(1 + i) > [(1 + g_1)(1 + g_2)]^{1/2}$.

Again, we have an ever-increasing path of welfare feasible, but also the possibility of a social collapse being "optimal." If $(1 + i)$ is greater than $(1 + g_2)$—the slow growing rate—but less than the geometric mean of the growth factors, the present value criterion will eliminate the slow-growing asset from the market while welfare improves from generation to generation. This is the case that perhaps people have in mind when they assert that removal of slow-growing assets is compatible with improving the lot of the future. However, this case is by no means guaranteed. It is also possible to have $(1 + i)$ smaller than $(1 + g_1)$ but still larger than the geometric mean of the growth factors. In that case, even though the rate of time preference is less than the fast-growing and ultimately market-dominating asset, the economy is headed for collapse from the first generation, if it follows the present value criterion. The mathematical details illustrate what was mentioned in chapter 7: the slow-growing asset is not eliminated immediately from the market by the iron law of the discount rate. Due to its growing scarcity value, it is eliminated gradually. Each generation eliminates a little more in order for the growth in scarcity value to compensate for its slow natural growth.

Perhaps "whales" is an inappropriate example of a slow-growing asset that is vital to social survival. Clean air might be a better one. In this case the air's capacity to cleanse itself may be too slow to keep up with the rate at which it is loaded with industrial pollutants. But in either case the point is that quite aside from externality problems—the failure of the market to price whales or air correctly—there is the tendency of the present value criterion to eliminate slow-growing assets, whether or not they are vital to survival.

The above two examples illustrate an abstract theoretical point: namely, that there is nothing in the present value criterion to prevent it from choosing social extinction as "optimal" even though continued survival and even continued improvement in well-being is feasible. There is nothing in the criterion itself to rule out a fantasy such as this one:

You are the director of the Office of Management and Budget. A proposal reaches your desk about a riskless project which will extract energy from the sun at an increased rate for 200 years. New production processes could use the energy to triple our GNP every year until 2180. Total project costs are negligible with one exception. The sun will explode [because of the project] and end life in 2180.

You reach for OMB circular A-94, THE word since 1969 regarding "Discount rates and procedures to be used in evaluating deferred costs and benefits." Sure enough, after discounting benefits and costs, the project's net present value is phenomenal! Within weeks our government heeds the unanimous advice of investment analysts and commences the project. You sleep with comfort at having lived in the twentieth century.[3]

Such a fantasy is not "silly" in a theoretical sense, but is it not silly in a practical sense? Surely a total demise would be valued at infinite cost and even a powerful discount rate working against a distant but infinite cost could not make the project have a favorable net benefit. Unfortunately, two observations render this response less reassuring. First of all, as can be seen by the mathematical examples, a primrose path to apocalypse is not the only path to ruin, under the present value criterion. There need be no sudden jump to infinite costs, but only a gradual worsening of the environment. All that is needed is for the present value criterion to recommend a slightly lower level of some vital asset from one period to the next. All that is needed is to accept each year a slightly worse air quality "for the sake of productivity."

Second, many of the projects to be evaluated by the present value criterion (in its version of benefit–cost analysis) carry with them probabilistic costs. If any project accepted by benefit–cost analysis has even the smallest risk of eventual social collapse, then that is evidence that the practitioners do not count such costs as infinite. An expected value with any positive weight on an ultimate disaster with infinite cost leads to infinite expected cost, assuming that no project has the potential of infinite benefits. This is true even for any weight on the Baysian prior of the uncertain probability. Actually, there appear to be several ultimate gambles which have already been taken.

On both a theoretical and practical level there is nothing in the present value criterion to prevent future social collapse. From a still more practical point of view, combining benefit–cost analysis with political decision making can lead to heavy discounting of future risk and the neglect of future risks.

Notes

1. Irving Fisher, *The Theory of Interest* (New York, Macmillan, 1930).

2. An indifference curve is the set of pairs (r_0, r_1) for which the function value $U(r_0, r_1)$ is constant. An indifference curve is the same as a level curve. All pairs (r_0, r_1) on an indifference curve are combinations of present and future consumption which leave the present generation equally well off.

3. James Doilney, "Equity, Efficiency, and Intertemporal Resource Allocation Decisions" (Ph.D. dissertation, University of Maryland, 1974) p. III-13.

Index